D0081675

# GARDENS AND GRIM RAVINES

154490

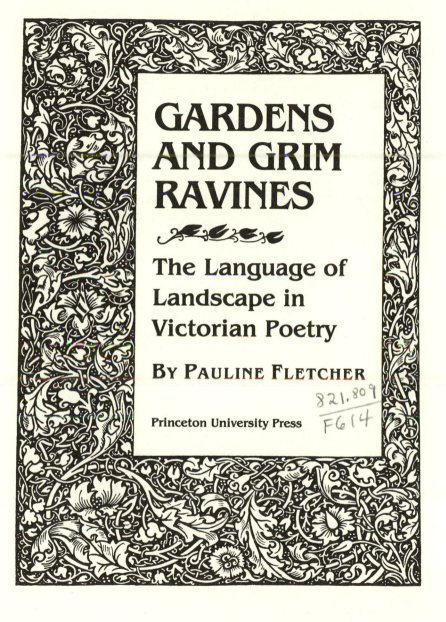

# GARDENS AND GRIM RAVINES

## The Language of Landscape in Victorian Poetry

BY PAULINE FLETCHER

821.809
F614

Princeton University Press

Alverno College
Library Media Center
Milwaukee, Wisconsin

Copyright © 1983 by Princeton University Press

Published by Princeton University Press, 41 William Street,
Princeton, New Jersey 08540
In the United Kingdom: Princeton University Press,
Guildford, Surrey

All Rights Reserved

Library of Congress Cataloging in Publication Data will be
found on the last printed page of this book

This book has been composed in Linotron Sabon and Benguiat

Clothbound editions of Princeton University Press books
are printed on acid-free paper, and binding materials are
chosen for strength and durability

Printed in the United States of America by Princeton
University Press, Princeton, New Jersey

# CONTENTS

v

# LIST OF ILLUSTRATIONS

(To follow p. 146)

1. John Martin, *Manfred on the Jungfrau*, courtesy of the City of Birmingham Museum and Art Gallery.
2. Thomas Rowlandson, *Doctor Syntax Tumbling into the Water*, illustration for *The Tour of Doctor Syntax, In Search of the Picturesque*, by William Combe.
3. A Victorian "wild" garden, from J. C. Loudon, *The Villa Gardener*, 2nd ed., 1850.
4. A Victorian garden with formal elements, from J. C. Loudon, *The Villa Gardener*, 2nd ed., 1850.
5. John Millais, *Ophelia*, courtesy of The Tate Gallery, London.
6. William Holman Hunt, *The Hireling Shepherd*, courtesy of the City Art Gallery, Manchester.
7. William Holman Hunt, *The Lady of Shalott*, illustration for the Moxon edition of Tennyson (1857), engraved by the Brothers Dalziel.
8. Dante Gabriel Rossetti, *St. Cecilia*, illustration for the Moxon edition of Tennyson (1857), engraved by the Brothers Dalziel.
9. Dante Gabriel Rossetti, *King Arthur and the Weeping Queens*, illustration for the Moxon edition of Tennyson (1857), engraved by the Brothers Dalziel.
10. Dante Gabriel Rossetti, *The Day Dream*, courtesy of the Victoria and Albert Museum, London.
11. Dante Gabriel Rossetti, *How They Met Themselves*, courtesy of the Fitzwilliam Museum, Cambridge.
12. Dante Gabriel Rossetti, *The Blessed Damozel 1871-1877*, courtesy of the Fogg Art Museum, Harvard University.

vii

# ACKNOWLEDGMENTS

I owe an enormous debt of gratitude to Professor George H. Ford for his enthusiastic support of this project, for his most valuable advice and criticism, and for his benign yet fierce scrutiny of my manuscript. Professor David G. Riede also read the manuscript, and I have benefited from his perceptive comments and suggestions.

Grateful acknowledgment is made to the editors of *Studies in Romanticism* for allowing me to use portions of my article, "Romantic and Anti-Romantic Gardens in Tennyson and Swinburne," the copyright of which is held by the Trustees of Boston University.

Finally, I should like to thank the following institutions and museums for allowing me to reproduce works in their collections: City of Birmingham Museum and Art Gallery (Fig. 1); City Art Gallery, Manchester (Fig. 6); the Tate Gallery, London (Figs. 5 & 13); Fogg Art Museum, Harvard University (Fig. 12); the Victoria and Albert Museum, London (Fig. 10); the Fitzwilliam Museum, Cambridge (Fig. 11); Walker Art Gallery, Liverpool (jacket illustration).

# PREFACE

The reader should be warned that it is not the purpose of this study to provide a general introduction to the Victorian poets. Other critics have performed that task admirably, and have left me free to take certain well-worn themes for granted. The limitations imposed by my chosen topic have meant that some very important poems receive little or no mention, simply because they are not concerned with landscape. The bulk of Browning's dramatic monologues, for example, fall into this category. Furthermore, I have imposed certain limitations on myself in the interests of brevity. It seemed to me to be beyond the scope of this study to include any discussion of the lengthy poetic dramas that so many Victorian poets produced. For this reason I have omitted Swinburne's *Atalanta in Calydon* and Hardy's *The Dynasts*. In any case, landscape figures very little in these works, and certainly not enough to warrant their inclusion. I make no apology for my omission of *Sordello*. Jane Carlyle may not have said the last word on that monster, but I shall leave it to others to challenge her judgment.

I could have included a chapter on Hopkins, who has as much right to be called a Victorian as Hardy does. My omission was largely a matter of personal choice, dictated partly by the length and shape of my book, and partly by the feeling that Hopkins is a highly idiosyncratic poet who demands separate treatment.

These omissions are balanced by the inclusion of many poems that make use of landscape only in a very marginal sense. The term "landscape," originally derived from painting, carries suggestions of a vista, a scene that is observed from a fixed viewpoint. But the poet, unlike the painter, is not tied to a fixed viewpoint; he may follow his characters as they move through the landscape and explore its hidden nooks. He may also follow them into the *paysage interieur*. I have therefore felt justified in extending the term to include such landscapes of the mind, as well as any description of the natural setting or environment in which a character in a poem may be placed.

Attitudes to landscape inevitably involve some consideration of attitudes to nature, and, indeed, it is sometimes impossible to separate the two. Wordsworth's description of the landscape near Tintern Abbey for example, is necessarily colored by his concept of Nature. On the other hand, there are many poems about nature and natural objects that do not include landscape: Arnold's "In Harmony with Nature," and Wordsworth's "My heart leaps up when I behold" might be cited as examples. But Wordsworth's sonnet "Composed upon Westminster Bridge" is surely a poem about landscape, even though it describes a view over the city. I have taken note of attitudes to nature as they affect landscape, but the concept of nature is not my chief concern. It has, in any case, been dealt with by other critics, such as Joseph Warren Beach in *The Concept of Nature in Nineteenth-Century English Poetry* (New York: Macmillan, 1936).

GARDENS AND GRIM RAVINES

# INTRODUCTION

My joy was in the wilderness,—to breathe
The difficult air of the iced mountain's top,
Where the birds dare not build, nor insect's wing
Flit o'er the herbless granite.
(Byron, *Manfred* II.ii, 62-69)

The Byronic hero reveals himself through his chosen landscape. The man for whom the alpine wilderness represents an ideal is implicitly rejecting all social values. He is *Manfred on the Jungfrau* (Fig. 1), a tormentd figure on the heights; he is a solitary rebel, testing his courage and endurance against natural forces, communing with his own soul or with the Infinite, a supreme example of the egotistical sublime. But one man's sublime wilderness is another man's dreary wasteland. Samuel Johnson would not have accepted the Byronic ideal. For him London was undoubtedly the "good place": "Why, Sir, you find no man, at all intellectual, who is willing to leave London. No, Sir, when a man is tired of London, he is tired of life; for there is in London all that life can afford."[1]

Johnson's city and Byron's wilderness represent two antithetical types of landscape, the social and the antisocial. The social includes all landscapes that are conducive to the life of man in the community, or that in some way reflect social values. Pastoral scenes, whether Arcadian or Georgic, fall most naturally into this group. The antisocial consists mainly of the great primeval wildernesses of mountain, sea, and forest. These are essentially heroic and romantic landscapes to which the terms "sublime" or "picturesque" may be applied.[2] There are,

[1] *Boswell's Life of Johnson*, edited by George Birkbeck Hill (Oxford: Clarendon, 1934), III, 178.
[2] According to Edmund Burke, the sublime is rooted in pain and associated with terror; its chief characteristics are vastness, power, and obscurity. *A*

3

in addition, antisocial landscapes that provide a more protective setting for the solitary figure, such as the woodland bower and other "secret and sheltered places, forests in moonlight, secluded valleys, and happy islands."[3] Such landscapes of refuge and retreat are isolated but are not in themselves hostile to man, and even their solitude may be modified. The bower is cut off from society, but it may provide a haven for a pair of lovers.

For most poets, however, the good place has been located at some point on a spectrum between the extremes of city and wilderness. Shakespeare's Forest of Arden is a retreat from the corrupt court, but it harbors a society in exile; Pope's garden at Twickenham is a refuge from London's sick hurry, but he expects to be visited by his friends and to exercise his filial piety there. The ideal is essentially social, and even his grotto is something to be shared with visitors. Wordsworth turns in spirit to the "sylvan Wye," but the "wild secluded scene" contains evidence of human activity in its hedgerows, "plots of cottage-ground," and "wreaths of smoke / Sent up, in silence, from among the trees."[4] Moreover, the poet turns to share the experience of this harmonious scene with his "dear, dear Sister." One of the most basic and revealing questions that may be asked of any man is what conception of the good place he holds.

I propose to ask this question of the major Victorian poets, and to use the typology outlined above as a tool for exploring

*Philosophical Enquiry into the Origin of Our Ideas of the Sublime and Beautiful*, pp. 58ff. The picturesque might be defined as a degenerate form of the sublime. Real terror has been replaced by a pleasurable *frisson* of horror, and genuine awe of nature's grandeur has given way to stereotyped reactions to a catalogue of picturesque objects. The history of these concepts has been dealt with by other critics. See, for example, Hipple, *The Beautiful, the Sublime, and the Picturesque in Eighteenth-Century British Aesthetic Theory*; Hussey, *The Picturesque*; and Marjorie Nicolson, *Mountain Gloom and Mountain Glory*.

[3] Frye, *Anatomy of Criticism*, p. 185. Frye describes such landscapes as belonging to "the phase of the collapse and disintegration of the comic society."

[4] Wordsworth, *Poetical Works*, ed. Hutchinson, p. 163.

their attitudes to landscape. The distinction between social and antisocial is particularly appropriate to the Victorians, since it reflects a dichotomy that is basic to an age that was divided between an inherited romantic subjectivism and an emerging consciousness of social problems. This division was expressed by one of the most representative figures of the age in terms of his attitude to landscape. John Ruskin had admired and defended Turner's paintings of sublime scenery, and written passionately of the beauty of the Alps. But he was eventually to turn his gaze from the grandeur of the mountain peaks to the squalor of the villages beneath them. With a touch of evangelical puritanism he decides that it is "not good for man to live among what is most beautiful." He continues:

> So that it is, in reality, better for mankind that the forms of their common landscape should offer no violent stimulus to the emotions,—that the gentle upland, browned by the bending furrows of the plough, and the fresh sweep of the chalk down, and the narrow winding of the copse-clad dingle, should be more frequent scenes of human life than the Arcadias of cloud-capped mountain or luxuriant vale.[5]

This is a pastoral and humanized landscape, close in spirit to the ideal landscapes of Homer, which, as Ruskin himself had noted earlier, always show a "quiet subjection of their every feature to human service."[6] The younger Ruskin had been indifferent to such humble scenery, but now he sees the dark underside of the romantic landscape and turns, as Rosenberg says, "from mountains to men, from art to society."[7]

Ruskin's awareness of the moral and social dimensions of

---

[5] Ruskin, *Works*, VI, 167-68.

[6] Ruskin, *Works*, V, 234-35.

[7] Rosenberg, *The Darkening Glass*, p. 22. In a recent article Wendell Stacy Johnson traces the movement in Ruskin's poetry from "Romantic celebrations of landscape" to flight into a "landscape of dead seas and gloomy mountains that is wholly passionless." "Memory, Landscape, Love: John Ruskin's Poetry and Poetic Criticism," *Victorian Poetry*, 19 (1981), 34. The movement in the poetry, then, does not seem to be from mountains to men, but from the glory to the gloom of the romantic landscape.

rural scenery represents an important early contribution to the sociology of landscape, and a significant departure from an earlier tradition of judging landscape in purely aesthetic terms. William Gilpin, one of the early theoreticians of the Picturesque, had deliberately rejected anything connected with cultivation of the land as unworthy to form part of an ideal landscape. "As to the appendages of husbandry," he wrote, "and of every idea of cultivation, we wish them totally to disappear."[8] Signs of human life were not necessarily banished from picturesque scenes, but in order to qualify for inclusion they had to have the quality of "roughness." Tumbledown cottages and ragged peasants were to be preferred to well-kept houses and sleek inhabitants—preferred, that is, on purely aesthetic grounds and not because the painter was suggesting that the material conditions of the peasantry ought to be improved. The connoisseur of the picturesque separated human need from aesthetic criteria. The ragged children that might form a colorful group in the corner of a landscape were merely objects of interest on a level with "Gothic cathedrals and old mills, gnarled oaks and shaggy goats, decayed cart horses and wandering gypsies."[9] Such an exaggerated rejection of all that was useful and civilized was easy to satirize. As early as 1799 Thomas Rowlandson had caricatured the frenzied hunt for scenic grandeur in his *Artist Travelling in Wales*, and he was later to do the illustrations for William Combe's comic poem, *The Tour of Doctor Syntax, In Search of the Picturesque* (Fig. 2). Like all fashionable crazes the cult of the Picturesque soon became outmoded.[10]

Ruskin's refusal to see the squalid mountain villages as picturesque adjuncts to scenery introduced a moral dimension into the judgment of landscape. However, he was not merely

---

[8] Quoted by Barbier in *William Gilpin: His Drawings, Teaching, and Theory of the Picturesque*, p. 112.

[9] Hipple, *The Beautiful*, p. 210.

[10] According to Manwaring, the cult of the Picturesque "rises into frequency by 1760, is general after 1780, and ridiculously hackneyed after 1800." *Italian Landscape in Eighteenth Century England*, p. 167.

moralizing on the landscape in the tradition of eighteenth-century topographical poetry. "In this poetry," writes John Barrell, "the landscape becomes a theatre where the poet's own moral reflections are acted out; where the objects do not so much give rise to the reflections, as the ready-made and waiting reflections justify the inclusion of this or that object in the poem."[11] Ruskin has no ready-made reflections to apply to what he sees. Instead, the poverty of the mountain people forces itself upon his attention in such a way that he is compelled, reluctantly, to judge the landscape in terms of its usefulness to human life.

It was Ruskin's social conscience that interfered with his enjoyment of mountain scenery, but other forces were also at work, turning the Victorians away from the sublime. As various critics have pointed out, the transcendent vision of the Romantics, the felt connection between God and Nature, was very largely lost during the nineteenth century.[12] In part it was undermined by scientific discoveries in biology and geology, but in any case, the cult of the Sublime, and the more frivolous cult of the Picturesque that developed from it, contained the seeds of their own destruction. As more and more people rushed off to the Alps to experience the right emotions, so those emotions became increasingly difficult to capture. The poet or painter could no longer enjoy the mountains in solitude, but must share them with boisterous groups of tourists and mountaineers. In 1864 Ruskin made biting reference to those who regarded the mountains "as soaped poles in a bear-garden, which you set yourselves to climb, and slide down again, with 'shrieks of delight.' "[13] These comments, as David Robertson has pointed out,[14] were no doubt unfair to those alpine enthusiasts who were also intelligent men of letters,

---

[11] Barrell, *The Idea of Landscape and the Sense of Place*, p. 35.

[12] See, for example, Beach, *The Concept of Nature*; and Hillis Miller, *The Disappearance of God*.

[13] Ruskin, *Sesame and Lillies, Works*, XVIII, 89.

[14] Robertson, "Mid-Victorians amongst the Alps," in *Nature and the Victorian Imagination*, p. 113.

such as Leslie Stephen and Frederic Harrison, but Stephen·
himself seems to echo Ruskin's criticism when he writes, "We
rushed with delight into that enchanted land; climbed peaks
and passes; made proselytes in every direction to the new
creed; and ended, alas! by rubbing off the bloom of early
romance, and laying the whole country open to the incursions
of the ordinary tourist."[15]

The tendency to reject mountain scenery was nowhere more
apparent than in the Victorian novel, which, as George Levine
says, "tended to find meaning and connection in the more
human landscapes of the lowlands and rivers."[16] Even Scott,
a lover of the mountains, was, like Ruskin, ambiguous in his
attitudes toward them: "In Scott's highlands, outlaws rebel
and conspire, their romantic excesses ultimately to be de-
stroyed by the civilization of the lowlands."[17] The idealism
of the heights was to be replaced by the idealism of the valleys,
as George Ford, also writing about the novel, suggests. The
lost paradise for the Victorians was to become "a blissful scene
of a green valley in which was nestled a scattered group of
thatch-roofed cottages, with lattice windows and winding paths
lined with hollyhocks and roses."[18]

To a certain extent it might be said that the Victorians
retreated from the mountains into the garden, but the garden
is the most complex and ambiguous of all landscapes. Man
finds the wilderness, although he may project his own emo-

---

[15] Stephen, "A Substitute for the Alps," in *Men, Books, and Mountains*,
p. 204. Both Stephen and Harrison wrote prolifically about their alpine ex-
periences. See, for example, Stephen, *The Playground of Europe* and Har-
rison, *My Alpine Jubilee, 1851-1907*.

[16] Levine, "High and Low: Ruskin and the Novelists," in *Nature and the
Victorian Imagination*, pp. 142-43.

[17] Levine, *The Realistic Imagination*, p. 208. Donald Stone also stresses
the twofold nature of Scott's influence on the Victorians: "Scott's later novels
reveal his dual impulse to search for new sources of romantic material even
while determining, in the end, to deflate or disavow the excesses and impli-
cations of romanticism." *The Romantic Impulse in Victorian Fiction*, p. 16.

[18] Ford, "Felicitous Space: The Cottage Controversy," in *Nature and the
Victorian Imagination*, p. 29.

tions onto it, but he creates the garden, and since it is created for pleasure rather than utility it embodies his own idea of himself, or of his society. In this respect it is a social landscape. However, there are many types of garden, and some of them are created specifically for antisocial purposes. Andrew Marvell's garden is an idyllic retreat for solitary contemplation, a model of Paradise, but without the annoying company of that root of all evil, woman: "Such was that happy garden-state, / While man there walked without a mate."[19] Wordsworth's garden at Dove Cottage was a "natural" paradise "reconstructed in harmony with the hills and planted with the wild and native things that grow in Nature's midst."[20] In contrast to the "wild" garden are the great formal gardens created for social display. The wide terraces and long straight walks of Versailles, for example, almost demand crowds of well-dressed ladies and gentlemen, groups of musicians, and parading coxcombs.

In their gardens, as in so much else, the Victorians were thoroughly eclectic, combining elements of different styles and periods.[21] Edward Kemp, for example, has this advice for gardeners in 1848: "On the whole the mixed style, with a little help from both the formal and the picturesque, is altogether best suited for small gardens."[22] Here an alpine rockery, there a formal parterre, and both springing from a sweep of

---

[19] "The Garden," in *The Poems and Letters of Andrew Marvell*, I, 53. Although it is clear that the garden continued to be associated with its paradisal archetype in *Genesis*, the nineteenth century had lost touch with the more complex and esoteric symbolism attached to the *hortus conclusus*, which was still a living tradition for Marvell. See Stewart, *The Enclosed Garden*.

[20] Noyes, *Wordsworth and the Art of Landscape*, p. 110.

[21] Many histories of landscape gardening exist, and I have not thought it necessary to give an account of the changes wrought in the eighteenth and nineteenth centuries by such well-known figures as "Capability" Brown and Humphry Repton, or of the debate between the Brown/Repton school and the "wild improvers," Payne Knight and Uvedale Price. See, for example, Clifford, *A History of Garden Design*; Hyams, *The English Garden*; and Manwaring, *Italian Landscape in Eighteenth Century England*.

[22] Kemp, *How to Lay Out a Garden*, p. 126.

lawn twenty feet across (Figs. 3 and 4)! This confusion of styles was intensifed by the craze for exotic plants. The Victorian garden became a showcase for the spoils of empire, and the new style, in which each plant specimen was displayed to best advantage, became known as the "Gardenesque." Exotic plants brought a new interest in color, and flowering shrubs and bedding plants came back into the garden in rich profusion. William Morris's garden at Red House exemplified just such a happy and flowery confusion: "the surrounding garden divided into many squares, hedged by sweetbriar or wild rose, each enclosure with its own particular show of flowers; on this side a green alley with a bowling green, on that orchard walks amid gnarled old fruit-trees: all struck me as vividly picturesque and uniquely original."[23]

But in spite of their lack of consistency, Victorian gardens were not without charm, as Derek Clifford points out:

> Seclusion was their greatest strength. But the cause of their seclusion, the encircling shrubbery, also gave by its contrasted tones and textures and because of the long shadows thrown at dawn and dusk a more effective setting to the English lawn than ever before. Their evergreen ramparts gave them a timelessness that even ephemeral bedding-out schemes could not dispel. They encircled and protected a world of green shadows, of croquet, and of afternoon tea.[24]

Such a landscape, like Pope's garden, is both social and antisocial. It is a private world, cut off from society by its "ramparts" of protective shrubbery, but it contains a small society of people who play croquet and drink tea. It is undoubtedly a place of privilege from which the laboring masses are excluded, but compared to the grand estates of the eighteenth century, or to the gardens of Versailles, it represents a democratic development. The encircling shrubbery provided pri-

[23] Vallance, William Morris, His Art, His Writings, and His Public Life, p. 49.
[24] Clifford, A History of Garden Design, p. 192.

vacy for a small estate or suburban garden; such a device was unnecessary for the owner whose land stretched almost to the horizon.

The nineteenth century was the age of the small gardener, and the publication of books such as Kemp's, quoted above, or Loudon's *Suburban Gardener and Villa Companion* (1838), marked a significant sociological change. According to Edward Hyams, "The small burgess was displacing the gentleman in social importance, and the Loudons realised it. Many great gardens were still to be made; but in the future the smaller owner was to be more important in the development of gardening."[25]

The ancestry of the suburban garden is amusingly suggested by Dickens in *Great Expectations*. Wemmick's tiny "castle" and garden, complete with moat and drawbridge, is a whimsical miniature of the great country estate. Of course, such a garden violates every principle of good taste; but as a source of innocent pleasure and of relief from the horrors of the urban wasteland, it illustrates the humane philosophy that lay behind the creation of the garden suburb.

The social conscience of the Victorians led to the creation of even more democratic gardens—the great city parks—which were "useful landscapes within the town for the use and enjoyment of the public at large."[26] The city park was a social landscape, but it provided opportunities both for enhanced sociability and for private retreat; the lawn was balanced by the winding path and the sequestered nook, as Arnold demonstrates in his "Lines Written in Kensington Gardens." According to Jay Appleton in *The Experience of Landscape*, such a balance between open prospect and place of refuge is a characteristic of the ideal landscape.

Appleton is one of a number of critics who have shown the value of a modern theoretical approach to the study of landscape. Whereas earlier literary historians had discussed eight-

---

[25] Hyams, *The English Garden*, p. 123.
[26] Chadwick, *The Park and the Town*, p. 19.

eenth-century landscape in terms of contemporary aesthetic theories formulated by such writers as Burke and Gilpin, Appleton makes use of the insights of modern biology, and in particular of habitat theory. "Habitat theory postulates that aesthetic pleasure in landscapes derives from the observer experiencing an environment favourable to the satisfaction of his biological needs."[27] An ideal landscape should provide a balance between open vistas and protective cover, so that it affords "both a good opportunity to see and a good opportunity to hide."[28] In a particular landscape, however, the balance may shift in favor of one or other of the necessary elements, and, using Appleton's terminology, we may describe the formal garden as "prospect-dominant," whereas the Victorian garden should probably be seen as "refuge-dominant."

Appleton's theory provides a valuable alternative to a narrowly Freudian interpretation of landscape. In *The Interpretation of Dreams*, Freud writes: "many landscapes in dreams, especially any containing bridges or wooded hills, may clearly be recognized as descriptions of the genitals." He quotes a description from a woman's dream: "Behind the church there was a hill and above it a thick wood," and annotates "hill" as *"mons veneris,"* and "wood" as "pubic hair."[29] In a post-Freudian age it is almost impossible to read a description of a wooded hollow without making the Freudian connection, but comparatively few critics have found it fruitful to interpret topographical features exclusively as genital symbols. Such an approach would obviously be too narrow.[30] Many critics, however, have made use of the psychological theories of Freud, Jung, and others in a more general manner when discussing

[27] Appleton, *The Experience of Landscape*, p. 73.

[28] Ibid., p. 74.

[29] *Works of Sigmund Freud*, V, 356, 366.

[30] It may however, be suitable for short articles. Paul Sheppard, Jr. discusses gorges as vagina symbols in "The Cross Valley Syndrome," *Landscape*, 10, No. 3 (1961), 4-8; and R. E. Hughes finds both male and female symbols in the landscape of Childe Roland; see "Browning's 'Childe Roland' and the Broken Taboo," *Literature and Psychology*, 9 (1959), 18-19.

landscapes that obviously represent states of mind rather than actual places. John Rosenberg's work on Tennyson, Frederick Crews' book on Hawthorne, and Carol Fabricant's feminist approach to eighteenth-century landscape may be quoted as examples.[31]

Biological and psychological theories have added valuable dimensions to our reading of the landscape, but because they are primarily concerned with our responses to basic, universal urges they tend to ignore the fact that the landscape is often part of a complex social and political structure. Can the grandiose gardens of Versailles, for example, best be read in terms of biological need or psychological theory? Or should they be seen as an expression of political dominance over both man and nature, an assertion of brute power, and a reflection of absolute monarchy?

In recent years several critics have discussed landscape in terms of its underlying political, economic, and social realities. Raymond Williams, in his important study of the pastoral tradition, *The Country and the City*, states that the idealization of pastoral or rural life is achieved "by conscious selection and emphasis"; it "depends, often, on just the suppression of work in the countryside, and of the property relations through which this work is organised."[32] George Ford reveals the reality beneath the sentimental myth of life in a country cottage.[33] John Barrell, in his study of the rural poor in English painting from 1730 to 1840, also exposes the dark side of the pastoral idyll: "For the most part the art of rural life offers us the image of a stable, unified, almost egalitarian society, so that my concern in this book is to suggest that it is possible

---

[31] Rosenberg, *The Fall of Camelot*; and "Tennyson and the Landscape of Consciousness," *Victorian Poetry*, 12 (1974), 303-10; Crews, *The Sins of the Fathers: Hawthorne's Psychological Themes*; Fabricant, "Binding and Dressing Nature's Loose Tresses: The Ideology of Augustan Landscape Design," *Studies in Eighteenth-Century Culture*, 8 (1979), 109-35.

[32] Williams, *The Country and the City*, pp. 31, 46.

[33] Ford, "Felicitous Space," pp. 29-48.

to look beneath the surface of the painting, and to discover there evidence of the very conflict it seems to deny."[34]

When Barrell looks beneath the surface of Constable's harmonious landscapes the results are sometimes surprising. Constable's ideal is clearly what I have called the social landscape, and Ruskin's description, quoted earlier, of some "gentle upland, browned by the bending furrows of the plough" might have been made for one of his paintings. However, as Barrell points out, Constable achieves the harmonious blending of man and landscape largely by reducing and distancing his figures, so that we cease to see them as individual men and women. "If," he writes, "they obtruded more, if they became less symbolic, more actualised images of men at work, we would run the risk of focussing on them as men—not as the tokens of a calm, endless, and anonymous industry, which confirm the order of society."[35] Barrell's analysis is a useful reminder that although Constable, in comparison with landscape painters such as Claude and Salvator Rosa, seems to be giving us a realistic depiction of the countryside, he is nevertheless still working within an idealizing pastoral tradition.

Another interesting treatment of "the politics of landscape" may be found in James Turner's book of that title. Turner discusses country-house and topographical poetry of the seventeenth century, and shows how the poets constantly denounce the evils of enclosure, the cruelty of the rack-renter, and the vanity of the rich, while at the same time emphasizing that their particular patrons are noble, just, and benevolent. Turner is "able to see the whole system of aesthetic *topographia*, and the myths that accompany it, as a superstructure founded on the relationships engendered by 'rents, labour, trade and tillage.' "[36] Poems such as Denham's *Coopers Hill* and Marvell's *Upon Appleton House* lend themselves to such an interpretation because they deal with landscape as it has been formed and shaped by the great landowners to express

[34] Barrell, *The Dark Side of the Landscape*, p. 5.
[35] Ibid., p. 149.
[36] Turner, *The Politics of Landscape*, p. 190.

their view of themselves and the world. Moreover, the poet himself is part of the superstructure he describes by virtue of his dependence on the patronage of the landowner; he takes his place in the network of relationships connected to the land, laboring not to till fields but to raise a poetic structure that mirrors and interprets the landscape.

But Turner's method does not lend itself to the analysis of landscape in Victorian poetry. The formal topographical poem was, for the Victorians, a dead genre, largely because its economic basis—the desire of the poet to flatter or instruct his patron—no longer existed. The Victorians were dependent on an anonymous middle-class readership for patronage, and had no direct economic link with rural life. This fact alone makes most Victorian poetry unsuitable for the kind of sociological and political criticism practiced by Williams, Barrell, and Turner. It is significant that Williams passes from the rural poetry of the eighteenth century and the Romantic period to a consideration of the novel in the nineteenth century. For him, "Clare marks the end of pastoral poetry, in the very shock of its collision with actual country experience," and he has nothing to say about Victorian poetry.[37] Barrell also ignores Victorian poetry, stating merely that "in poetry and painting the countryside comes to take on the simply negative virtue of not being the city. It is no longer a place of tension, as we will find it to be in the work of Gainsborough, Morland, and Constable, but one defined as empty of tension; a place of refreshment and recreation."[38]

Barrell finds no tension in Victorian poetic landscapes largely because his ideological and critical tools will not allow him to see the tensions that undoubtedly exist, but that may be unrelated to questions of property ownership and the ex-

[37] Williams, *The Country and the City*, p. 141. Richard Feingold gives an even earlier date for the disappearance of the pastoral. "But after 1800 the pastoral was something to be either contemned or rescued, and the georgic simply disappeared." *Nature and Society: Later Eighteenth-Century Uses of the Pastoral and Georgic*, p. 1.

[38] Barrell, *The Dark Side of the Landscape*, p. 32.

ploitation of rural labor. They may arise from precisely that sense of the country as "a place of refreshment and recreation." The country then becomes an escapist paradise which is perceived as offering only a temporary haven. And even that haven might be purchased at the price of guilt and isolation. Victorian landscapes may not reflect the class struggle so much as the internal struggle between duty and desire, or between the need for human companionship and the need to escape social pressures. Or the conflict may be at even deeper levels of the psyche, where consciously repressed fears and desires are expressed through landscapes that exist only in the mind.

Each of the critical approaches that I have discussed illuminates a valuable aspect of landscape, but each clearly has its limitations. I propose to adopt an eclectic approach that draws on the insights provided by various schools of criticism. Such an approach best meets the needs of an eclectic age, and should allow for a reading of the rich language of landscape in Victorian poetry without limiting the text in advance. It will enable me to enter the *paysage interieur* and other antisocial landscapes of refuge or retreat, but it will also permit me to see the landscape as an expression of social and political values. Above all, a flexible approach is needed for the exploration of those shadowy areas of tension where conflicting signals are given by the landscape. We have already seen how Ruskin heard the voices of social conscience and guilt as well as the romantic voice of the sublime from his beloved alpine scenery. We have seen, too, how the Victorian garden developed toward the small, secluded, and private world on the one hand, and toward the great public park on the other. The tension between social responsibility and private necessity, between engagement and withdrawal, is one of the central dramas of the age. It is, according to Levine, even reflected in the realistic novel: "That responsibility [to the community] is the primary surface concern of the realists, for whom the figure on the mountain, ambiguously beautiful, is deadly and demonic even in its possible purity. His seductiveness, and the novelists' repressed Alpine longings, quietly energize the very literature which keeps its back to the mountains."[39]

For the poet, however, less committed than the novelist to a realistic account of life in the community, the tensions may be different. The figure on the mountain may be more seductive, or more terrifying; the pastoral valleys may offer escapist havens, responsible community life, or merely suffocating dullness. But tensions, both social and psychological, will still make themselves felt through the landscapes of poetry, and the Victorian poets should reveal both themselves and much about their society through their chosen landscapes.

[39] Levine, *The Realisic Imagination*, p. 212.

CHAPTER I

# TENNYSON:
# THE PRIMAL WILDERNESS

Tennyson's early poetry shows, more than that of any other Victorian poet, the lingering taste for the sublime and the picturesque. His skill as a verbal landscape painter has often been admired, though some critics have dismissed this aspect of his art as mere ornamentation.[1] More recently, critics have paid much attention to his use of certain landscapes as the equivalents of psychological states, or have seen him as a transitional figure between the picturesque school and the modern tendency to depict *le paysage interieur*.[2] Both these types of landscape, the picturesque and the psychological, are, as will be shown, largely antisocial landscapes of withdrawal, and they are mostly to be found in the earlier Tennyson. As he matured, Tennyson moved away from such antisocial landscapes toward landscapes that included or reflected human society.

In this chapter I propose to show how, after an early enchantment with romantic scenery, Tennyson rejected the sublime and the picturesque. Increasingly, the various types of wilderness (mountain, sea, and forest), came to be seen as barbaric wastelands that a man of sense should avoid.

The youthful Tennyson had cultivated sensibility rather than sense, however. He was a worshiper of Byron, and when the

[1] For example, Douglas Bush writes that Tennyson "lives mainly as a painter of landscape and water," but sees his landscapes as merely decorative. *Mythology and the Romantic Tradition*, p. 197. John Dixon Hunt also stresses Tennyson's use of picturesque landscape in "The Poetry of Distance: Tennyson's 'Idylls of the King,' " in *Victorian Poetry*, ed. Bradbury and Palmer, pp. 89-121.

[2] McLuhan expresses this view in "Tennyson and Picturesque Poetry," in *Critical Essays on the Poetry of Tennyson*, ed. Killham, pp. 67-85.

18

great Romantic poet died in 1824, Tennyson was profoundly affected, feeling that "the whole world was at an end; I thought that everything was over and finished for everyone, that nothing else mattered."[3] Many of Tennyson's early poems show the influence of Byron, and also of Scott. He spoke later of how, at the age of twelve, he had written "an epic of six thousand lines à la Walter Scott,—full of battles, dealing too with sea and mountain scenery."[4] The epic has not survived, and most of the early, published poems that show a love of wild, romantic scenery were not reprinted by the poet after 1827. "On Sublimity" may stand as a fairly representative example of the type:

> O tell me not of vales in tenderest green,
>     The poplar's shade, the plantane's graceful tree;
> Give me the wild cascade, the rugged scene,
>     The loud surge bursting o'er the purple sea:
> On such sad views my soul delights to pore.[5]

This is a piece of literary apprenticeship; "wild cascade" and "rugged scene" suggest Salvator Rosa, and the hackneyed language indicates that Tennyson was not responding to a deeply felt personal experience.

Another early poem, "The Lover's Tale," seems to strike a more genuine note. It opens with a description of a distant view in which trite phrases have been replaced by greater freshness and accuracy of perception:

> Here far away, seen from the topmost cliff,
> Filling with purple gloom the vacancies
> Between the tufted hills, the sloping seas
> Hung in mid-heaven, and half-way down rare sails,
> White as white clouds, floated from sky to sky.
>
> (TW, 301)

---

[3] Quoted by Ricks, *Tennyson*, p. 14.
[4] Hallam Tennyson, *Alfred Lord Tennyson: A Memoir*, I, 12.
[5] *The Poems of Tennyson*, ed. Ricks, p. 116. Hereafter cited as *TW* with page numbers.

A lingering element of the sublime is contained in "purple gloom," but the scene has the qualities of a somewhat melancholy, twilit Claude instead of the more dramatic contrasts of a Salvator. It is calm and tranquil, tending toward the beautiful rather than the sublime.

Mountain scenery is used in "The Lover's Tale" for dramatic effect, but it is never more than an adjunct to the human story. The lover tells how he and Camilla once climbed the mountains together:

> The path was perilous, loosely strewn with crags:
> We mounted slowly; yet to both there came
> The joy of life in steepness overcome,
> And victories of ascent, and looking down
> On all that had looked down on us; and joy
> In breathing nearer heaven.
> (*TW*, 314)

The predominant feeling in the passage is not awe of the sublime, but the sense of human companionship and the shared triumph of a difficult climb. Moreover, the moment of exhilaration on the mountain top is short-lived and illusory. The companions descend to a woodland nook where Camilla confesses that she loves another man. The hero than retreats into the solitude of the forest, and the landscape of heroic endeavor and of exaltation is replaced by the landscape of melancholy withdrawal.[6] Indeed, the gloomy cavern within the wood closely resembles a tomb, and it induces a deathlike inertia in the hero: "All day I sat within the cavern-mouth, / Fixing my eyes on those three cypress-cones / That spired above the wood" (*TW*, 331). The landscape of withdrawal or seductive ease was, as we shall see, to represent a particularly strong temptation for Tennyson, but in this poem happiness is not to be found in the solitude of the cavern in the woods; the speaker

---

[6] Or, to use the terminology devised by Appleton, a prospect-dominant landscape has given way to a refuge-dominant landscape. Appleton would also describe the cavern within the wood as the reduplication of refuge symbols. *The Experience of Landscape*, p. 73ff. and p. 270.

20

is only there because he cannot marry the woman he loves and join the normal life of the community. There is no question of viewing the woods as a place of spiritual regeneration and rebirth. Nor is the wilderness seen as a place where a man might learn to hear the still sad music of humanity.

Wordsworthian transcendence has fled. But Tennyson still found mountains, and the Pyrenees in particular, "a continual source of inspiration."[7] "Oenone" was one result of that inspiration, written after the 1830 visit to the Pyrenees of Tennyson and Hallam. The poem, first published in 1832, was heavily revised later, and it is significant that nearly all the revisions tend to make the landscape softer. The movement is away from the sublime and the picturesque toward more pastoral and humanized scenery. The 1832 version opens with thirteen lines of scenic description:

> There is a dale in Ida, lovelier
> Than any in old Ionia, beautiful
> With emerald slopes of sunny sward, that lean
> Above the loud glenriver, which hath worn
> A path through steepdown granite walls below
> Mantled with flowering tendriltwine. In front
> The cedarshadowy valleys open wide.
> Far-seen, high over all the Godbuilt wall
> And many a snowycolumned range divine,
> Mounted with awful sculptures—men and Gods,
> The work of Gods—bright on the darkblue sky
> The windy citadel of Ilion
> Shone, like the crown of Troas.
> (*TW*, 385n.)

By 1842 this had become:

> There lies a vale in Ida, lovelier
> Than all the valleys of Ionian hills.
> The swimming vapour slopes athwart the glen,
> Puts forth an arm, and creeps from pine to pine,

[7] Hallam Tennyson, *A Memoir*, I, 54-55.

21

And loiters, slowly drawn. On either hand
The lawns and meadow-ledges midway down
Hang rich in flowers, and far below them roars
The long brook falling through the cloven ravine
In cataract after cataract to the sea.
Behind the valley topmost Gargarus
Stands up and takes the morning: but in front
The gorges, opening wide apart, reveal
Troas and Ilion's columned citadel,
The crown of Troas.
                    (*TW*, 385)

The "swimming vapour" that "creeps" and "loiters, slowly drawn" in the second version invests the scene with languid beauty. The gentle downward progress implied by "loiters" has replaced the more dramatic contrast of the earlier version, where the "emerald slopes . . . lean / Above the loud glen-river." The "steepdown granite walls" of 1832 have given way to more pastoral "lawns and meadow-ledges" that "hang rich in flowers." Cataracts and gorges do still provide a dramatic contrast in this softened landscape, but the "Godbuilt wall" of snowy mountains, with its "awful sculptures" has disappeared. Instead, "Gargarus / Stands up and takes the morning." The image suggests calm serenity and beauty, without the touch of terror that makes for the sublime.

When Tennyson visited the Pyrenees again in 1861, this time accompanied by his family, he wrote "In the Valley of the Cauteretz" (*TW*, 1123), a poem in which the emphasis has shifted from the beauty of the scenery to its particular human associations. The voice of the stream has become "as the voice of the dead," and the chief significance of the valley for the poet is that it was there that "I walked with one I loved two and thirty years ago."

Jerome Hixson comments that "the difference between the same scenery in 'Oenone' and that in 'All along the valley' is the difference between vivid Keatsian imagery in 'Oenone' and deeply felt symbolism in the poem composed on his return

22

in 1861."[8] Hixson is surely right about the shift from Keatsian imagery to symbolism, but what comes across even more strongly is the subordination of landscape to human feeling. One might say that this landscape does achieve transcendence for Tennyson, but it is a quite un-Wordsworthian transcendence. Similar scenery had, for the great Romantic poet, become:

> like workings of one mind, the features
> Of the same face, blossoms upon one tree;
> Characters of the great Apocalypse,
> The types and symbols of Eternity,
> Of first and last, and midst, and without end.[9]

If Tennyson sees the features of any face in the rocks and flashing mountain stream of the Cauteretz, it is the face of Hallam rather than that of Eternity. "Rock and cave and tree" only achieve eternity for him because they make the "voice of the dead" a "living voice to me."

In the same way, the spirit of Hallam pervades all types of landscape in *In Memoriam*:

> Thy voice is on the rolling air;
> I hear thee where the waters run;
> Thou standest in the rising sun,
> And in the setting thou art fair.
> (*TW*, 979)

In such lines there is a resemblance between Hallam and Wordsworth's Lucy, who becomes one with the "rocks, and stones, and trees" (*Wordsworth*, p. 149). There is also a very important difference between the two: Lucy has no very clear existence apart from the natural objects with which she is identified both before and after her death; one cannot even be sure that this "thing that could not feel / The touch of earthly years" is or was a real person. For Wordsworth, it is

[8] Hixson, "Cauteretz Revisited," *Tennyson Research Bulletin*, 2 (1975), p. 147.
[9] Wordsworth, *Works*, p. 537.

23

Nature that gives reality and permanence to Lucy; for Tennyson, Hallam was the greater reality, and it is his presence that may sometimes sanctify nature and render it sublime. However, more often the cosmic landscapes of *In Memoriam* lack this human significance, and are terrifyingly bleak manifestations of nature's indifference:

"The stars," she whispers, "blindly run:
A web is woven across the sky;
From out waste places comes a cry,
And murmurs from the dying sun."
                    (*TW*, 866)

The influence of the new scientific discoveries, particularly Lyell's geology, on Tennyson's attitude to nature has been dealt with so often that it is not necessary to discuss it here. What is important is not only that nature came to be seen as brutal and cruel in many of its moods, but that in turning away from the Wordsworthian concept of Nature, Tennyson had to replace it with faith in human or divine love.[10]

Small wonder, then, that alpine scenery, which is the most inhuman of all types of landscape, should so often have been rejected by Tennyson. The movement away from the sublime is most perfectly expressed in the famous lyric from *The Princess* in which the shepherd exhorts the maid (or "Jungfrau") to descend from the mountain heights to the pastoral valleys:

"Come down, O maid, from yonder mountain height:
What pleasure lives in height (the shepherd sang)
In height and cold, the splendour of the hills?
But cease to move so near the Heavens, and cease
To glide a sunbeam by the blasted Pine,
To sit a star upon the sparkling spire;
And come, for Love is of the valley, come,

[10] This conclusion was also reached by Valerie Hollis: "What he came to realize between 1832 and 1842 was that beautiful natural imagery, unless it is related to some aspect of the human experience, is not of lasting significance." "Landscape in the Poetry of Tennyson," p. 100.

For Love is of the valley, come thou down
And find him; by the happy threshold, he,
Or hand in hand with Plenty in the maize,
Or red with spirted purple of the vats,
Or foxlike in the vine; nor cares to walk
With Death and Morning on the silver horns,
Nor wilt thou snare him in the white ravine,
Nor find him dropt upon the firths of ice,
That huddling slant in furrow-cloven falls
To roll the torrent out of dusky doors:
But follow; let the torrent dance thee down
To find him in the valley; let the wild
Lean-headed eagles yelp alone, and leave
The monstrous ledges there to slope, and spill
Their thousand wreaths of dangling water-smoke,
That like a broken purpose waste in air;
So waste not thou; but come; for all the vales
Await thee; azure pillars of the hearth
Arise to thee; the children call, and I
Thy shepherd pipe, and sweet is every sound,
Sweeter thy voice, but every sound is sweet;
Myriads of rivulets hurrying through the lawn,
The moan of doves in immemorial elms,
And murmuring of innumerable bees."
(*TW*, 835-36)

The lonely figure on the mountain inevitably recalls such romantic prototypes as Byron's Manfred or Frankenstein's monster, but Tennyson has replaced the demonic masculine figure with a female figure whose chief act of rebellion is that she clings to her sexual purity. In Mary Shelley's *Frankenstein* Levine notes the "ambiguities in the tension between domesticity and Prometheanism," and points out the lack of a final "lowland resolution."[11] The major tension in Tennyson's *Princess* is between domesticity and virginity, and the seductive masculine call is made from the valleys, not the heights.

[11] Levine, "Ruskin and the Novelists," p. 147.

It is the masculine figure who endorses the values of the community and who reminds the lonely maiden that "the children call." We are left with the conviction that a "lowland resolution" is both right and inevitable.

Another source of tension is present, however, and it is not so easily resolved. It is suggested in the sense of frustration conveyed through the description of the mountain waterfalls that never reach their destination, but "like a broken purpose waste in air." It is tempting to speculate whether Tennyson might not have had in mind the wasted effort of his Spanish adventure in the Pyrenees in 1830. He and Arthur Hallam had set out with high political idealism, but their attempts to aid the Spanish revolutionaries had had to be abandoned. In much the same way, the princess abandons her high revolutionary purpose for the love of the valleys. The lyric seems to endorse her decision, but there is a dreamy seductiveness in the last two lines that echoes the languid rhythms of "The Lotos-Eaters." In abandoning the life of strenuous activity on the heights, the princess, like the mariners, may be opting for a life of present ease that carries the taint of corruption. As Ricks has pointed out, it is Love who speaks in this lyric, and his words are "suggestive, but irresponsible, insinuating, certainly not monopolizing the poem's values. To Love (and to the urgent lover) the heights are sterile. But Tennyson conveys their dignity and their potent reminder."[12]

Further comparison between this poem and "The Lotos-Eaters" shows how Tennyson can use similar landscapes to create different emotional effects. Both landscapes contain the basic elements of the sublime: mountain peaks, pine trees, waterfalls, and mountain ledges. In "The Lotos-Eaters," however, all these features are softened so as to hide the threat of strenuous and heroic endeavor usually implied by such scenery. Although the "Three silent pinnacles of aged snow" might seem to stand as a call to action, they are reassuringly "far off," and their peaks are "sunset flushed" (*TW*, 430),

[12] Ricks, *Tennyson*, p. 203.

which implies both warmth and the decline into old age. The pines on these mountains are not blasted, as in "Come down, O Maid," but are "shadowy" and "dewed with showery drops" (*TW*, 430). The streams in both poems are transformed into smoke that hardly falls, but in "The Lotos-Eaters" there is no hint of a broken purpose, and the soporific rhythm allows no time for thoughts of action: "And like a downward smoke, the slender stream / Along the cliff to fall and pause and fall did seem."

In the lyric from *The Princess*, on the other hand, there is no softening of the mountain landscape. Instead, its harshness is used to enhance the desirability of the lush valleys. One may ask to what extent Tennyson shared the shepherd's rejection of the cold heights. After the tour with Moxon he grumbled that although the crags pleased him, "mountains, great mountains, disappointed me. I couldn't take them in, I suppose, crags I could."[13] Years later, in 1880, Tennyson was to make another unfavorable comment on mountains, and, significantly, his rejection of them is linked with his rejection of Shelley, a hero of his romantic youth: " 'The Revolt of Islam' is splendid, but it gives me a headache—it's fatiguing—all mountain tops and glories."[14] This is the remark of an old man, and should perhaps not be given too much weight; when he wrote "Come down, O Maid," Tennyson had preserved a more careful balance: "Love is of the valley," but "Death and Morning" walk together on the silver mountain tops. The valley is the safe way, the middle way; both the danger and the glory of youth belong to the peaks.

This way of looking at landscape implies a reading of it in allegorical or moral terms derived from human experience. Nature is no longer the Great Universal Teacher; instead, it is man who bestows meaning on natural scenery, and for Tennyson mountains are almost always associated with high idealism or heroic endeavor. The mystic experiences of Sir

[13] Quoted ibid., p. 186.
[14] Quoted by Charles Tennyson, in *Alfred Tennyson*, p. 451.

Galahad, for example, are associated with mountain heights and waste places:

> I leave the plain, I climb the height;
> No branchy thicket shelter yields;
> But blessèd forms in whistling storms
> Fly o'er waste fens and windy fields.
>
> (*TW*, 612)

In his later version of the Grail legend, however, Tennyson shows much less admiration for Galahad's heroic quest in the wilderness. The bouncy rhythm and assertive action of "I leave the plain, I climb the height," give way to the painful vision which is part horror, part triumph:

> and never yet
> Hath what thy sister taught me first to see,
> This Holy Thing, failed from my side, nor come
> Covered, but moving with me night and day,
> Fainter by day, but always in the night
> Blood-red, and sliding down the blackened marsh
> Blood-red, and on the naked mountain top
> Blood-red, and in the sleeping mere below
> Blood-red.
>
> (*TW*, 1675)

Galahad achieves his vision, but, as Arthur points out, he brings back nothing of value for the community; indeed, his flight across the wasteland in pursuit of the grail is a flight away from social responsibility and toward mystical self-an-nihilation. He is last seen "on the great Sea, / In silver-shining armour starry-clear" (*TW*, 1676), but this personal triumph is set against the crumbling ruin that Camelot becomes during the absence of the questing knights.

It is fitting that Galahad should finally disappear into the sea. Like the mountains, the sea is antisocial; it is a type of sublime wilderness that provides a particularly good testing ground for the romantic hero. This was pointed out by W. H. Auden, who, in *The Enchafèd Flood*, differentiates between classical and romantic attitudes to the sea. In Auden's terms, the classical hero chooses the life of the shore, with its social responsibilities and ties, whereas the romantic hero chooses the sea. He lists the distinctive items in the romantic attitude:

1. To leave the land and the city is the desire of every man of sensibility and honor.
2. The sea is the real situation and the voyage is the true condition of man.
3. The sea is where the decisive events, the moments of eternal choice, of temptation, fall, and redemption occur. The shore life is always trivial.
4. An abiding destination is unknown even if it may exist: a lasting relationship is not possible nor even to be desired.[15]

Tennyson's Ulysses is, as Auden points out, "the typical Romantic Marine hero," who views the shore life as trivial, and who commits himself to the antisocial quest on the sea. Telemachus represents the classical ideal within the poem, the man of the shore and of civilization:

> discerning to fulfil
> This labour, by slow prudence to make mild
> A rugged people, and through soft degrees
> Subdue them to the useful and the good.
> Most blameless is he, centred in the sphere
> Of common duties, decent not to fail
> In offices of tenderness, and pay
> Meet adoration to my household gods,
> When I am gone. He works his work, I mine.
> (TW, 564)

Most critics have felt that Ulysses damns Telemachus with faint praise, and there has been much debate about the degree to which the poet identifies himself with the point of view of

[15] Auden, The Enchafèd Flood, pp. 13-14.

his speaker.[16] What is surely significant is that the young man represents the classical ideal of the settled community, while the old man emerges as the romantic rebel. This reversal of the normal roles might suggest that although Tennyson himself identifies somewhat uneasily with his aging hero, he also recognizes that the future belongs to Telemachus. Or, as Harold Bloom expresses it, "Tennyson's Ulysses is the Romantic quester grown old and perfect in his solipsism, a Child Harold who has lived too long and now secretly loathes his own belatedness."[17]

In his later poetry Tennyson obviously moved closer to the classical ideal. In "The Holy Grail" Arthur represents that ideal. Like Telemachus, he is the man who stays at home, but he is treated without condescension, and his warnings about the evil consequences of the quest are justified. Tennyson's changing attitudes may be illustrated by the different ways in which he handles the "enchafèd sea" that his questers face in "Ulysses" and in "The Holy Grail."

For Ulysses, "the deep / Moans round with many voices" (TW, 565), and these voices express the basic ambiguities of the poem. Some of the voices of the sea are dark intimations of mortality, whispering to Ulysses of the Happy Isles of death where he may rejoin Achilles. But the sea is also invitingly broad, and its "scudding drifts" and "sounding furrows" (TW, 562, 565) speak to him of adventure, and suggest possibilities of personal enrichment and opportunity. The sea has been glamorized, or "romanticized" in Auden's sense.

This is not so in "The Holy Grail." Galahad and Percivale confront a dreary wasteland:

A great black swamp and of an evil smell,
Part black, part whitened with the bones of men,

[16] See, for example: Baum, Tennyson Sixty Years After, pp. 301-303; Chiasson, "Tennyson's 'Ulysses'—A Re-interpretation"; and Robson, "The Dilemma of Tennyson," in Critical Essays, ed. Killham, pp. 164-73, 155-63, respectively.
[17] Bloom, A Map of Misreading, p. 156.

Not to be crost, save that some ancient king
Had built a way, where, linked with many a bridge,
A thousand piers ran into the great Sea.
(*TW*, 1676)

Galahad's frantic race across the bridge which "as quickly as
he crost / Sprang into fire and vanished" is the desperate flight
of the hysterical mystic, accompanied by "thunder such as
seemed / Shoutings of all the sons of God" (*TW*, 1676). Per-
civale's description of the dreadful apotheosis of Galahad bril-
liantly combines classical horror of the sea with romantic
exaltation.

When Lancelot faces the sea on his quest, the exaltation
has gone; the sea is merely dreadful, and Lancelot is a madman
for committing himself to it:

and then I came
All in my folly to the naked shore,
Wide flats, where nothing but coarse grasses grew;
But such a blast, my King, began to blow,
So loud a blast along the shore and sea,
Ye could not hear the waters for the blast,
Though heaped in mounds and ridges all the sea
Drove like a cataract, and all the sand
Swept like a river, and the clouded heavens
Were shaken with the motion and the sound.
And blackening in the sea-foam swayed a boat,
Half-swallowed in it, anchored with a chain;
And in my madness to myself I said,
"I will embark and I will lose myself,
And in the great sea wash away my sin."
(*TW*, 1683)

At best, the sea faced by Lancelot might cleanse him of
guilt. It has become a penitential wilderness rather than a field
for heroic endeavor, and this less romantic sea reflects Ten-
nyson's critical attitude toward the knights who leave Camelot
in search of the grail. Their mission is destructive, contributing

nothing to the quality of life in Camelot; most of the knights fail even at the personal level, and those who succeed do so at the cost of their social identity. Through Arthur, Tennyson endorses the values of the community and of the social landscape, rejecting the egotism of the romantic quester in the wilderness.

It has been argued by various critics that Arthur is too insipid to embody such values successfully.[18] Certainly, his civilizing mission fails in the end, and its failure may in part reflect a continuing conflict in Tennyson. It is significant that after the failure of his Telemachean effort on the shore, Arthur assumes something of the Ulysses role and commits himself to the sea. In so doing he becomes a quest hero, but whereas the other quest heroes who confronted the sea—Ulysses, Galahad, and Lancelot—hoped to bring nothing back for the society they had abandoned, Arthur's quest is linked to his social role. He becomes the god-king who journeys to the underworld in order to heal himself and so regenerate a dying civilization. Admittedly, the hope that he will return from Avilion is faint, and his own mind "is clouded with a doubt" (TW, 1753); the "great deep" may simply be a euphemism for death, the end of all social and human effort. The dark barge that takes Arthur is, above all, a ship of death, bearing him on "the long journey towards oblivion."[19]

The link between the sea and death is one that occurs frequently in Tennyson, the best-known example being undoubtedly the poem that he desired to be placed last in all editions of his works, "Crossing the Bar." In this poem there is no question of the sea representing a call to heroic action; this is "such a tide as moving seems asleep" (TW, 1458), and it offers death as a peaceful haven. One may draw a parallel between the ship in this poem, which carries the soul to its true home beyond the grave, and the "Fair ship" of In Me-

[18] Swinburne, for example, dubbed the Idylls the "Morte d'Albert," and accused Tennyson of "reducing Arthur to the level of a wittol." "Under the Microscope" (1872), in Jump, ed., Tennyson: The Critical Heritage, p. 319.
[19] Lawrence, "Ship of Death," in The Complete Poems, III, 177.

*moriam,* that "Sailest the placid ocean plains" (*TW,* 872), bringing Hallam home to his final resting place in England. In both cases the sea might be described as an antisocial landscape, since it represents a realm beyond the demands of the life of the shore. To commit oneself to the "boundless deep" may also involve the possibility of an afterlife, perhaps in the Happy Isles, or on the Isle of Avilion, or in the heaven of the Christian mystic; all of these may be seen as ultimate escapist paradises in which the ordinary problems of society are transcended or forgotten.

In some of Tennyson's early poems, the sea represented a different form of escapist paradise, more closely resembling the "kind sea-caves" of Matthew Arnold. "The Merman" and "The Mermaid" are playful evocations of such underwater havens, whose inhabitants laugh and play and kiss in what Howard Fulweiler describes as "an introspective and subjective realm of escape":[20]

> Under the hollow-hung ocean green!
> Soft are the moss-beds under the sea;
> We would live merrily, merrily.
> (TW, 194)

In "The Sea-Fairies" the erotic pleasures of this watery lotos-land are offered to weary mariners, but there is no real suggestion that these sirens are sinister and dangerous. In "The Kraken," however, Tennyson gives us an altogether different type of seascape:

> Below the thunders of the upper deep;
> Far, far beneath in the abysmal sea,
> His ancient, dreamless, uninvaded sleep
> The Kraken sleepeth: faintest sunlights flee
> About his shadowy sides: above him swell
> Huge sponges of millenial growth and height;
> And far away into the sickly light,

[20] Fulweiler, "Tennyson and the 'Summons from the Sea,' " *Victorian Poetry,* 3 (1965), 25.

From many a wondrous grot and secret cell
Unnumbered and enormous polypi
Winnow with giant arms the slumbering green.
There hath he lain for ages and will lie
Battening upon huge seaworms in his sleep,
Until the latter fire shall heat the deep;
Then once by man and angels to be seen,
In roaring he shall rise and on the surface die.

(*TW*, 247)

It is tempting to suggest that this is the same erotic world of the mermaids viewed from a different, and much sterner, angle. The Kraken, a wondrous, apocalyptic beast, lurks in the depths of the subconscious, in "the twilight world of myth in which consciousness and unconsciousness intersect."[21] Whatever interpretation we give to the poem, it is at least clear that the great deep was, for Tennyson, not merely the realm of death, but also the dwelling place of strange and terrible forms of life. Above all, it is a realm beyond man's control, where social laws are totally irrelevant. As such, it is viewed by the poet both with fascination and with a certain degree of horror.

Tennyson's feeling for the sea is revealed in comments on it in notebooks and diaries, which are more enthusiastic than his comments on mountains. Fitzgerald remembered him saying, "Somehow water is the element which I love best of all the four," and Hallam Tennyson adds that his father always had a passionate love for the sea.[22] When the poet visited Cornwall in 1848 he fell over a wall onto "fanged cobbles" in his eagerness to see the sea, and his diary has entries such as "Glorious grass-green monsters of waves," and "Saw the long green swell heaving on the black cliff."[23] Such descriptions evoke the world of "The Kraken," written years earlier,

[21] Rosenberg, "Tennyson and the Landscape of Consciousness," *Victorian Poetry*, 12 (1974), 303. See also Richard Preyer, "Tennyson as an Oracular Poet," *Modern Philology*, 55 (1958), 239-51, for a similar view.
[22] Fitzgerald, "Some Recollections of Tennyson's Talk from 1835 to 1853," p. 142.
[23] Cited by Hallam Tennyson, *A Memoir*, I, 274-76.

and point to Tennyson's continuing fascination with the terrible aspects of the deep. He could be merely dismissive about Mont Blanc, saying that the glance he gave it "did not by any means repay me for the toil of travelling to see him," but when he heard that the waves at Bude were bigger than at any other part of the British coast, he felt the need to go there and "be alone with God."[24]

Tennyson's love of the sea was no doubt partly based on happy childhood memories of the coast at Mablethorpe, although when he revisited these scenes in later life he sometimes met with disillusion. In the fragment, "Here often, when a child, I lay reclined," he contrasts his early "delight in this locality" with his present disappointment:

> And here again I come, and only find
> The drain-cut levels of the marshy lea,—
> Gray sandbanks, and pale sunsets,—dreary wind,
> Dim shores, dense rains, and heavy-clouded sea!
>
> (*TW*, 500)

The childhood magic has fled, but the bleak landscape, viewed with adult melancholy, is still a source of poetic inspiration.

Indeed, as "Break, break, break" indicates, the sea lent itself to the expression of melancholy, and was therefore a more congenial type of wilderness to a man of Tennyson's temperament. Moreover, the sea had not been subjected over the years to the mindless enthusiasm of connoisseurs of the picturesque; unlike the mountains, it had not been tainted by what Carlyle described as the "epidemic, now endemical, of Viewhunting."[25] In addition, the work of the geologists had done much to rob the mountains of their transcendental mystery. The lesson of Nature's cruel indifference is largely read in the fossils of "scarpèd cliff and quarried stone" (*TW*, 911). The hills themselves are impermanent, and therefore not fitting symbols of the Deity:

[24] Ibid., 233, 287.
[25] Carlyle, *Sartor Resartus*, p. 117.

35

The hills are shadows, and they flow
From form to form, and nothing stands;
They melt like mist, the solid lands,
Like clouds they shape themselves and go.
(*TW*, 973)

But what the hills flow into is "the stillness of the central sea"
(*TW*, 973). Since all is flux, the sea, as the primordial flux
itself, paradoxically becomes the only possible symbol of eter-
nity and stability, a conclusion that, as we shall see, was later
to be echoed by Swinburne, another great poet of the sea.
Man comes from the deep and, like the hills, he must return
to it. Moreover, as the reservoir of his most profound fears
and subconscious desires, it retained for Tennyson that aspect
of the sublime which the mountains had largely lost. It is not,
however, the realm of ordinary life, which must be lived on
the land between the mountains and the sea.

Even in the valleys and plains of this middle region there
are many landscapes that are still hostile to man, and Ten-
nyson is one of the great poets of the wasteland. Sometimes
the wasteland is a pitiless desert, such as the "land of sand
and thorns" (*TW*, 1674) in "The Holy Grail." As Percivale
rides through this desolate land, he is tormented by visions
of paradisal landscapes of great beauty and fertility:

And on I rode, and when I thought my thirst
Would slay me, saw deep lawns, and then a brook,
With one sharp rapid, where the crisping white
Played ever back upon the sloping wave,
And took both ear and eye; and o'er the brook
Were apple-trees, and apples by the brook
Fallen, and on the lawns. "I will rest here,"
I said, "I am not worthy of the Quest;"
But even while I drank the brook, and ate
The goodly apples, all these things at once
Fell into dust, and I was left alone,
And thirsting, in a land of sand and thorns.
(*TW*, 1673)

Like the tropical island of the lotos-eaters, this landscape is a snare and a delusion, tempting Percivale away from his heroic quest. But its fruit turns to dust in his hands. Earthly joys can have no reality for the man obsessed with other worldly desires. At the same time it is made clear that Percivale is not ready for a spiritual reward; his vision of a holy city also turns to dust. As John Reed comments, "like Browning's Childe Roland, Percivale is surrounded by the externalized wilderness of his own doubt."[26] However, nature is not simply seen as an extension of the human consciousness in "The Holy Grail." Even Galahad, sure of his spiritual reward, rides through a dreadful landscape of swamp and marsh that cannot be seen as "the externalized wilderness of his own doubt." Nature itself is something to be overcome; it is the hostile environment against which man must defend his spiritual identity.

This is particularly true of *The Idylls of the King*, in which a very sharp line is drawn between man's civilizing effort and the brute nature that surrounds and threatens Camelot. When Arthur becomes king he inherits a wasteland ruled by wolf, boar, and bear, and his great accomplishment is to drive back the wilderness; he "slew the beast, and felled / The forest, letting in the sun, and made / Broad pathways for the hunter and the knight" (*TW*, 1472). There is no romantic primitivism here. The forest is consistently seen as the realm of evil and the heart of darkness. This attitude is very close to that of the Greeks and the Romans. The Greek word *hyle* "denotes the chaos antecedent to the operation of Form, but literally means 'forest' "; and the Latin *silva* is seen "as original chaos and as the abode of the darker instincts."[27] In the *Idylls*, the forest is inhabited by beasts and lawless knights. It serves, as Jerome Buckley expresses it, "both as setting for personal error, passion, and self-will and as a symbol of bewilderment and frustration."[28] So, when Geraint is suffering from neurotic jealousy and mistrust of his wife, his cry is "To the wilds!" (*TW*,

[26] Reed, *Perception and Design in Tennyson's "Idylls of the King,"* p. 92.
[27] Piehler, *The Visionary Landscape*, pp. 75, 76.
[28] Buckley, *Tennyson: The Growth of a Poet*, p. 187.

1552), and it is only when they emerge from the woods into
a pastoral landscape that his heart softens toward her:

> So through the green gloom of the wood they past,
> And issuing under open heavens beheld
> A little town with towers, upon a rock,
> And close beneath, a meadow gemlike chased
> In the brown wild, and mowers mowing in it:
> And down a rocky pathway from the place
> There came a fair-haired youth, that in his hand
> Bare victual for the mowers; and Geraint
> Had ruth again on Enid looking pale.
>
> (*TW*, 1556)

There is no mistaking the relief of the "open heavens" after
the "green gloom," and the sight of a settled community and
of normal human activity acts, temporarily at least, like a
healing balm on Geraint to restore human compassion.

Even when the court, the center of civilization, is corrupt,
there is no relief to be obtained from the wild woods, no
version of the Robin Hood myth, or of the Forest of Arden.
Balin, the savage man, sees Lancelot and the Queen in the
garden, and flees from his own evil suspicions into the forest.
But there he meets the even more corrupt Vivien, and, listening
to her lies, renounces both his knighthood and his humanity:

> here I dwell
> Savage among the savage woods, here die—
> Die: let the wolves' black maws ensepulchre
> Their brother beast, whose anger was his lord.
>
> (*TW*, 1589)

Finally he is killed by and kills his own brother, thus destroy-
ing one of the most basic bonds necessary for the functioning
of any society. In the character of Balin, Tennyson comes close
to producing a Noble Savage, but his rages, though springing
from a partly justified sense of outrage, are shown to be too
undisciplined to bring about anything but his own destruction.
The woods do not offer him spiritual relief; they merely mirror

his own savagery. As Rosenberg has pointed out, "the land-scape is a spatialization of Balin's consciousness, Balin the animate point at which the landscape comes into focus."[29]

The various landscapes of the *Idylls* unite to form a remarkably orderly topography that might be arranged on a scale from the least to the most civilized, or of Nature versus Art. At one extreme are the hostile wastelands, swamps, and forests; in the middle are fertile plains and pastoral valleys; rising from the plain is the city of Camelot, an achievement of a high and complex art, a city "built / To music, therefore never built at all" (*TW*, 1491). It is the ideal city of men's aspirations, but it carries the seeds of its own destruction because it is set in total opposition to the wild nature that surrounds it. If that were all, Camelot might survive, but the enemy is also within. The beast lurks in the dark forests of the heart of man, and it is partly Arthur's failure to accommodate the beast in man that causes his whole idealistic enterprise to "Reel back into the beast, and be no more" (*TW*, 1708).

The hierarchy of beast, man, and angel is clearly set out in the sculpture that decorates the hall built by Merlin:

And in the lowest beasts are slaying men,
And in the second men are slaying beasts,
And on the third are warriors, perfect men,
And on the fourth are men with growing wings,
And over all one statue in the mould
Of Arthur, made by Merlin, with a crown,
And peaked wings pointed to the northern star.
(*TW*, 1669)

Arthur, the god-king, is depicted in angelic form, and his whole purpose is to transform men into angels, eliminating the beast altogether. No alternative to slaying is given: either man kills the beast, or the beast kills man. The framework is

[29] Rosenberg, *The Fall of Camelot*, p. 77. Clyde de L. Ryals makes the same point in *From the Great Deep*, p. 186.

too rigid to admit the possibility of compromise; if it does not succeed it must break. At least Shakespeare's Prospero sets Caliban to work, and takes ultimate responsibility for him when he declares, "this thing of darkness I / Acknowledge mine" (*The Tempest* V.i.275-76).

Camelot does not work with nature; it is, in the strictest sense, supernatural, and often has the quality of an illusion. It is a "dim rich city" (*TW*, 1668), and Arthur, seeing it wreathed in thunder-smoke, fears "lest the work by Merlin wrought, / Dreamlike, should on the sudden vanish" (*TW*, 1669). When Gareth first sees the city it has the unreal quality of a mirage:

> At times the summit of the high city flashed;
> At times the spires and turrets half-way down
> Pricked through the mist; at times the great gate shone
> Only, that opened on the field below:
> Anon, the whole fair city had disappeared.
> (*TW*, 1489)

Camelot has obvious connections with the Holy City, and like the New Jerusalem it is a city devoted to spiritual perfection. It is a "high city," its spires wreathed in the clouds. It is also, of course, a Victorian Gothic palace, and Gothic architecture takes its inspiration from natural forms: first, from the forest, with its canopy of interlocking branches, and second, from the soaring spires of the mountains. Ruskin had recognized this, and in 1853 he had taught the Victorians to see "this look of mountain brotherhood between the cathedral and the Alp."[30] Moreover, he listed "Savageness" and "Naturalism" as characteristics of the Gothic.[31] It is somewhat ironic, therefore, that Camelot, man's attempt to drive out the savage altogether, should be a Gothic rather than a cool, classical structure. With its spires and turrets in the clouds it very much resembles a distant cluster of alpine peaks, and

[30] Ruskin, *Works*, X, 188.
[31] Ibid., p. 184.

one might say that it is an attempt to redeem through Art the mountains that had lost their significance as Temples of the Infinite, or the forests of brute nature that were seen as a threat in their original form. Furthermore, the palace is decorated with the forms of the fabulous and terrifying beasts that haunt the forests. When the city is destroyed, all that remains are the fragments of these beasts, "hornless unicorns, / Cracked basilisks, and splintered cockatrices" (*TW*, 1681), amongst the ruins. Man's attempt to conquer the beast by transforming it into art has failed; the beast, instead of being slain by man, triumphs over him. The fall of Camelot has apocalyptic overtones, and Tennyson may well have intended a parallel with the fabulous beast of the apocalypse, of whom it was written: "And all that dwell upon the earth shall worship him" (Rev. 8:8).

However, the last line of the Idylls strikes a less apocalyptic note: "And the new sun rose bringing the new year" (*TW*, 1754). Camelot, the idealistic enterprise on the heights, may have failed, but Tennyson does not deny all hope. Finally, as in *The Princess* and "The Palace of Art," the call is for the soul to come down from the heights, natural or man-made, to the fertile valleys and plains. Here the wilder elements, both of nature and of man's own passions, have been subjected to some degree of control and cultivation. At the same time, the inhabitants of the pastoral valleys must work with nature rather than attempting to exclude it.

CHAPTER II

# TENNYSON: FROM ESCAPIST PARADISE TO SOCIAL LANDSCAPE

The pastoral valleys of which the shepherd sings in "Come down, O maid," imply the presence of settled communities and domestic happiness. But the younger Tennyson was strongly drawn to valleys of a more secluded nature, such as the vale of Ida in which Oenone's bower is situated. This is a place of paradisal beauty, wild, uncultivated, and remote from society, but it is not a threatening wilderness.

> Then to the bower they came,
> Naked they came to that smooth-swarded bower,
> And at their feet the crocus brake like fire,
> Violet, amaracus, and asphodel,
> Lotos and lilies: and a wind arose,
> And overhead the wandering ivy and vine,
> This way and that, in many a wild festoon
> Ran riot, garlanding the gnarlèd boughs
> With bunch and berry and flower through
> and through.
> (*TW*, 390-91)

The vines may run riot, the crocuses may flame, but they are not hostile to man. The smooth sward is kind to the naked feet of the goddesses, and the exuberant growth of ivy softens and clothes the gnarlèd boughs with festive garlands. In many respects this is an Arcadian landscape, and Douglas Bush and others have pointed out the extent of Tennyson's debt to Theocritus and Virgil.[1] Tennyson draws on the classical tra-

---

[1] Bush, *Mythology and the Romantic Tradition*, pp. 197-228. See also Mustard, *Classical Echoes in Tennyson*, and the excellent notes in Rick's edition of Tennyson.

ditions of the pastoral love-poem, with Oenone, the deserted lover, lamenting the loss of her shepherd-prince, Paris. But Oenone's bower also takes its place in a very English tradition. It looks back to Spenser and Milton, and it foreshadows the Pre-Raphaelite love-bower, overpoweringly decorated and "embroidered." Above all, it has the lush quality of Keats, and recalls such landscapes as the bower of Adonis in "Endymion":

> Above his head,
> Four lily stalks did their white honours wed
> To make a coronal, and round him grew
> All tendrils green, of every bloom and hue,
> Together intertwined and tramelled fresh:
> The vine of glossy sprout; the ivy mesh,
> Shading its Ethiop berries; and woodbine,
> Of velvet leaves and bugle-blooms divine.[2]

This has a swooning richness that overpowers consciousness and that leads on to the woodland bower in the "Ode to the Nightingale," where the connection between such luxuriance and death is made plain. In the "embalmèd darkness" of Keats's "verdurous glooms and winding mossy ways" the temptation is to be "half in love with easeful death" (*Keats*, pp. 528-29). It is a temptation that was well understood by Tennyson, but it was Keats, as George Ford points out, who "offered an example of a sort of poetry which made such an escape not only permissible but desirable."[3]

In "Oenone" Tennyson stops short of the surrender to oblivion, but the potential for death, treachery, and betrayal is hidden beneath the beauty of the Arcadian landscape; the Trojan war is inherent in the pastoral idyll. Everything in this lush and erotic setting urges Paris to reject the stern gifts of power and wisdom offered by Herè and Pallas Athene, and to choose Aphrodite's soft promise of love. The choice of love destroys love, and the deserted Oenone is left in a ruined bower:

[2] *Keats: The Complete Poems*, ed. Allott, pp. 179-80.
[3] Ford, *Keats and the Victorians*, p. 35.

They came, they cut away my tallest pines,
My tall dark pines, that plumed the craggy ledge
High over the blue gorge, and all between
The snowy peak and snow-white cataract
Fostered the callow eaglet—from beneath
Whose thick mysterious boughs in the dark morn
The panther's roar came muffled, while I sat
Low in the valley.
(*TW*, 395-96)

The removal of softening foliage transforms what had been a sensuously feminine landscape into one that is harshly masculine, its craggy ledges and snowy peaks starkly revealed.

This process is continued in "The Death of Oenone," where the fertile vale has become a wasteland, and Oenone has retreated, like the hero of "The Lover's Tale," into a cave:

Oenone sat within the cave from out
Whose ivy-matted mouth she used to gaze
Down at the Troad; but the goodly view
Was now one blank, and all the serpent vines
Which on the touch of heavenly feet had risen,
And gliding through the branches overbowered
The naked Three, were withered long ago,
And through the sunless winter morning-mist
In silence wept upon the flowerless earth.
(*TW*, 1427)

The tomblike cave revealed at the heart of what was once an idyllic landscape suggests that for Tennyson, as for Keats, the escapist paradise is closer to death than its fertility would suggest. This might be seen as a variation on the classical theme, "et ego in Arcadia," but it is, in fact, very different. Death is present not merely as the flaw in paradise, but as the desirable end to which the nineteenth-century escapist paradise is tending. This becomes clear in "The Lotos-Eaters," where a tropical island paradise offers the temptation of "dark death, or dreamful ease" (*TW*, 433).

44

I have already commented on the way in which the pictur-esque landscape of this island is subverted, denied its custom-ary strenuousness. There are barren peaks, but the lotos blooms beneath them, and they will never be climbed; there is the restless sea surrounding the island, but the melancholy Lotos-eaters treat it as a spectacle rather than a challenge:

> Only to hear and see the far-off sparkling brine,
> Only to hear were sweet, stretched out beneath the pine.
> (*TW*, 435)

The vegetation of the island is as rich as it was in the vale of Ida, but it lacks the vitality of the flamey crocuses and rioting vines of Oenone's bower. The island vines do not riot, they creep:

> Here are cool mosses deep,
> And through the moss the ivies creep,
> And in the stream the long-leaved flowers weep,
> And from the craggy ledge the poppy hangs in sleep.
> (*TW*, 432)

Time drifts slowly in this somnolent land where it seems to be always afternoon, and the Lotos-eaters are as languid as the air that swoons round them. Like the Garden of Eden, the island requires no arduous labor from its inhabitants, and offers them the perfection of unceasing fertility. But the land-scape is not totally static, and its fertility is close to decay:

> Lo! sweetened with the summer light,
> The full-juiced apple, waxing over-mellow,
> Drops in the silent autumn night.
> All its allotted length of days,
> The flower ripens in its place,
> Ripens and fades, and falls, and hath no toil,
> Fast-rooted in the fruitful soil.
> (*TW*, 433)

In fact, the land of the Lotos-eaters is about as far from Eden as it could possibly be. Eden was filled with morning light, with freshness and innocence, whereas Tennyson's island is a land of afternoon, a refuge for the jaded and the world-weary. To eat of the fruit in Eden was to fall from innocence and to enter the outside world of self-consciousness, pain, toil, and death. The weary mariners eat the Lotos in order to escape from such a world. But they do not regain innocence, and the paradise they enter is a false one with death as its most potent reward:

> All things have rest, and ripen toward the grave
> In silence; ripen, fall and cease:
> Give us long rest or death, dark death, or
> > dreamful ease.
> > (*TW*, 433)

Tennyson both desired and feared the sensuous richness of such landscapes. He could not have written such a poem had he not felt the strong pull of oblivion, but he does remain aware that the desire of the mariners for rest is self-indulgent, and in his revisions of 1842 he inserted a lengthy reminder of the society, the duties, and obligations that are being denied.

In "Tithonus" the desire for death is more profound. The first version of the poem was written after Hallam's death, and it has been described by Christopher Ricks as "Tennyson's subtlest and most beautiful exploration of the impulse to suicide."[4] Ricks's point is just, but the Tithonus myth provided Tennyson with a vehicle through which he could also express a yearning for the processes of ordinary life. The immortality of Tithonus defies the natural cycle of life and death. He decays, but cannot die, and the cruel irony of his situation is emphasized by the landscape that surrounds him:

> The woods decay, the woods decay and fall,
> The vapours weep their burthen to the ground,
> Man comes and tills the field and lies beneath,
> And after many a summer dies the swan.
> > (*TW*, 1114)

---

[4] Ricks, *Tennyson*, p. 129.

The woods, the husbandman, and the swan age like him, echoing his decay, but they at least finally have rest and "ripen toward the grave." The desire for oblivion is strong, but it is balanced by a desire that differs sharply from the easy escapism of "The Lotos-Eaters." Tithonus asks only to share the fate of "the kindly race of men"; his sharpest envy is reserved for "happy men that have the power to die," and the description of the "grassy barrows of the happier dead" contains a reminder that by giving his body to the earth man becomes part of the cycle of death and renewal. This cycle is perfectly illustrated by the role of Eos in the poem. She has eternal youth, but only because she submits to the natural process, dying each day that she may awaken each morning "with a heart renewed." There is nothing static about her immortality. Her cheek "begins to redden," her "sweet eyes brighten," her wild team of horses "arise, / And shake the darkness from their loosened manes, / And beat the twilight into flakes of fire." Each coming of the dawn is a miraculous triumph over the forces of night and death.

In the final analysis "Tithonus" is not an escapist poem; Tithonus rejects the escapism of his earlier desire for immortality and demands instead the common fate of all things. But he is condemned to wander forever in the unreal landscape of immortality:

> Here at the quiet limit of the world,
> A white-haired shadow roaming like a dream
> The ever-silent spaces of the East,
> Far-folded mists, and gleaming halls of morn.
>                    (*TW*, 1114)

Set against this is the pastoral image of men that till the fields in an infinitely enviable world of change, toil, and death. In this world steam rises from the "dim fields" in response to the coming of the dawn. Tithonus, on the other hand, trapped in the "glimmering thresholds" of eternity, remains cold even though he is bathed in the dawn's "rosy shadows."

Before he learned to envy the lives of men who toil and die,

Tennyson wrote many poems that do express a simple desire for escape. Remote Arcadian valleys and tropical or magic islands, such as the garden-isle of the Hesperides, are favorite escapist paradises.[5] Even more common is the enclosed garden, such as the "High-wallèd gardens green and old" of the "Recollections of the Arabian Nights" (*TW*, 206). These are gardens of elaborate artifice with "deep inlay / Of braided blooms," and "Imbowered vaults of pillared palm"; they are described in Tennyson's most ornate and decorative style:

> Above through many a bowery turn
> A walk with vary-coloured shells
> Wandered engrained. On either side
> All round about the fragrant marge
> From fluted vase, and brazen urn
> In order, eastern flowers large,
> Some dropping low their crimson bells
> Half-closed, and others studded wide
> With disks and tiars, fed the time
> With odour in the golden prime
> Of good Haroun Alraschid.
> (*TW*, 207)

The speaker passes through this garden into a lemon grove, where

> In closest coverture upsprung,
> The living airs of middle night
> Died round the bulbul as he sung;
> Not he: but something which possessed
> The darkness of the world, delight,
> Life, anguish, death, immortal love,
> Ceasing not, mingled, unrepressed,
> Apart from place, withholding time.
> (*TW*, 208)

[5] Stange describes the island of "The Hesperides" as "both a type of the Garden of Eden and a figure of the poet's secret life." He links it with the garden of "The Poet's Mind." "Tennyson's Garden of Art: A Study of *The Hesperides*," in *Critical Essays*, ed. Killham, p. 109.

Because the poet dwells so lovingly on the rich surface, the reader tends to accept the song of the bulbul as merely another sensuous detail, but Culler has pointed out that this song is at the heart of the poem's significance: "Thus at the center of the poem and as the true object of its quest stands, not an amorous object, but the voice of the artist."[6] The bulbul, then, would be the equivalent of Keats's nightingale, but it is significant that it sings in a dark garden rather than a woodland bower. Art, for Tennyson, is associated with culture, and there is no impulse to "fade away into the forest dim" (*Keats*, p. 526).

The image of the bulbul as the poet's soul places the gardens of "The Arabian Nights" in the same category as the gardens of the mind in such poems as "Ode to Memory" and "The Poet's Mind." In "The Arabian Nights" the garden is not yet identified as being the poet's mind; it is an exotic garden visited by the poet in imagination, in which he hears the bulbul singing of "Life, anguish, death, immortal love." In the "Ode to Memory," the poet first uses the phrase "garden of the mind" (*TW*, 211), but this garden is one largely made up of memories of the poet's youth. The speaker rejects the picturesque and exotic landscapes that he had often used in his earlier poems, presumably because they are not personal memories, but were part of his borrowings from literary sources:

> Thou comest not with shows of flaunting vines
>     Unto mine inner eye,
>     Divinest Memory!
> Thou wert not nursèd by the waterfall
> Which ever sounds and shines
>    A pillar of white light upon the wall
> Of purple cliffs, aloof descried.
>           (*TW*, 212)

Instead, he bids memory come from the woods and "The seven elms, the poplars four / That stand beside my father's door." According to Ricks, this landscape is based upon the coun-

---

[6] Culler, *The Poetry of Tennyson*, p. 33.

tryside surrounding Somersby; a second landscape of "heapèd hills that mound the sea," suggests the seacoast near Mablethorpe, and a third depicts the Somersby garden.[7] Tennyson is quite consciously making a statement about the sources of his poetic inspiration, rejecting outside influences, and rooting his poetry in his own experience. He will use the familiar landscape of Lincolnshire, sometimes bleak and flat, but often richly pastoral, rather than the more dramatic scenery of Scott and Byron;[8] he will dwell in the garden of his own mind rather than in the garden of literature. In this poem, the retreat into his own mind is made in the interests of poetic integrity; it is not really an attempt to escape from the world.

It is in "The Poet's Mind" that the garden of the mind does become a retreat from a hostile world. The "Dark-browed sophist" (TW, 224) is warned to keep away from the holy ground, a sacred enclosure hedged round with laurels. But it is a fairly short step from the garden as a fortress against the sneering critic to the garden as a prison in which all human contact is denied. "The Poet's Mind" is linked thematically with the poems in which Tennyson uses the "High-born maiden" symbol, discussed by Lionel Stevenson.[9] These poems, which include "Mariana," "The Lady of Shalott," and "The Palace of Art," all take as their central symbol the figure of a lonely maiden in a tower or palace, and in all of them there is at least a vestigial garden. In "Mariana" the garden has become a dreary wasteland, yet there are enough details to suggest that it was once the idyllic enclosed garden of a noble house. Its blackened flower-plots, neglected pear tree, and unlifted latch are desolate reminders of beauty, fruitfulness, and sociability. If, with Stevenson and Bloom, we see Mariana as a

---

[7] See Rick's notes on the poem, TW, 212-13.

[8] For descriptions of the Lincolnshire countryside, see Rawnsley, "Tennyson and Lincolnshire" in Tennyson and His Friends, ed. Tennyson; also Church, The Laureate's Country; Walters, In Tennyson Land; and Charles Tennyson, Alfred Tennyson, pp. 35-36.

[9] Stevenson, "The 'High-Born Maiden' Symbol in Tennyson," in Critical Essays, ed. Killham, pp. 126-36.

projection of the poet's own soul, then the garden of the mind that she inhabits no longer contains a crystal clear fountain like that in "The Poet's Mind"; it has become a "sluice with blackened waters" (*TW*, 189), and the imprisoned soul, instead of exulting in its romantic isolation, longs for "him" to come.[10] "Mariana" is in some respects Tennyson's most romantic poem, but it also contains the seeds of a revulsion from the egotistical sublime.

In "The Lady of Shalott," more obviously an allegory of the poetic consciousness, the gray towers "Overlook a space of flowers" (*TW*, 355); the river serves as a moat. The suggestion of an enclosed garden was even stronger in the 1832 version of the poem: "The little isle is all inrailed / With a rose-fence, and overtrailed / With roses" (*TW*, 355n.). This garden, like the world outside, is perceived by the Lady only as a reflection in the mirror. The Lady has withdrawn from the comparative openness of the garden into the innermost retreat of the tower within the garden.

"The Palace of Art" has a garden that is similarly diminished, being reduced to four lawns in each courtyard, "wherefrom / The golden gorge of dragons spouted forth / A flood of fountain-foam" (*TW*, 402). The soul is more fortunate than the Lady of Shalott, however, since she has a view of distant lands from her gallery, and she may wander from room to room viewing various landscapes depicted on the tapestried walls. Nevertheless, vivid as these tableaux are, they are one step further removed from reality than the folk that the Lady of Shalott sees reflected in her mirror, and the soul begins to feel "Deep dread and loathing of her solitude" (*TW*, 415).

In all these poems the gardens are places of isolation, imprisonment, or withdrawal; in all of them the poet identifies with a feminine persona inside the garden. Most of these gardens have a strange, fantastic quality, or are frankly sym-

---

[10] Bloom says of Mariana that she is "a poetess and she sings a Dejection Ode that Tennyson scarcely ventured to write in his own person. Her disease is Romantic self-consciousness, and no bridegroom can come to heal her." *The Ringers in the Tower*, p. 148.

bolic of the mind, whereas real gardens are usually attached
to houses and are therefore part of the social fabric. In these
early poems the garden is an antisocial enclosure in which the
soul suffers the imprisonment of solipsism. Later, Tennyson
shifts his perspective: instead of identifying with the maiden
in the tower/garden, he identifies with the lover outside, who
tries to end the romantic isolation by breaking into the en-
closure. This entails a different view of the garden: it is now
a social fact, usually attached to a great house, and the drama
enacted within it is social rather than metaphysical.

"Margaret," although somewhat saccharine, is an interest-
ing transitional poem. It goes beyond its companion poem,
"Adeline," in giving an active role to the speaker, who be-
comes the lover pleading with the maiden to break her iso-
lation:

> O sweet pale Margaret,
> O rare pale Margaret,
> Come down, come down, and hear me speak:
> Tie up the ringlets on your cheek:
>  The sun is just about to set,
>  The arching limes are tall and shady,
>   And faint, rainy lights are seen,
>    Moving in the leavy beech.
> Rise from the feast of sorrow, lady,
>   Where all day long you sit between
>    Joy and woe, and whisper each.
> Or only look across the lawn,
>   Look out below your bower-eaves,
> Look down, and let your blue eyes dawn
>   Upon me through the jasmine-leaves.
>            (*TW*, 456)

The garden is seen as a neutral zone between the maiden's
enclosure and the world outside; it has been entered by the
lover, but he seems unable to climb to the bower eaves where
his lady luxuriates in her sorrow, and the final barrier must
be broken by Margaret herself. His call to her to "Come

down" is echoed later in both *The Princess* ("Come down, O Maid,") and in *Maud* ("Come into the garden, Maud"). The garden in "Margaret" is still without real social significance, however, since we are told nothing about the lady's or the lover's circumstances.

These circumstances are less vague in "Oh! That 'Twere Possible," which was later revised and included in *Maud*. In both versions of the poem the lovers meet in the garden:

Alas for her that met me,
That heard me softly call—
Came glimmering through the laurels
At the quiet even-fall,
In the garden by the turrets
Of the old Manorial Hall.
(*TW*, 600)

Here the social context that was to be so richly filled out in *Maud* is present in embryo. The garden has become the adjunct of the Manorial Hall, a symbol of the exclusive power of wealth and birth, and the secret assignation suggests that the lover is a socially unacceptable intruder.

This view of the garden as linked to social status is in some respects a return to a traditional concept. Paul Piehler describes the enclosed garden of medieval allegory as a "symbol of social exclusiveness," and adds that such a garden "thus became for a number of reasons the natural symbol of the private morality of an exclusive class."[11] A more positive version of this concept is to be found in Pope's garden poems. These are partly in the "retirement" tradition, going back through Andrew Marvell to the Roman poets; but Pope's ideal, embodied in "The Epistle to Burlington," is not merely of the garden as a recovery of pastoral or prelapsarian innocence, but as an expression of high civilization, good taste, humane values, and correct philosophical principles. Pope's own house, garden, and grotto at Twickenham were, as May-

---

[11] Piehler, *The Visionary Landscape*, pp. 101, 105.

nard Mack writes, an expression of "the poet's sense of himself as spokesman for an idealized community, a way of life, a point of view."[12] The way of life is essentially aristocratic, and it is as an accepted member of that world that Pope offers advice to the Earl of Burlington.

The hero of *Maud*, on the other hand, reflects the aspirations and bitterness of a more democratic age, and perhaps some of the personal bitterness of the man who was not considered good enough for Rosa Baring, and who had to wait many years for Emily Sellwood.[13] Tennyson's protagonist is the outsider who must stand at the garden gate because he is "nameless and poor" (*TW*, 1049). He is also the romantic rebel who would break down the social hierarchy, enter the enclosed garden, and proclaim the primacy of passion over economic privilege. He wishes to detach the garden from its social background, and to recreate it as a paradise of primal innocence. This attempt to recover Eden is expressed in lyrics such as "Come into the garden, Maud" (*TW*, 1075), and "Maud has a garden of roses" (*TW*, 1064). Alas, Eden has become private property, and the speaker can only recover it in imagination by deliberately ignoring the fact that Maud's garden really belongs to her brother, the "Sultan," whose nickname reminds us that death was the usual punishment accorded to intruders.

This modern Sultan grants access to his garden only to the wealthy. The new lord who has come to woo Maud gains admission with money from coal mines, so that instead of representing the pastoral retreat of the unworldly, the garden has become the crowning reward of the industrial capitalist. It may be said that Tennyson is merely exposing the reality behind the myth, and that even in Pope's age gardens had been built with wealth acquired at the expense of a dispossessed peasantry. As Raymond Williams points out, the land-

---

[12] Mack, *The Garden and the City*, p. 9.
[13] For an excellent account of *Maud* as autobiography, see Rader, *Tennyson's "Maud": The Biographical Genesis*.

scape gardeners of the eighteenth century created "a rural landscape emptied of rural labour and of labourers."[14]

If, in *Maud*, the garden has become the exclusive preserve of the rich, the lovers can at least retire to the wild woodland outside the enclosure. The "woody hollows in which we meet" now become "the valleys of Paradise" (*TW*, 1077). But even this Eden fails, because behind the wood is "the dreadful hollow" and its ledges "drip with a silent horror of blood" (*TW*, 1040). The wood is a place of violence; its freedom from unjust human laws or social codes means that the even harsher law of nature prevails:

> For nature is one with rapine, a harm no preacher can heal;
> The Mayfly is torn by the swallow, the sparrow speared by the shrike,
> And the whole little wood where I sit is a world of plunder and prey.
> (*TW*, 1049)

Such an environment can only provide a temporary and very dangerous retreat for the lovers.

Although Tennyson's sympathies are with these lovers in their battle against society, one is reminded that in other poems less innocent lovers meet in the woods; it is there that Vivien seduces Merlin, and that Pelleas sees and falls in love with the haughty and corrupt Ettarre. In the *Idylls* in particular, the woods are most often the realm of corrupt sensuality and lawless passion. Even in an early poem, "A Dream of Fair Women," the woodland bower is seen as a sinister place. The dreamer in this poem wanders into a wood in which "Growths of jasmine turn'd / Their humid arms festooning tree to tree" (*TW*, 444). An excess of fertility has produced its own antidote, and the forest is so covered with vines that the "Gross darkness of the inner sepulchre / Is not so deadly still." In this tomblike atmosphere the dreamer sees Helen, Cleopatra, and

---

[14] Williams, *The Country and the City*, p. 125.

others, all of whom recount their tragedies of violence and passion.

The hero of *Maud* would really prefer the safety of the garden to the dubious haven offered by the woods; he wants his romantic love to be given social sanction. This is strongly implied in the serenely beautiful lyric, "I have led her home, my love, my only friend" (*TW*, 1067), in which the images suggest the calm fulfillment of domestic happiness rather than the excitement of passion:

> And never yet so warmly ran my blood
> And sweetly, on and on
> Calming itself to the long-wished-for end,
> Full to the banks, close on the promised good.
>
> (*TW*, 1067)

The garden to which Maud has been led is yet another Eden, where the cedar sighs for its "Forefathers of the thornless garden" (*TW*, 1068), but the achievement of Paradise is fleeting; modern gardens are not "thornless," and bliss gives way to "some dark undercurrent woe" (*TW*, 1070). Man cannot recreate Eden in a garden that is part of the social world, and therefore subject to the laws of that world. It is also part of the larger, natural world, and must obey Nature's laws, too. If Nature is "red in tooth and claw," then its fangs will show, even in the garden.

Indeed, many of the gardens in *Maud*, though beautiful and desirable, carry sinister overtones of blood and violence. This is partly achieved through the symbolism inherent in the flowers. As E.D.H. Johnson points out, Tennyson exploits the traditional associations of lily and rose with purity and passion, but as the poem progresses the rose comes to symbolize "not only the passion of love, but also the violence to which ... that passion had been tending from the outset."[15] Not only do the roses frequently suggest blood; the birds and

[15] Johnson, "The Lily and the Rose: Symbolic Meaning in Tennyson's *Maud*," *PMLA*, 64 (1949), 1,225.

flowers assume an anthropomorphic quality that is very threatening. The birds in the Hall-garden call a warning or a threat to Maud when she meets her lover in the woods. The flowers in Section xxii hear the music of the ball, and are addressed by the hero; they have a foreknowledge of events that destroys any suggestion of primal innocence:

> The red rose cries, "She is near, she is near;"
>   And the white rose weeps, "She is late;"
> The larkspur listens, "I hear, I hear;"
>   And the lily whispers, "I wait."
>                         (*TW*, 1077)

One may object that this is merely an extreme form of the pathetic fallacy, and that the speaker is projecting his disturbed mental state onto his surroundings, but the fact remains that the garden does not provide the hero with a retreat, either from the world or from his own psychosis. Again and again he attempts to see the garden as a refuge, but each time disturbing suggestions enter and gradually destroy his paradise. In Section xiv he starts with flat, simple statements that operate at the level of cliché to create an idyll: "Maud has a garden of roses / And lilies fair on a lawn" (*TW*, 1064). This is followed almost immediately by his exclusion from the garden as he stands "by her garden gate," and by the violent passion implicit in the motif over the gate: "A lion ramps at the top, / He is clasped by a passion flower." The idyll is further shattered by the mention of Maud's brother and his "roystering company," and by the speaker's doubts about Maud's affection. Finally, he sees the "death-white curtain drawn" round the house, and feels a horror creep over himself. Later, in his madness, the speaker remembers Maud's garden as beautiful but sterile, and the roses have turned to blood:

> But I know where a garden grows,
> Fairer than aught in the world beside,
> All made up of the lily and rose
> That blow by night, when the season is good,

To the sound of dancing music and flutes:
It is only flowers, they had no fruits,
And I almost fear they are not roses, but blood.
(TW, 1089)

What emerges from Maud is a very interesting paradox. We are constantly reminded that the garden is an attempt to recreate Eden. These reminders firmly establish it as potentially the ideal landscape. But in actuality, the various gardens of the poem are all less than Edenic because they are seen as part of an imperfect world in which, as James Kincaid expresses it, "Eden is beyond recall."[16] Tennyson has sacrificed the idyllic quality of the garden, but he has gained immeasurably in the richness of suggestion now invested in this ancient symbol.

The gardens of "Aylmer's Field" and "Enoch Arden" also exploit this wider social resonance, and they explore the same basic theme of the intruder in the garden. In "Aylmer's Field" the garden is first seen as the paradise of childhood in which Leolin

Had tost his ball and flown his kite, and rolled
His hoop to pleasure Edith, with her dipt
Against the rush of air in the prone swing,
Made blossom-ball or daisy-chain, arranged
Her garden, sowed her name and kept it green
In living letters, told her fairy-tales.
(TW, 1163)

But as they emerge from childhood, differences in social status and wealth disrupt the idyll, and the garden becomes a place where the lovers can make a "perilous meeting under the tall pines / That darkened all the northward of her Hall" (TW, 1171).

Leolin, exiled as a law student in London, sometimes gains solace as he walks in the Temple gardens, "the gardens of that rival rose" (TW, 1172), but the reminder that this is the

[16] Kincaid, Tennyson's Major Poems, p. 125.

garden in which the red and white roses of the warring houses of York and Lancaster were picked, hardly acts as a consoling thought. Meanwhile Edith is a virtual prisoner, "Kept to the garden now, and grove of pines" (*TW*, 1175). After the deaths of Edith and Leolin, disaster overtakes the family, and the once proud and exclusive garden becomes the domain of the humblest creatures:

Then the great Hall was wholly broken down,
And the broad woodland parcelled into farms;
And where the two contrived their daughter's good,
Lies the hawk's cast, the mole has made his run,
The hedgehog underneath the plantain bores,
The rabbit fondles his own harmless face,
The slow-worm creeps, and the thin weasel there
Follows the mouse, and all is open field.
(*TW*, 1183)

The transformation of the enclosed garden into the open field represents a breakdown in civilization that is in some respects analogous to the triumph of the wilderness over Camelot. But the civilization represented by the Hall in "Aylmer's Field" enshrined no high ideals, and the wild animals that usurp the ancient family seat are fairly harmless creatures that bear little resemblance to the "beast" of the *Idylls*. The poles of Art and Nature are still present in "Aylmer's Field," but they have been scaled down, and in a world where Art is represented by corrupt social values based on a materialistic law of the jungle, then Nature can be seen to be preferable. On a lesser scale, however, the animals that inherit the Hall and garden will continue the predatory traditions of its former owners, with hawk set against rabbit, and the weasel pursuing the mouse. The conclusion to the poem invites comparison with the projected fate of Timon's villa in Pope's "Epistle to Burlington":

Another age shall see the golden Ear
Imbrown the Slope, and nod on the Parterre,

Deep Harvests bury all his pride has plann'd,
And laughing Ceres re-assume the Land.[17]

But Pope allows a rich pastoralism to triumph; Tennyson's
ending is not so optimistic.

In "Enoch Arden" the intruder in the garden is the returned
husband instead of the socially unacceptable lover. Enoch
Arden watches the domestic idyll of his wife and children with
his rival and successor, Philip, from the darkness of a bleak
little garden:

but behind,
With one small gate that opened on the waste,
Flourished a little garden square and walled:
And in it throve an ancient evergreen,
A yewtree, and all round it ran a walk
Of shingle, and a walk divided it:
But Enoch shunned the middle walk and stole
Up by the wall, behind the yew.
(*TW*, 1147)

Unlike Maud's garden of roses and lilies, this garden is
devoid of any erotic overtones, unless we take the single yew
tree as a phallic symbol. However, it is more likely to be a
symbol of the husband's lonely endurance and exclusion from
the happiness within the house, and may be compared with
the single poplar that Mariana sees from her casement, which
"gnarled and alone on the level waste, encapsulates her spir-
itual isolation."[18] The single yew is also a symbol of the social
law of monogamy that makes it impossible for Enoch Arden
to reveal himself to his wife. He cannot even call to her to
come to him in the garden, but must shun the middle walk
and steal along the wall like a thief in the night. This "little
garden square and walled" offers no generous shrubberies or
winding lanes for clandestine meetings. It is a formal garden,

[17] Pope, *Poetical Works*, ed. Davis, p. 320.
[18] Lourie, "Below the Thunders of the Upper Deep: Tennyson as Romantic
Revisionist," *Studies in Romanticism*, 18, No. 1 (1979), 16.

scaled down both to the social position of its owners, and also to the rather smug exclusiveness of narrow domestic propriety.

In at least two poems the intruder succeeds in winning the maiden. The first is "The Day-Dream," a version of the Sleeping Beauty fairy tale. The second, which is more interesting because it has a contemporary setting, is "The Gardener's Daughter." In this poem Tennyson creates the kind of Eden that consistently eluded the hero of *Maud*, but he does it largely by ignoring all social facts. One may presume that a gardener's daughter does not occupy a forbiddingly high position in society, but in any case no mention is made of either her status or of the hero's. No parents or brothers interfere in this romantic and accessible garden, which blooms "Not wholly in the busy world, nor quite / Beyond it" (*TW*, 510). Such a degree of remoteness perfectly expresses Tennyson's ideal, and it is also the ideal behind the creation of the garden suburb. Sufficiently isolated to provide a retreat, and to be free of the world's artificial social standards, this garden is still within reach of human company:

News from the humming city comes to it
In sound of funeral or of marriage bells;
And, sitting muffled in dark leaves, you hear
The windy clanging of the minster clock;
Although between it and the garden lies
A league of grass, washed by a slow broad stream,
That, stirred with languid pulses of the oar,
Waves all its lazy lilies, and creeps on,
Barge-laden, to three arches of a bridge
Crowned with the minster-towers.
(*TW*, 510)

Idyllic and pastoral, this is no retreat in the deep solitude of the embowering woods, such as Keats or Rossetti would have sought for their lovers. The sounds of the humming city enhance rather than disturb its peaceful quality, and provide the security of a settled, organized community close at hand.

61

On a scale of romantic passion, this garden occupies a place midway between those of *Maud* and that of "Enoch Arden." The gardens in *Maud* are more romantic but less secure. Instead of the chimes of the minster clock that provides hourly reminders of a sanely ordered communal life, the hero of *Maud* hears from his "own dark garden" the sounds of "the tide in its broad-flung shipwrecking roar" and "the scream of a maddened beach dragged down by a wave" (*TW*, 1048). At the other extreme is the unromantic garden of "Enoch Arden," which has its position in a tightly knit community of properly married couples who know each other's business. Its geometric regularity does not admit the turbulence of passion.

Whereas in "Enoch Arden" marriage figures prominently, in "The Gardener's Daughter" an idyll is achieved by cultivating ambiguity in everything relating to social and economic laws. Most critics assume that the hero marries the gardener's daughter, but marriage is never mentioned in the poem. Certainly, she gives herself to him, and it may seem most unlikely that Tennyson would celebrate an illicit love affair, but at that point when the affair would have become respectable and subject to social approval, the poet draws a veil of vagueness across the story. He speaks of "meetings, of farewells" (*TW*, 520), and of "difference, reconcilement, pledges given, / And vows, where there was never need of vows, / And kisses" (*TW*, 521), but of nothing that is specific to marriage. Nor do the last lines really settle anything, except that the relationship lasted for some time:

My first, last love; the idol of my youth,
The darling of my manhood, and, alas!
Now the most blessed memory of mine age.
(*TW*, 521)

Whether we are right or not in assuming that he married her, it would seem that marriage was too harsh a social and economic fact for the poet to risk mentioning it specifically. The garden is too fragile an Eden to bear the weight of a social system. Tennyson's omissions are particularly interesting if

62

one accepts Rader's view that Rose, the gardener's daughter, was based on Rosa Baring.[19] The poet would have had good reason to ignore the barriers that existed in reality between himself and an idyllic union with Rosa.

It is perhaps because it is not seen as part of a social system involving marriage that the Somersby garden can evoke such happy memories in *In Memoriam*. In lyric CII the poet takes leave of the beloved place in which his "boyhood sung / Long since its matin song," and in which he wandered with his "lost friend among the bowers" (*TW*, 955). It is also in this garden that the poet has one of his most significant experiences of Hallam, described in lyric XCV. In this section the garden setting is carefully exploited:

By night we lingered on the lawn,
  For underfoot the herb was dry;
  And genial warmth; and o'er the sky
The silvery haze of summer drawn;

And calm that let the tapers burn
  Unwavering: not a cricket chirred:
  The brook alone far-off was heard,
And on the board the fluttering urn.
                              (*TW*, 945)

The calm tranquillity of the summer evening, its "genial warmth," and "silvery haze," all contribute to that peace of soul in the poet which is a necessary prerequisite for communion with the dead. At the same time, there is a reassuring sense of human companionship and normal activity; this garden is not an introspective realm of grief into which the poet has withdrawn. The emphasis is on "we," and the homely mention of the "fluttering urn" and the burning tapers suggests the proximity of domestic comforts. Nor is the poet so absorbed in his grief that he cannot join in the hearty singing of "old songs that pealed / From knoll to knoll," while "couched

---

[19] Rader, *Tennyson's "Maud,"* pp. 30-31. Ricks takes the same view in his notes on the poem, *TW*, 507-508.

at ease, / The white kine glimmered." The garden impercep-
tibly blends with the surrounding pastoral landscape. When
his companions withdraw, it is with a quiet tact that contrib-
utes to the overall sense of calm:

> But when those others, one by one,
>   Withdrew themselves from me and night,
>   And in the house light after light
> Went out, and I was all alone.
> (TW, 946)

The perfect setting and the right frame of mind in the poet
have been created for the mystical experience that follows, in
which "The living soul was flashed on mine." Then, returning
from this ecstatic communion in a cosmic landscape of "em-
pyreal heights," the poet becomes aware once more of the
glimmering cows and the dark trees. These lines (51-52) are
an exact repetition of lines 14 and 15, thus enclosing his
supernatural experience within a frame of quiet, unchanging,
pastoral nature. But immediately afterwards, the garden seems
to vibrate in sympathy with him as the dawn trembles into
life:

> And sucked from out the distant gloom
>   A breeze began to tremble o'er
>   The large leaves of the sycamore,
> And fluctuate all the still perfume,
>
> And gathering freshlier overhead,
>   Rocked the full-foliaged elms, and swung
>   The heavy-folded rose, and flung
> The lilies to and fro, and said
>
> "The dawn, the dawn," and died away;
>   And East and West, without a breath,
>   Mixt their dim lights, like life and death,
> To broaden into boundless day.
> (TW, 947)

The rose in this passage is not used as a symbol of sexual
passion. Its "still perfume" has contributed to the hushed

mystique of the night, and its "heavy-folded" bud promises new life. The Somersby garden was associated by Tennyson with his childhood and with his friendship for Hallam. It has no disturbing erotic overtones, and it does not have to take account of social status, marriage, or economics; it can therefore be seen as an Edenic landscape, although suffused with the nostalgia of lost happiness.

In associating Hallam with such an idyllic landscape Tennyson is building on the traditions of the pastoral elegy, a fact that has been recognized by various critics.[20] It should be stressed, however, that Tennyson's Golden Age does not exist in some mythical past but in the years he shared with Hallam. Moreover, the landscape need not be Arcadian in any traditional sense in order to be sanctified by memory:

I climb the hill: from end to end
Of all the landscape underneath,
I find no place that does not breathe
Some gracious memory of my friend.
(*TW*, 953)

[20] Arthur J. Carr summarizes the traditional elements to be found in *In Memoriam*: "It opens with a formal invocation to a higher power and closes with an epithalamium. It describes the funeral procession (the voyage of the ship returning Hallam's body to England) and the mourning of nature, which is a kind of death. The poet himself represents the mourners. In accordance with the sophisticated tradition of the elegy, Tennyson launches forth on sober and noble themes, both personal and general, concerning the meaning of history, the nature of nature, and his personal destiny as man and as poet. The poem draws to a close with a lengthy apotheosis that dismisses the mood of grief, settles the perplexities, and issues upon a higher plane." "Tennyson as a Modern Poet," in *Critical Essays*, ed. Killham, p. 61. Priestley sees "the traditional classical elegiac form" as being the core of *In Memoriam; Language and Structure in Tennyson's Poetry*, p. 120. Sendry argues for close links between two great elegies in " 'In Memoriam' and 'Lycidas,' " *PMLA*, 82 (1967), 437-43. However, Bradley says the conventions of the classical pastoral elegy "occur in *In Memoriam* only here and there, and perhaps generally with a jarring effect": *A Commentary on Tennyson's "In Memoriam,"* p. 102; and Pattison states that although Tennyson uses the convention, he sees the pastoral "as a restricting form that, even at the price of suffering, must be overcome": *Tennyson and Tradition*, p. 118.

Even the bleakest landscape, the "gray old grange," the "low morass," or "sheepwalk up the windy wold" is blessed because it "reflects a kindlier day." In themselves such landscapes are nothing. "Their consolation," as David Shaw writes, "does not depend on the successful transfer of a quality from landscapes to the mind."[21] Even the Somersby garden must draw its quality from being loved and watched by those who can bring the richness of association to it, as Tennyson makes clear in lyric CI, "Unwatched, the garden bough shall sway" (*TW*, 954). Somersby only becomes a "sacramental landscape"[22] because it has an intensely personal significance for Tennyson. For this reason it remains an essentially private landscape, closer in some respects to the early escapist gardens than to the gardens of *Maud* or "Enoch Arden"; it cannot be made to reflect a wider social or political reality.

It is in *The Princess* that the garden attains its highest development as an embodiment of social and political values. The poem is set in a garden frame, with the story of Princess Ida being recounted by a group of young people in Sir Walter Vivian's park on a fine summer's day. The park is, of course, an aristocratic preserve, but it has been made democratic, at least temporarily, by being thrown open to the local populace for the day. For this brief period the garden represents the possibilities of social harmony, and of inclusion rather than exclusion. In addition, the garden contains many fossils and other natural curiosities as ornaments, so that the wilderness too is represented, but controlled, and the "images of nature's awesome destructive power are thus made safe and manageable in the domestic atmosphere."[23] Nor is the machine excluded from this garden: amidst the rolling lawns and Gothic ruins are mechanical fountains, mock cannons, telescopes, steamboats, and other contrivances to amuse and instruct the populace. Such events were fairly common during the 1840s,

[21] Shaw, *Tennyson's Style*, p. 141.
[22] Ibid., p. 141.
[23] Kincaid, *Tennyson's Major Poems*, p. 78.

and Killham gives an account of the festivals organized by various mechanics' institutions, one of which, held at the country estate of Edmund Lushington, was attended by Tennyson himself. The festivals "were not only intended to provide rational amusement, 'the diffusion of the most useful knowledge,' but also to further 'the promotion of better feelings among all classes.' "[24]

In the conclusion to the poem the garden setting is deliberately given a political significance:

> So I and some went out to these: we climbed
> The slope to Vivian-place, and turning saw
> The happy valleys, half in light, and half
> Far-shadowing from the west, a land of peace;
> Gray halls alone among their massive groves;
> Trim hamlets; here and there a rustic tower
> Half-lost in belts of hop and breadths of wheat;
> The shimmering glimpses of a stream; the seas;
> A red sail, or a white; and far beyond,
> Imagined more than seen, the skirts of France.
> "Look there, a garden!" said my college friend,
> The Tory member's elder son, "and there!
> God bless the narrow sea which keeps her off,
> And keeps our Britain, whole within herself,
> A nation yet, the rulers and the ruled—."
> (*TW*, 842-43)

The peace and harmony of this view of rural England as a garden should not blind us to the fact that the philosophy expressed is not merely conservative, but fairly authoritarian, and that it entrenches social inequality. The garden is used here as an image of order and the preservation of the status quo; it has nothing in common with the romantic gardens of escape in Tennyson's early poems, or the erotic gardens of *Maud*. The "gray halls" stand almost like fortresses amidst their "massive groves," dominating the pastoral landscape in

[24] Killham, *Tennyson and "The Princess,"* p. 59.

which "trim hamlets" know their place. This is indeed a land of "rulers and the ruled," and the symbolic opening of the park on one day a year is a small concession to democracy. The poet, however, takes a more progressive view than the Tory member's son; he sees in this one day of openness a possible pattern for the future: "For me, the genial day, the happy crowd, / The sport half-science, fill me with a faith" (*TW*, 843).

Within this frame of the aristocratic garden is the even more exclusive feminist garden created by the Princess Ida. This garden is first invaded by the prince and his friends disguised as women, and then thrown open by Ida herself for use as a hospital. The bridegroom has to come, not as a conquering knight, but either in the form of a woman, or as an invalid. Even the poetic plea, "Come down, O Maid," is spoken by Ida herself. Although many unfair pressures are brought to bear on the princess, finally her garden must be surrendered, not invaded. This marks a radical difference between *The Princess* and some of the other poems in which the isolated maiden theme appears. The garden in *The Princess* is not dominated by father, husband, or brother; it is not part of the social fabric. It is a romantic garden representing Ida's own heroic resolve, a symbol of her high, if perhaps mis-guided, purpose, and therefore it is she who must open its gates. Ida is closer to the Lady of Shalott than to Maud. In coming down from the heights, however, she kills not herself, but her woman's college.

The Lady of Shalott is lured away by the bold and assertive sexuality of Sir Lancelot. Ida is won by a pity for the sick prince that reveals her own womanly tenderness to herself. Her sexual awakening is expressed in the delicate eroticism of a "garden poem" that she herself reads to the prince in low tones. This famous lyric suggests tender sensuality and the fulfillment of surrender:

> Now sleeps the crimson petal, now the white;
> Nor waves the cypress in the palace walk;

Nor winks the gold fin in the porphyry font:
The fire-fly wakens: waken thou with me.

Now droops the milkwhite peacock like a ghost,
And like a ghost she glimmers on to me.

Now lies the Earth all Danaë to the stars,
And all thy heart lies open unto me.

Now slides the silent meteor on, and leaves
A shining furrow, as thy thoughts in me.

Now folds the lily all her sweetness up,
And slips into the bosom of the lake:
So fold thyself, my dearest, thou, and slip
Into my bosom and be lost in me.

(TW, 834-35)

The gardens of *The Princess* fit one inside the other like a nest of Chinese boxes. We pass from the outer, political garden of the frame to Ida's more personal but ideological garden, until we finally penetrate to the erotic center in the garden of this lyric.

Ida's surrender, finally, is neither violent nor forced. Its quality is conveyed in the gentle verbs of the lyric: things slide and slip into each other, or droop and glimmer. They lie open, but also fold up: they sleep, and waken, with a slow rhythm that culminates in the fulfillment of "be lost in me." By contrast, the roses in Maud's garden are busy, wakeful, and knowing, denied the rich peace that is suggested in the sleeping petals of crimson and white. However, although suggestive of a new mood in Ida, the lyric is not part of the narrative, and the garden it describes has no existence outside the imagination. As a "happy garden" it exists rather in hope for the future than in present achievement, and the seductive promise of the lyric must be balanced against Ida's sense of failure in her high mission. We cannot make the easy assumption that Eden has been achieved, because we are too well aware of what has been sacrificed. In this respect, the garden of the lyric resembles the limited achievement of the garden that frames the poem, which on one day a year symbolizes a harmonious and open society.

The movement in Tennyson from the garden of the mind to the garden of the country estate is a movement toward a social landscape from one of romantic isolation. For many critics this represents a betrayal on Tennyson's part of his romantic inheritance and of his "true" nature as a poet. Harold Bloom writes that the "Tennyson who counts for most . . . is certainly a Romantic poet," and he traces the "conflict in Tennyson's earlier poetry between a Romantic imagination and an emergent societal censor."[25] What I have traced in Tennyson's use of the garden as a locus is, however, not an emerging societal censor but an increasing awareness of social complexity. The escapist gardens of the early poems are fascinating products of the romantic imagination, and Mariana's wasted garden must remain one of the most haunting images in Tennyson's poetry. But there is a sense in which those early gardens are one-dimensional. They lack the resonance of the gardens in *Maud*, for example, where the traditional image of the garden as Eden is played off against the poet's awareness that the garden is part of both nature and of the social structure, partaking of the violence of one and the corruption of the other. Such a view of the garden has nothing to do with social censorship, the Victorian compromise, or a timid retreat from romanticism.

Other poets before Tennyson had seen the garden as a microcosm of society. But the tendency had been to use the garden for the purposes of overt moralizing; this is what hap-

---

[25] Bloom, *Ringers in the Tower*, pp. 146, 147. Bloom is echoing the judgment of Harold Nicolson that Tennyson was forced to "trim his sails to the vacillating breezes of public taste"; *Tennyson: Aspects of His Life, Character and Poetry*, p. 229. Buckley, on the other hand, rejects the distinction between the public and private Tennyson: "from the beginning he felt some responsibility to the society he lived in, and until the end he remained obedient to the one clear call of his own imagination"; *Tennyson: The Growth of a Poet*, p. 255.

pens in the famous garden passage in *Richard II* (III.iv), for example, and Pope quite deliberately uses the garden to teach a lesson on the proper use of riches. Tennyson avoids such overt moralizing;[26] his gardens are simply used as settings in various poems. But in each case, the nature of the garden itself suggests, with great subtlety, much about the kind of society of which it forms a part, and embodies many of the conflicts in that society. This represents a significant development in the use of landscape in poetry, and in particular, in the use of that enduring symbol, the garden.

[26] With some exceptions, of course. The references to gardens in "Locksley Hall Sixty Years After" are more overtly moralizing. Here Tennyson links the taming of the landscape with the killing of "every serpent passion" in man, and yearns for a state in which "every grim ravine" has been transformed into a garden. He also places a garden on the planet Venus, and speculates that it, being closer to the sun, may be a "world of never fading flowers" (*TW*, 1366). Eden, taking advantage of the new astronomy, has been transferred to another planet; such a transfer no doubt reflects Tennyson's increasing pessimism about the possibility of achieving paradise on earth.

CHAPTER III

# ARNOLD:
# THE FOREST GLADE

To turn from a consideration of Tennyson's landscapes to those of Matthew Arnold is to recognize immediately that Arnold is a more limited figure. Tennyson takes the landscape of isolation through to its logical conclusion: the dreary wasteland of Mariana's self-absorption. At the other end of the spectrum he gives us the landscape of social significance: the country estate thrown open to the public, symbolic at once of aristocratic privilege and democratic progress. Arnold's landscapes fall between these two extremes; they are never as bleak in their solitude, and when his protagonist abandons that solitude (as in the "Obermann" poems) it is not in order to create a landscape that reflects society. As a man, Arnold committed himself to the struggle in society in a very practical manner, but as a poet, his constant desire is to escape, even temporarily, from a world in which he feels himself to be an alien, to some green, sequestered spot where he might reestablish, through the healing powers of Nature, contact with his own deepest being.

His debt to Wordsworth is obvious, but he was not merely a disciple. "Throughout a long and varied career," writes Leon Gottfried, "Matthew Arnold never tired of admiring, criticizing, imitating, and rebelling against William Wordsworth."[1] He took much from Wordsworth, but he developed his own particular brand of romanticism. Although Arnold's attitudes are complex and variable, he did tend, like Tennyson, to move away from the sublime and the picturesque, rejecting the stern-

[1] Gottfried, *Matthew Arnold and the Romantics*, p. 6. Arnold's debt to Wordsworth has been discussed by many critics. See, for example, Jamison, *Arnold and the Romantics*, pp. 30-57, and James, *Matthew Arnold and the Decline of English Romanticism*, pp. 30-56.

72

er aspects of romanticism but preserving a love for the softer,
although still romantic, landscapes of refuge and retreat.

He shared Wordsworth's deep love of the English country-
side, and had spent many hours roaming the hills surrounding
Fox How, the family home in the Lake District. His tribute
to Wordsworth in "The Youth of Nature" is also a tribute to
the beauty of the scenery they both knew so well:

Raised are the dripping oars,
Silent the boat! the lake,
Lovely and soft as a dream,
Swims in the sheen of the moon.
The mountains stand at its head
Clear in the pure June-night,
But the valleys are flooded with haze.
Rydal and Fairfield are there;
In the shadow Wordsworth lies dead.
So it is, so it will be for aye.
Nature is fresh as of old,
Is lovely; a mortal is dead.[2]

One cannot doubt Arnold's feeling for the quiet beauty of the
landscape, but the passage invites comparison and contrast
with the famous episode in *The Prelude*, also involving a boat,
lake, and mountains:

When from behind that craggy steep till then
The horizon's bound, a huge peak, black and huge,
As if with voluntary power instinct
Upreared its head. I struck and struck again,
And growing still in stature the grim shape
Towered up between me and the stars, and still,
For so it seemed, with purpose of its own
And measured motion like a living thing,
Strode after me.
    (I.377-85)

[2] *The Poems of Matthew Arnold*, ed. Allott, pp. 259-60. Hereafter cited
as *AW* with page numbers.

Wordworth's landscape is sublime, and the huge mountain peak strikes awe into the heart of the boy; Arnold's mountains are merely beautiful; no terrible "voluntary power" attaches to them, and nowhere in his poetry are they invested with such power. Moreover, the Wordsworth most admired and praised by Arnold is not the Wordsworth of this passage from *The Prelude*, but a less sublime poet whose calm serenity is reflected in the landscape of Arnold's "The Youth of Nature."[3] His "soothing voice" is heard in "Memorial Verses" as the voice of one who

> laid us as we lay at birth
> On the cool flowery lap of earth,
> Smiles broke from us and we had ease;
> The hills were round us, and the breeze
> Went o'er the sun-lit fields again;
> Our foreheads felt the wind and rain.
> Our youth returned; for there was shed
> On spirits that had long been dead,
> Spirits dried up and closely furled,
> The freshness of the early world.
> (*AW*, 242)

The emphasis in this poem is on youthful freshness and on the more gentle and pastoral aspects of nature. This is not the Wordsworth of the Simplon Pass, hardly even the poet who listens to the still, sad music of humanity. Arnold praises "Wordsworth's sweet calm" (*AW*, 139), but seems to ignore his sterner qualities. However, it is only fair to point out that he did greatly admire "Michael" for the grand simplicity of its language, and, one suspects, for its stoicism.

It is interesting to compare Arnold's view of Wordsworth with that of J. C. Shairp, Arnold's Balliol friend, who pub-

[3] In his essay on Wordsworth, published in 1879, Arnold did not rank *The Prelude* amongst the poet's best works. However, as Allott suggests (*AW*, 259), Arnold may have read *The Prelude* shortly before starting to write "The Youth of Nature" in 1850, and he would have found many passages more soothing than the one I have quoted.

lished *On Poetic Interpretation of Nature* in 1877. In his chapter on Wordsworth, Shairp hardly mentions him as a mountain poet, and does not even refer to the Simplon Pass passage. He quotes, with apparent approval, Macaulay's comment on *The Prelude*: "There are the old raptures about mountains and cataracts."[4] It is a comment in which the well-bred yawn is barely stifled. Shairp values Wordsworth not for his raptures, but for showing us that "Nature is to man a supporting, calming, cooling, and invigorating power."[5] Both Arnold and Shairp took from the great Romantic poet only what they most needed, his "healing power" (*AW*, 242). They were unable to share his feeling for the sublime, that sense of awe or even terror that sometimes overcame him in the presence of nature's most powerful phenomena, particularly the mountains.

Arnold did, however, share Wordsworth's love of the mountains; they enter his poems frequently, but instead of attaining a Wordsworthian transcendence, they are most often given a symbolic value. In fact, almost all landscape has a symbolic value for Arnold, who evolved a private mythology out of landscape types for the interpretation of human experience. This mythology has been explored by Culler in his book *Imaginative Reason: The Poetry of Matthew Arnold*, and by Alan Roper in *Arnold's Poetic Landscapes*, and one cannot write about Arnold's landscapes without being heavily indebted to these critics. Culler isolates three main regions, which he calls "the Forest Glade, the Burning or Darkling Plain, and the Wide-Glimmering Sea."[6] He explains that the "first is a period of joyous innocence when one lives in harmony with nature, the second a period of suffering when one is alone in a hostile world, and the third a period of peace in which suffering subsides into calm and then grows up into a new joy, the joy of active service in the world."[7] Moreover,

---

[4] Shairp, *On Poetic Interpretation of Nature*, p. 244.
[5] Ibid., p. 260.
[6] Culler, *Imaginative Reason*, p. 4.
[7] Ibid.

the three regions correspond to three ages in the life of man: childhood, maturity, and old age or death. Very often the forest glade will be situated on the slopes of a mountain where the River of Life has its source, but the mountain peak itself is not included in Culler's basic scheme, although he does mention that the high-placed City of God or Throne of Truth, which is reached "by strenuous effort, not by drifting down a stream," may be an alternative to the wide sea.[8]

The germ of Arnold's symbolic landscape is to be found in a poem by his father, Thomas Arnold, written in 1839 but until recently unpublished. The poem describes a peaceful upland vale with infant stream, and in the distance the mightly sea of eternal life. The stream longs to join the sea, but must first cross the busy world where it will become soiled. All this is closely paralleled in Matthew Arnold's poetry. Where Dr. Arnold differs from his son is in the joy with which he obeys the call to duty on the plains:

> Better thy sullied Stream
> Than thy clear Waters in thy upland Vale!
> Better that ceaseless Din than thy blithe Song
> Answering the mountain Gale!
>
> Thy sullied Waters tell
> Of others' Stains which thou hast wash'd away;
> Thy straightened Course shows that where Duty calls
> Thou wilt not play.[9]

It is also significant that for Dr. Arnold the mountains are a region of youthful peace and irresponsible joy, in striking contrast to the use his son makes of them in "Rugby Chapel," where life's pilgrimage is symbolized by an arduous climb through alpine passes:

> We, we have chosen our path—
> Path to a clear-purposed goal,

[8] Ibid., p. 6.
[9] AW, Appendix B, p. 675.

Path of advance!—but it leads
A long, steep journey, through sunk
Gorges, o'er mountains in snow.
Cheerful, with friends, we set forth—
Then, on the height, comes the storm.
Thunder crashes from rock
To rock, the cataracts reply,
Lightnings dazzle our eyes.
Roaring torrents have breached
The track, the stream-bed descends
In the place where the wayfarer once
Planted his footstep—the spray
Boils o'er its borders! aloft
The unseen snow-beds dislodge
Their hanging ruin; alas,
Havoc is made in our train!
                    (AW, 486)

This is an impressive alpine description, but even here the
mountains are not "instinct" with "voluntary power," nor
are they valued for what they are in themselves. The Words-
worthian experience was denied to Arnold, but like Tennyson
in "The Holy Grail," he has found a way of redeeming the
sublime landscape for poetic use by transforming it into al-
legory. In "Rugby Chapel" the mountains are seen as a place
of trial, and the winding track is the hard path of duty which
leads only to the shelter of the "lonely inn 'mid the rocks; /
Where the gaunt and taciturn host / Stands on the threshold"
(AW, 486). A somewhat dubious reward for the arduous climb,
one might feel, and although the poem ends on the positive
and rousing note of "On, to the City of God," the lonely inn
remains a more haunting image of the final goal of the journey.
It is as though even in this poem dedicated to his father's
memory, Arnold remained in some doubt about the value of
the hard climb up the path of duty.

The symbolic significance of the mountains does not remain
constant in Arnold's poetry. The journey in "Rugby Chapel"

might be regarded as a version of the romantic quest, although strangely transformed by Victorian earnestness, but in other poems the heights are associated with classic repose and calm serenity. Such qualities belonged to Shakespeare:

> For the loftiest hill,
> Who to the stars uncrowns his majesty,
> Planting his steadfast footsteps in the sea,
> Making the heaven of heavens his dwelling-place,
> Spares but the cloudy border of his base
> To the foiled searching of mortality.
> (*AW*, 39-40)

Sophocles too, "saw life steadily and saw it whole" (*AW*, 111), as though from a great height. Lesser natures, however, cannot easily bear the solitude of such heights, and in the two "Obermann" poems Arnold deals with such a nature. The earlier poem, "In Memory of the Author of 'Obermann,' " opens with a description of romantic, alpine scenery that has more than a touch of the sublime:

> In front the awful Alpine track
> Crawls up its rocky stair;
> The autumn storm-winds drive the rack,
> Close o'er it, in the air.
> (*AW*, 136)

The lines are an invitation to strenuous activity, and we are in the world of "Rugby Chapel," where it is our duty to toil up the mountain.

That call to duty receives its first check as the speaker turns the pages of *Obermann* and feels the "air of languor, cold, and death, / Which brooded o'er thy soul" (*AW*, 137). The really startling word is "languor," which fights against the bracing alpine air. It is important to note that Obermann's retreat is not on the bare mountain tops but in a secluded alpine dell. He is not a Shakespeare or a Goethe, both of whom earned the right to survey the world from a vantage point. He lacks both their classical repose and also the demonic urge of the romantic quester (or even the earnest energy of the Victorian headmaster), for whom the mountains would have presented a challenge. Paralyzed by despair, Arnold's Obermann has no heart for the quest, and never attempts to climb the peaks. For him the mountains represent a denial of life. Toward the end of the poem Arnold tries to disguise the sterility of Obermann's life by giving his alpine retreat some of the warmth and beauty of a pastoral idyll. "Balms" float on the mountain air, "the slopes are green" and "With the pale crocus starred"; the distant peaks are flushed with rosy light, and Obermann, listening to "accents of the eternal tongue" feels himself grow young again (*AW*, 141). It is really a disguised attempt on Arnold's part to create a haven for himself and to recover the Wordsworthian vision of his boyhood;[10] but he is too honest to deceive himself, and dismisses both dream and Obermann, who is, after all, but a "sad guide":

> Away the dreams that but deceive
> And thou, sad guide, adieu!
> I go, fate drives me; but I leave
> Half of my life with you.
> (*AW*, 142)

Finally, he bids Obermann farewell in "this stern Alpine dell" (*AW*, 144), and the phrase embodies the basic contradictions of the poem. "Stern" echoes the call to duty and action associated with the mountain imagery of "Rugby Chapel," whereas a "dell" is the kind of secluded nook into which a child might creep in order to avoid such duties. One is reminded that in Thomas Arnold's poem the mountain was a symbol, not of action or of the mature mastery of life, but of childish irresponsibility. Arnold himself seems to have held both views almost simultaneously. In a letter to Clough in 1848, Arnold had written that he "took up with Obermann, and refuged myself with him in his forest against your Zeit

[10] The poem is dated 1849, when Arnold was twenty-seven, but it is obvious that he was already feeling the loss of youthful enthusiasm.

Geist," but in the same paragraph he speaks of becoming "calm in spirit, but uncompromising, almost stern."[11] He is stern in rejecting the kind of poetry of ideas and social concern that Clough was writing, but his sternness takes the form of escape into the forest. Shortly after writing this letter, however, Arnold renounced the indulgence of this forest retreat, and returned to the battle with the Zeit Geist in the cities of the plains. Ambiguities multiply, and many of them seem to be outside the poet's conscious control, springing from internal tensions that he was unable to resolve. As Arnold himself puts it in another letter to Clough in 1849, "I have never yet succeeded in any one great occasion in consciously mastering myself."[12]

There is a further ambiguity in the significance of the mountain when one considers that for Arnold it is sometimes the source of the River of Life, and therefore associated with youth and freshness, and sometimes the site of the City of God toward which one must toil over rocky wastes. It is both Life and Death, the beginning and the end, the call of duty and the escape into childhood.

"Obermann Once More," written almost twenty years later, contains some of the ambiguities of the earlier poem, but in general it is less complex. The image of the mountain as pastoral retreat predominates. The vision of Obermann is framed by descriptions of alpine scenery that are rich and soft, with "Full-foaming milk pail" and Jaman "delicately tall / Above his sun-warmed firs" (AW, 561, 562). The Poet comes quite unambiguously to this idyllic landscape in a mood of escapism:

Yes, I forget the world's work wrought,
Its warfare waged with pain;
An eremite with thee, in thought
Once more I slip my chain,

[11] *Letters to Clough*, edited by Lowry, p. 95.
[12] Ibid., p. 110.

And to thy mountain-chalet come,
And lie beside its door,
And hear the wild bee's Alpine hum,
And thy sad, tranquil lore.
(AW, 562)

These are beautiful lines, but a little too easy in their gentle melancholy and nostalgia. Arnold has grown used to his chain and forgotten the tense ambiguities of his earlier attitude to Obermann. Only when Obermann speaks does anything emerge to contradict our sense of this as a happy pastoral retreat:

"O thou, who, ere thy flying span
Was past of cheerful youth,
Didst find the solitary man
And love his cheerless truth—

Despair not thou as I despaired,
Nor be cold gloom thy prison!"
(AW, 573)

But almost immediately Obermann passes into a prophecy of uncharacteristic optimism about the dawning of a new age. Tranquillity has been achieved in this poem, one feels, at the cost of poetic power, and the mountains, robbed of their fierceness and terror, have acquired an ideal picture-postcard beauty.

Switzerland was associated not only with Obermann, but also with a certain freedom from the restraints of English life. In 1857 Arnold wrote to his sister: "I have a positive thirst to see the Alps again, and two or three things I have in mind which I cannot finish till I have again breathed and smelt Swiss air."[13] Almost ten years earlier, in Thun, Arnold had first met the mysterious "Marguerite," who was to inspire a series of haunting love lyrics, and who remained inextricably bound up with his memories of Switzerland. However, for Arnold as for Tennyson, love belongs to the valleys rather than to

[13] *Letters of Matthew Arnold 1848-1888*, edited by Russell, I, 63.

ARNOLD

the mountain peaks, and Marguerite is, as Culler says, a "goddess of the forest glade."[14] She is associated, in "Parting" (AW, 124-27), with "some wet bird-haunted English lawn" and with "some sun-flecked mountainbrook"; the mountains, on the other hand, represent the speaker's life apart from her, a "cold distant barrier" against the passionate life.

Landscape motifs are developed throughout the poem, and intensified by the alternating verse forms. The speaker is drawn away from the soft beauty of Marguerite and her surroundings to the storm-winds, "ice-cumbered gorges," and "vast seas of snow," torrents, avalanches, and pine-woods. "I come, O ye mountains! / Ye torrents, I come!" he cries, in what sounds like an ecstatic surrender to passion, but is actually the opposite.[15] The ruling paradox of this poem is that all the stormy, passionate imagery is on the side of solitude, while Marguerite is seen in terms of pastoral serenity, even of the "home" of English lawns. Does he flee from her to the mountain heights of quiet contemplation, or to the stormy and solitary battle with his own ego? In a letter to Clough written on the occasion, Arnold says, "tomorrow I carry my aching head to the mountains," but this promises only a brief respite, and in three or four days he will "try how soon I can ferociously turn towards England."[16] The "ferociously" implies that England represented the burning plains of duty, but what do the mountains represent here? Their storms and avalanches would seem to be merely a proving ground for the battles of the plain.

Ronald Becht suggests that in "his appeal to the mountains, the speaker is, in fact, voicing a death-wish, a desire to lose himself in cosmic forces that lie outside and dominate the world."[17] Certainly the speaker is seeking the death of passion

[14] Culler, Imaginative Reason, p. 123.
[15] Or, as Culler expresses it somewhat comically: "He flings off up the mountains to take refuge in the arms of Mother Nature"; "Arnold and Etna," in Victorian Essays: A Symposium, p. 45.
[16] Letters to Clough, p. 111.
[17] Becht, "Matthew Arnold's 'Switzerland': The Drama of Choice," Victorian Poetry, 13 (1975), 40.

82

in the mountains, but not quite the death of self. He begs the mountains to "calm me, restore me / And dry up my tears," and Nature is asked to "Fold closely . . . / Thine arms round thy child." The mountains are being asked to perform the soothing Wordsworthian function of calming and refreshing the weary soul. And yet there seems to be an inherent contradiction in asking the bleak snowfields, winds, torrents, and avalanches to provide the almost infantile comfort suggested in the image of the encircling arms.

"Parting" would be a complex enough poem if that were all, but Arnold's habit of embodying his own tensions in ambiguous metaphors gives rise to what must be some of the strangest lines in English poetry. After a tender description of Marguerite's beauty, the speaker turns away from her:

Ah! with that let me go
To the clear, waning hill-side,
Unspotted by snow.
(AW, 125)

Presumably Marguerite, or the region she inhabits, is "spotted with snow." Yet she has been associated with English lawns and pastoral landscapes, and the speaker goes from her to the snow and ice of the high mountains. In the poem as a whole, snow symbolizes the purity and austerity of the solitary life. Here one is surprised by its use as an image of corruption; it foreshadows his accusations against Marguerite in the second half of the poem. These accusations, that "the lips, ah! of others" have been pressed to hers, seem to me to be a very cheap way of resolving the tensions of the poem and of justifying his action in abandoning her. But the metaphor he has used makes nonsense of the accusation; it is as if he were saying, "You are spotted with purity." This is perhaps an unconscious expression of Arnold's own moral unease. The earlier sections of the poem in which her beauty and exquisite natural freshness are described, carry much more poetic conviction than the later charges brought against her. Alan Roper says, "the poem has changed directions sharply and has run

ARNOLD

out of control in doing so,"[18] which is, I think, true; but I
would also concur with the kinder judgment of Lionel Trilling
that the "very contradictions attest to the actuality of the
affair."[19]
   In the next poem of the series, "Isolation. To Marguerite,"
the speaker is quite sure that it is all her fault. He was constant,
she unworthy of him, and he addresses his lonely heart:

Which never yet without remorse
Even for a moment didst depart
From thy remote and spheréd course
To haunt the place where passions reign—
Back to thy solitude again!
                    (AW, 128)

Having settled the question of Marguerite's culpability in his
own mind, the speaker now sees the mountain solitude not
as stormy but as "remote and spheréd"; he has achieved the
calm detachment of a Shakespeare or a Sophocles, but only
by convincing himself that the passionate life, as represented
by Marguerite, was tainted with corruption.
   It is interesting to compare the topography of the "Ober-
mann" poems with that of the "Marguerite" poems. Both
Marguerite and Obermann occupy settings that are midway
points between the alpine peaks and the level plains, but there
the similarity ends. Marguerite is associated with the town of
Thun and its lakeside community; Obermann is a solitary
recluse in a remote alpine valley.[20] When Arnold's protagonist
leaves Marguerite he goes up into the mountains; when he
leaves Obermann he descends to the plains. This important

---

[18] Roper, *Arnold's Poetic Landscapes*, p. 152.
[19] Trilling, *Matthew Arnold*, p. 122. Culler also takes a more sympathetic
view. He suggests that Arnold's disillusionment with Marguerite was the
result of his "discovering underneath the illusion of Romantic love the fact
of sex." "Arnold and Etna," p. 46.
[20] Arnold stated that the first Obermann poem was "conceived, and partly
composed, in the valley going down from the foot of the Gemmi Pass towards
the Rhone"; quoted by Allott, *AW*, 123n.

84

difference should indicate that it is a mistake to identify Marguerite and Obermann too closely, as some critics have done. For example, Culler writes that Marguerite "represents the same spiritual morbidity as did Obermann."[21] This is only a fleeting comment in an otherwise excellent essay, but it seems to me to represent a serious misjudgment. The "spiritual morbidity" surely belongs to Arnold (or his protagonist) and to Obermann, not to Marguerite. Obermann is the "patron saint of impotence";[22] his icy despair and solitude make him the antithesis of the passionate Marguerite. Indeed, it may be said that Arnold's protagonist leaves Marguerite for Obermann, since the first "Obermann" poem was conceived on the projected trip to the mountains of which the poet speaks in "Parting." Arnold, leaving "Marguerite," took his aching head to the mountains, where he identified with the lonely author of *Obermann*, and at the same time bid him farewell. Within the space of a week he abandoned both the passionate life and the life of solitary contemplation. These alternatives, though very different, were both associated with Switzerland, and Arnold renounces both for England and duty.

In his poem "Heine's Grave," Arnold identifies with another writer who escapes temporarily from the world into the solitude of the mountains. Indeed, as Allott has pointed out, Arnold falsifies the record in order to make Heine a Romantic solitary: he describes him standing "at nightfall, alone!" on the "roof of the Brocken-tower" (*AW*, 515), whereas Heine himself had made it clear that he was with a group of students, workmen, and "worthy citizens with their worthy wives and daughters, who all came to see the sun set."[23] But although solitary, Arnold's Heine does at least have a heart "Freshened and light with the May," so that his mountain retreat, unlike Obermann's, is associated with youthful enthusiasm. Arnold

[21] Culler, "Arnold and Etna," p. 49. And Bonnerot writes, "Obermann et Marguerite sont étroitement unis." *Matthew Arnold: Poète*, p. 58.
[22] This, according to Culler, was how George Sand described him; "Arnold and Etna," p. 48.
[23] Quoted from Heine's "Die Harzreise" by Allott, *AW*, 515n.

identifies with the young Heine, but rejects the mature poet, master of bitter wit and scorn, even more surely than he rejected Obermann.

A more austere alpine retreat is that represented by the Carthusian monastery in "Stanzas from the Grande Chartreuse." The travelers to the monastery pass from lush alpine meadows into the forests of the mountainside, "Past limestone scars with ragged pines," up the stony paths until "At last the encircling trees retire" (*AW*, 302). The trees have acted as a protection from which the travelers now emerge into a more bleak alpine setting above the tree line. This journey up the mountain is reminiscent of the one in "Rugby Chapel"; it is the path of duty to the City of God, and the monastery is a preparation for that City. Here the monks lead a life of stern renunciation, "where no organ's peal / Invests the stern and naked prayer" (*AW*, 303). Yet the speaker sees the monastery predominantly as a refuge from the world; what he seeks is protection rather than austerity:

> Oh, hide me in your gloom profound,
> Ye solemn seats of holy pain!
> Take me, cowled forms, and fence me round,
> Till I possess my soul again.
>               (*AW*, 306)

The austerity is still there, of course, but the monks are asked to fence him round, shutting out both the world and the bleak alpine winds. They form a kind of protective enclosure for him, a "stern Alpine dell," indeed.

In the final section the poet imagines himself, and others like him who are unable to join the brave new world of Victorian progress, to be "shy recluses" (*AW*, 310), almost as retired as the Carthusians:

> We are like children reared in shade
> Beneath some old-world abbey wall,
> Forgotten in a forest-glade,
> And secret from the eyes of all.

> Deep, deep the greenwood round them waves,
> Their abbey, and its close of graves!
> (*AW*, 309)

Encircling trees have replaced the ring of cowled forms, and the abbey wall offers both shelter and seclusion. This imaginary abbey in a forest glade is a more comfortable place than the Carthusian monastery on its bleak mountain. The journey to the City of God has been tacitly dropped; the abbey is a refuge set amongst "secluded dells" (*AW*, 311), rather than a way-station on the path of duty.

However, a touch of Carthusian austerity remains: pleasure has been renounced along with action, and the speaker asks only that both banners and bugles should pass, "And leave our desert to its peace!" (*AW*, 311). Like Obermann's retreat, this secluded nook represents both self-denial and self-indulgence. Arnold remains deeply divided in his attitude to such solitary landscapes.

Nowhere is this divided attitude made clearer than in "Empedocles." Empedocles identifies the mountains with the loneliness of creative effort, but he renounces his laurel wreath while at the same time ascending the mountain. He complains that the devotee of Apollo is brought face to face with himself: "He hears nothing but the cry of the torrents, / And the beating of his own heart" (*AW*, 195). There is an interesting parallel between these lines and Browning's definition of the subjective poet as one who "selects that silence of the earth and sea in which he can best hear the beating of his individual heart"; but the alternative offered by Browning of becoming an objective poet who "chooses to deal with the doings of men" was not possible for Empedocles.[24] The busy chatter of ordinary men, so fascinating to Browning, keeps Empedocles divided from himself:

[24] Browning, "An Essay on Percy Bysshe Shelley," reprinted in *Victorian Poetry and Poetics*, ed. Houghton and Stange, p. 357. Both this essay and Arnold's "Empedocles" were first published in 1852.

And he will fly to solitude again,
And he will find its air too keen for him,
And so change back; and many thousand times
Be miserably bandied to and fro
Like a sea-wave, betwixt the world and thee,
Thou young, implacable God! and only death
Can cut his oscillations short.
                              (AW, 196)

At least Arnold managed to cut his own oscillations short without recourse to suicide. "Empedocles on Etna" inevitably recalls *Manfred on the Jungfrau* (Fig. 1) and in many ways Etna is an extreme form of the sublime, and Empedocles an extreme form of the Byronic hero. But Arnold's poem is also about the failure of the Romantic Sublime. Only Callicles, the happy, pastoral singer of the woodland groves, feels the beauty of the "brilliant mountain-crests" (AW, 157), whereas for Empedocles himself Etna is "this charred, blackened, melancholy waste" (AW, 186). Faced with such a loss of the transcendent vision, this Byronic hero can only throw himself into the volcano. In so doing, he recovers the sublime for a brief moment before extinction:

                    The numbing cloud
Mounts off my soul; I feel it, I breathe free.
Is it but for a moment?
—Ah, boil up, ye vapours!
Leap and roar, thou sea of fire!
My soul glows to meet you.
                         (AW, 203-204)

All too often, critics write about the Victorians as if they had somehow betrayed their Romantic inheritance. "Empedocles" should not be seen as a betrayal, but rather as a tragic recognition on Arnold's part that the Romantic vision could not have been maintained. Wordsworth, gazing on the "beauteous forms" of Nature, could achieve that blessed state in which "we are laid asleep / In body, and become a living soul"

("Tintern Abbey," ll.45-46). For Empedocles such a state of
oneness with nature could only be achieved by the desperate
action of leaping into the volcano, an action that establishes
him as a new kind of romantic hero. His soul, confronted
with the molten heart of the earth, "glows to meet" it as he
finally surrenders his separate identity and the burden of con-
sciousness.

When Arnold, unlike Empedocles, descends to the burning
plains, he descends to a wasteland, but the values that draw
him down are social. His quest in the wasteland is not that
of the lonely romantic hero; he goes to labor among men. But
he does not become an objective poet, writing about men.
Nor does he transform his landscapes, as Tennyson trans-
formed his gardens, so that they reflect the life of man in
society. Instead, the landscape to which he would like to re-
treat goes underground, and at rare intervals, "A man becomes
aware of his life's flow, / And hears its winding murmur; and
sees / The meadows where it glides, the sun, the breeze" ("The
Buried Life," *AW*, 291). The natural landscape from which
man draws spiritual sustenance has had to become internal-
ized to protect it from the corruption of the outside world. It
has something in common with the internal landscapes of
Tennyson's early poems, but whereas these were gardens, con-
taining both art and artifice, Arnold's are pastoral or wild
(but not rugged) landscapes. Most often his *locus amoenus* is
an enclosed, green space such as the forest glade already noted
in "Stanzas from the Grande Chartreuse." Culler's description
of this type of landscape is worth quoting in full:

> The first region of Arnold's world is usually presented as
> a place of deep or variegated shadow, cool and well-
> watered, with clear-running streams or bubbling foun-
> tains. Usually it is set on the shoulder of a mountain, but
> it may be in the corner of an upland field or in some sun-
> dappled meadow deep in the woods. It may even be on
> an open heath so that it is screened by trees or protected
> by some depression in the land. For its main character-

istic, apart from the spring-like and virginal quality of its vegetation, is that it is secluded from the world, withdrawn and remote, and that the persons who inhabit it, who are mostly youths and children, live there in pristine innocence, untroubled by the problems that will later shake them in the world.[25]

Such landscapes of refuge are fairly common in Victorian poetry. Almost all of Dante Gabriel Rossetti's landscapes are enclosed, protected spaces, although unlike Arnold's, they can also, as will be shown later, include some hidden danger or sinister attribute. Amongst women poets the landscape of refuge seems to be particularly common. It is to be found in many of Elizabeth Barrett Browning's early poems, such as "An Island," "The Deserted Garden," and "The Soul's Travelling."

In "The Deserted Garden," for example, the *locus amoenus* is a "circle smooth of mossy ground / Beneath a poplar tree" which can only be reached by creeping "beneath the boughs." It is in a deserted and overgrown garden which has now become "my wilderness," and a very private place:

The trees were interwoven wild,
And spread their boughs enough about
To keep both sheep and shepherd out,
    But not a happy child.[26]

In this "child's nest so greenly wrought" she can curl up and read or dream, safe from adult intrusion. It is a "wilderness," cut off from the demands of society, but it is also a safe wilderness which even the relatively harmless sheep cannot invade. It has close affinities, even in this matter of the exclusion of the sheep, to the woodland glade in Arnold's "Kensington Gardens," to be discussed more fully later.

Christina Rossetti also describes a secret woodland covert in "Spring Quiet":

[25] Culler, *Imaginative Reason*, p. 6.
[26] Elizabeth Barrett Browning, *The Poetical Works*, p. 34.

Full of fresh scents,
And whispering air
Which sayeth softly:
"We spread no snare;

"Here dwell in safety,
Here dwell alone,
With a clear stream
And a mossy stone."[27]

But such woodland places may also be the haunts of vicious little goblin men, and in the end Christina was to withdraw to the further refuge of a heavenly landscape "in a distant place."[28] In poems such as "Earth and Heaven," she writes of the superiority of the heavenly to the earthly paradise.

There is no similar movement toward a heavenly paradise in Arnold, for whom heaven was perhaps too closely associated with the sternly dutiful religion of his father. The "gaunt and taciturn host" (*AW*, 486) of "Rugby Chapel" may offer the weary travelers a refuge from the storm, but it is unlikely to be a paradisal nook. Arnold is too sure that his intrusive parent will be a presence in that "far-shining sphere," and that he will be "Prompt, unwearied, as here" (*AW*, 484), asking awkward questions about the tasks still unperformed.

It is only in the forest glades and flowery nooks of this world that Arnold can find his refuge. The speaker in "The Scholar-Gipsy" waits in just such a place, surrounded by poppies and convolvulus, and bowered from the August sun by lindens. He waits for the "shepherd," who, in accordance with the conventions of the pastoral elegy, probably represents Clough. However, this shepherd does not inhabit the fragile world of Arcady; nor does he spend his days piping ditties to pretty shepherdesses. The poem opens with the command that he should go and deal with the very real demands of his flock:

[27] Christina Rossetti, *The Complete Poems*, I, 120.
[28] Christina Rossetti, "From House to Home," *Poems*, I, 88.

Go, for they call you, shepherd, from the hill;
Go, shepherd, and untie the wattled cotes!
No longer leave thy wistful flock unfed,
Nor let thy bawling fellows rack their throats,
Nor the cropped herbage shoot another head.
(*AW*, 358)

The pastoral world, far from representing an escape from
toil, stands here for the duties and responsibilities of ordinary
life, and the shepherd can devote only his evening hours to
the quest for the Scholar-Gipsy. The pastoral convention is
further subverted by the advice given to the gipsy to flee even
the contact of the seemingly innocent country folk, and to
"plunge deeper in the bowering wood" (*AW*, 367). The com-
mand, "Fly hence, our contact fear," both echoes and con-
trasts with the stern "Go," addressed to the shepherd in the
opening stanzas. Neither shepherd nor gipsy can rest in Ar-
cady; one must flee to greater solitude in the woods, the other
must submit to the call of duty.

The speaker himself seems to have been granted a brief
respite. He can enjoy the beauty of the Oxfordshire country-
side without apparently having to share the labors of shepherd
or reaper. Nor does he feel compelled to flee with the gipsy,
whom he imagines:

With a free, onward impulse brushing through,
By night, the silvered branches of the glade—
Far on the forest-skirts where none pursue.
(*AW*, 367)

He remains in his sheltered nook, a midway point between
civilization and wilderness, where he is hidden from the world
but can allow his eye to travel "down to Oxford's towers"
(*AW*, 359). He will return to the world of duty and toil, but
he allows himself a moment out of time in order to contem-
plate the probable fate of the gipsy, his alter ego, who has
become a romantic quester in the wilderness. The gipsy is that

part of himself that Arnold had had to suppress or reject. He is, as Wilson Knight says, "at home with the shadows of night-time or the underworld, and with nature wild and un-trimmed."[29] A. E. Dyson makes the same point when he calls the gipsy a "primitivist, attempting to realise the myth of the noble savage," although it is somewhat misleading to call Arnold's gentle, melancholy scholar a savage, noble or other-wise.[30] Nor is there any suggestion that the woods to which he flees are the realm of dangerous passions or eroticism, as they were for Tennyson in *Maud* and *The Idylls of the King*.

Arnold's woods are not dragon-haunted, and in general they are not even seen as the meeting place of lovers, except in "Tristram and Iseult." Tristram says, "I will think, we've lived / In the green wood, all our lives, alone" (*AW*, 222), but in fact they have not done so. His words are a wistful evocation of a life of love and innocence in natural surroundings. Vivian does seduce Merlin in the woods, as in Tennyson's version, but Arnold's description of the sylvan glade where this hap-pens is completely free of any sinister overtones:

You saw the bright-eyed squirrels dart along
Under the thorns on the green sward; and strong
The blackbird whistled from the dingles near,
And the weird chipping of the woodpecker
Rang lonelily and sharp; the sky was fair,
And a fresh breath of spring stirred everywhere.
Merlin and Vivian stopped on the slope's brow,
To gaze on the light sea of leaf and bough
Which glistering plays all round them, lone and mild
As if to itself the quiet forest smiled.
Upon the brow-top grew a thorn, and here
The grass was dry and mossed, and you saw clear
Across the hollow; white anemones

---

[29] Wilson Knight, "The Scholar Gipsy," in *Neglected Powers*, p. 240.
[30] Dyson, "The Last Enchantments," *Review of English Studies*, NS 8 (1957), 263.

Starred the cool turf, and clumps of primroses
Ran out from the dark underwood behind.
No fairer resting-place a man could find.
                              (*AW*, 236-37)

Tennyson made the woods into a psychological equivalent of
Vivien's corrupt passion; for Arnold the woodland glade merely
provides a setting, and the contrast between its innocent beauty
and Vivian's world-weariness is not even pointed ironically.
Nor is Arnold making the point, as Hardy might have done,
that nature is indifferent to man. For Arnold, as for Hopkins,
there "lives the dearest freshness deep down things" that man's
actions cannot spoil.[31]

This is largely because Arnold, in general, sees the forest
glade as a presexual paradise. Perhaps he was a little too well-
bred and fastidious to harbor monsters in the forests of his
imagination. His temperament was altogether cooler than
Tennyson's, and his forest landscapes are correspondingly tamer.
The woods which lie behind the aging couple in "The Youth
of Man" contain no blood-stained hollows; they are merely
"the woods / Which sheltered their childhood" (*AW*, 267).
The woods continue to shelter something of Arnold's child-
hood too, in that they are chosen by him as the refuge for his
surrogate, the Scholar-Gipsy, guardian of his youthful ideal-
ism. But he knows that his own life must be lived in the real
world, in the cities of the plain. It is precisely because he has
renounced the primal innocence of the woodland bowers that
his descriptions of them are suffused with the beauty of nos-
talgia.

His elegy for his friend Clough exploits this nostalgia.
"Thyrsis" might be described as a lament for Arnold's own
lost youth, and a memorial to the beauty of the Cumner hills
that he and Clough loved as young men. The landscape is
described with a keen sense of its subjection to time and change:

[31] Hopkins, "God's Grandeur," *The Poems of Gerard Manley Hopkins*,
ed. Gardner and Mackenzie, p. 66.

94

And we shall have him in the sweet spring-days,
With whitening hedges, and uncrumpling fern,
And blue-bells trembling by the forest-ways,
And scent of hay new-mown.
                    (*AW*, 542)

The present participles catch the plants in the act of growth. The hedges are whitening with spring blossom, just as they will later whiten with snow. The fern uncrumples with new life; later it will crumple with decay. The delicate bluebells tremble with fragile life, and the message of death is carried in the scent of new-mown hay.

The poem as a whole is, of course, largely in the tradition of the classical pastoral elegy. Arnold himself referred to Theocritus, "whom I have been much reading during the two years this poem has been forming itself," and Allott notes the debt to "The Lament for Bion" and to Virgil.[32] At the same time the poem is very English. Arnold "needed neither Theocritus nor Virgil to tell him 'what white, what purple fritillaries' grew by Ensham or by Sandford."[33] His feeling for the reality of the Cumner hills makes the brittle fictions of Arcady irrelevant, and classical pastoral gives way to English georgic; the "Dorian water's gush divine" (*AW*, 543) has been replaced by the familiar Thames. Thyrsis and Corydon tried their shepherd pipes among quiet English fields, walked along the track by Childsworth Farm, and looked down onto "that sweet city with her dreaming spires" (*AW*, 539). The use of English places and names within a classical frame of reference achieves a double purpose. The poets, Arnold/Corydon and Clough/Thyrsis, are heirs to the classical tradition but at the same time they are exiled from that tradition, born into an unpoetic age on some distant northern shore. Proserpine will not respond to Arnold's song:

[32] See Allott's notes to the poem. Arnold's comment is also quoted by Allott.
[33] Tinker and Lowry, *The Poetry of Matthew Arnold: A Commentary*, p. 218.

95

She loved the Dorian pipe, the Dorian strain,
But ah, of our poor Thames she never heard!
Her foot the Cumner cowslips never stirred;
And we should tease her with our plaint in vain!
(*AW*, 544)

As always, Arnold is caught between two worlds: his values are derived from classical Greece, but he must sing of the English countryside he knows and loves. Moreover, he is now an exile even from that countryside, which belongs essentially to his youthful Oxford days, and which is threatened by change. Unlike Obermann's safe retreat, this is a landscape populated by country folk and showing many signs of man's presence. Some of those signs are welcome: the cottage gardens, with their "jasmine-muffled lattices," snapdragons, and Sweet-William in abundant profusion, are lovingly evoked, as is the "scent of hay new-mown" (*AW*, 541, 542). But the pastoral activities of the country folk can also destroy the countryside as he knew it, especially the wild and flowery slopes of uncultivated land:

I know these slopes; who knows them if not I?
But many a dingle on the loved hill-side,
    With thorns once studded, old, white-blossomed
        trees,
    Where thick the cowslips grew, and far descried
    High towered the spikes of purple orchises,
        Hath since our day put by
The coronals of that forgotten time;
    Down each green bank hath gone the ploughboy's
        team,
    And only in the hidden brookside gleam
Primroses, orphans of the flowery prime.
(*AW*, 544)

The wilderness has had to retreat in the face of progress, represented here by the plough. Proud and towering spikes of royal purple have given way to the humble primroses, safe only on the "hidden brookside." Part of the poignancy of Arnold's writing comes from his sense of a shared fate with the wild flowers, and with all that has disappeared from the well-loved scene.

We have seen how Arnold is tempted by the seclusion of Obermann's alpine dell, midway between the sick hurry of the plains and the bleak grandeur of the heights. The pastoral landscape of "Thyrsis" is also a midway point, set between the populous city and the signal tree, "Bare on its lonely ridge" (*AW*, 546). Just as Obermann avoided the mountain peaks, so the poet puts off the pilgrimage to the elm for another day. The bare and lonely ridge with its single tree is a landscape of stoic endurance, much like that of "Resignation." The tree, like the "solemn hills," the "strange-scrawled rocks, the lonely sky," seems to "bear rather than rejoice" (*AW*, 100). The poet, having glimpsed this symbol of endurance, goes down into the valley to endure his own dutiful struggle in the "great town's harsh, heart-wearying roar" (*AW*, 550). He has been rejuvenated by his brief retreat into the wild and flowery nooks, but no permanent escape is possible.

In the heart of the great city itself Arnold can still find his pastoral retreat, and the woodland glade described in "Lines Written in Kensington Gardens" gives the perfect illusion of being untouched by man:

In this lone, open glade I lie,
Screened by deep boughs on either hand;
And at its end, to stay the eye,
Those black-crowned, red-boled pine-trees stand!
(*AW*, 269)

Although surrounded by the "girdling city's hum," the glade retains its primal innocence. Significantly, the only intruder is the occasional child, and the "active life" that takes place in the enclosure is that of the birds, the "blowing daisies" and "fragrant grass" (*AW*, 270). Even the sheep do not seem to enter the glade, although the sound of their cries tells of a pastoral world surrounding it. The title reminds us that this

97

little paradise is man-made, but it has none of the social significance or tensions of Tennyson's gardens. It is, nevertheless, a product of society, only made possible by the fact that the Victorians had created public gardens within the city. The illusion of wildness speaks of a nostalgia for romantic landscapes, but Arnold does not have to go to the banks of the Wye, or to the Cumberland hills in order to experience the soothing power of nature. Indeed, Kensington Gardens may be more soothing than the Lake District, as the harsh landscape of "Resignation" suggests.

Although Arnold's woodland glades are not erotic, they are, as Culler suggests, "intensely feminine and maternal."[34] Culler also stresses the similarity between the forest glade and the underwater landscapes of such poems as "The Forsaken Merman," but the sea caverns do have definite erotic overtones:

> Sand-strewn caverns, cool and deep,
> Where the winds are all asleep;
> Where the spent lights quiver and gleam,
> Where the salt weed sways in the stream,
> Where the sea-beasts, ranged all round,
> Feed in the ooze of their pasture-ground;
> Where the sea-snakes coil and twine,
> Dry their mail and bask in the brine.
>
> (AW, 102)

In this poem the symbolic significance of the sea as a realm of sensuous pleasure is fairly unambiguous, as it was for Tennyson in such poems as "The Merman." The stern path of Christian duty lies in the white-walled town, but joy and love are in the beautiful caverns of the merman, an infantile and pre-Christian paradise filled with languid beasts who surrender to the hypnotic rhythms of the ocean. Arnold's sea beasts would seem to be first cousins of Tennyson's Kraken, but they lack its apocalyptic quality. Lazily basking and coiling, they do not seem to have such reserves of terrible power.

[34] Culler, *Imaginative Reason*, p. 7.

Nevertheless, like the mountains, the sea is basically an ambivalent symbol for Arnold. Its womblike interior contains the "kind sea-caves" (AW, 103), the ultimate escape from the world of responsibility; its stormy surface, however, may represent the same kind of arduous challenge presented by the mountain peaks. In "A Summer Night" the choice is not between the life of duty in the town and the retreat to an underwater paradise; it is between a life of meaningless toil on the land, and an even more arduous commitment to the romantic quest on the sea, in which the pale mariner is seen:

With anguished face and flying hair
Grasping the rudder hard,
Still bent to make some port he knows not where,
Still standing for some false, impossible shore.
                                        (AW, 285)

The ambiguity of the sea is also apparent in "Dover Beach." It is first seen as serenely beautiful, but beneath its calm surface is the destructive force that eats away at the land, flinging the pebbles on the strand with a "grating roar" (AW, 255). The speaker turns from the contemplation of this bleak landscape to his human companion. The sea is no longer a "Sea of Faith," but a symbol of desolation.

It can also be a symbol of alienation, as in "Tristram and Iseult" and in "To Marguerite—Continued," where it is an actual physical barrier between the lovers. They are like islands surrounded by "The unplumbed, salt, estranging sea" (AW, 131), but "unplumbed" reminds us that in other poems Arnold does write of the underwater caverns as a meeting place for lovers. In his farewell to Marguerite the speaker chooses to see only the estranging surface of the sea, and not the hidden depths of its buried life. The sea caves, home of the erotic and sensuous life, had perhaps proved to be too dangerous. It was not safe to visit them for the kind of spiritual rejuvenation that Arnold derived from the more innocent forest glade.

The forest glade, or protected green hollow, remains for

Arnold a *locus amoenus* where a man may retire temporarily from the busy world, but it is not a place where one may live permanently. Nor does it function as in any sense an image of the world, either as it is, or as it should be. For this reason, it is a more limited symbol than Tennyson's gardens. It is also more limited in that, unlike Tennyson's gardens, the glade remains a fairly constant symbol in Arnold's poetry, almost always being associated with youth, innocence, and freshness. It represents an escape from duty, even, one might say, a place where one may hide from the stern father. It is often a solitary, antisocial landscape, but even when it includes human figures it includes only those who will not shatter the idyll: children, gipsies, pastoral folk, or a trusted companion.

Arnold's forest glade lacks the tensions to be found in most of Tennyson's landscapes. Tennyson was attracted by wild landscapes, but he also feared them, projecting the terrors and desires of his own deeply passionate nature onto them. Arnold suffuses his wild, secluded nooks with a gentle, flowery nostalgia which is very romantic in its way, but Tennyson's romanticism is deeper, more urgent; his wild places are haunted by the monsters of the subconscious.

# CHAPTER IV

# BROWNING:
# THE HUMAN LANDSCAPE

The folly of any attempt to reduce the rich diversity of Victorian poetry to a neat generalization is well illustrated by the contrasting styles and interests of Matthew Arnold and Robert Browning. Arnold spent his life laboring among men in the cities of the plain, and with excellent practical results for the British educational system, but the poet in him yearned constantly for the solitude of the forest glade, or the rural simplicity of pastoral landscapes. Browning, totally impractical in all worldly matters, was at the same time strongly drawn to urban life and the world of men and women. He is the least Wordsworthian of the Victorian poets. A friend of Browning's once asked: "You have not a great love for nature, have you?" He replied, "Yes, I have, but I love men and women better."[1]

Landscapes are not entirely absent from Browning's poetry, but they are greatly reduced in significance. Temperamentally, he found more to interest him in the crowded human scene, although he was not indifferent to the beauties of nature, as such poems as "Home-Thoughts, from Abroad" and "De Gustibus—" suggest. Whereas the first shows a yearning for the quiet loveliness of the English countryside, the second expresses a preference for the more dramatic scenery of Italy:

> What I love best in all the world
> Is a castle, precipice-encurled,
> In a gash of the wind-grieved Apennine.[2]

[1] Quoted by Orr, *Life and Letters of Robert Browning*, p. 316.
[2] *The Works of Robert Browning*, ed. Kenyon, III, 175. Hereafter cited as *BW* with volume and page numbers.

Such a landscape is remote and solitary, very much in the
tradition of Salvator Rosa; but it does not remain the speaker's
final choice. He directs his old friend to look for him:

> In a sea-side house to the farther South,
> Where the baked cicala dies of drouth,
> And one sharp tree—'t is a cypress—stands,
> By the many hundred years red-rusted,
> Rough iron-spiked, ripe fruit-o'ercrusted,
> My sentinel to guard the sands
> To the water's edge. For, what expands
> Before the house, but the great opaque
> Blue breadth of sea without a break?
> (*BW*, III, 175-76)

The "one sharp tree" is used here as a symbol of solitude in
much the same way as it was used by Tennyson in "Mariana"
and "Enoch Arden." But Browning's protagonist is no Mar-
iana; he cannot endure the silent emptiness of sand and sea
for long. Gradually, life creeps into the poem: first, the frescoes
in the house crumble "From blisters where a scorpion sprawls";
then, "A girl bare-footed" brings fruit and, more important,
news from the great world. The poem ends with the speaker
contentedly listening to her gossip. Like Tennyson's ideal in
"The Gardener's Daughter," this landscape lies "Not wholly
in the busy world, nor quite / Beyond it" (*TW*, 510).

Browning's love of Italy was more characteristically a love
of Italian culture and town life than a love of the countryside.
He gives humorous expression to this in his antipastoral poem
"Up at a Villa—Down in the City," one of the few Victorian
poems in praise of urban life. The speaker, an "Italian Person
of Quality," contrasts the boredom of country life with the
interest supplied by the city square:

> Well now, look at our villa! stuck like the horn of a bull
> Just on a mountain-edge as bare as the creature's skull,
> Save a mere shag of a bush with hardly a leaf to pull!
> —I scratch my own, sometimes, to see if the hair's turned
> wool.

But the city, oh the city—the square with the houses!
Why?
They are stone-faced, white as a curd, there's something
to take the eye!
Houses in four straight lines, not a single front awry;
You watch who crosses and gossips, who saunters, who
hurries by.

(BW, III, 155-56)

The delight taken by the speaker in the orderly geometry and
white freshness of the city architecture is a deliberate rejection
of the picturesque. Moreover, a fountain and accompanying
nymph, stock properties of the rural *locus amoenus*, have been
brought into the city square, providing the cool splash of
water, but no retreat from the crowds. Nor does the speaker
desire such a retreat. He delights in the noisy bustle:

*Bang-whang-whang* goes the drum, *tootle-te-tootle* the
fife;
No keeping one's haunches still: it's the greatest pleasure
in life.

(BW, III, 158)

Nothing could be further removed in spirit from Arnold's
retreat within the city, Kensington Gardens, than this cheerful
vulgarity.

However, it may be objected that neither Browning's poem,
nor his somewhat comic speaker, is intended to be taken se-
riously, whereas Arnold's "Kensington Gardens" is. A more
serious comparison might be drawn between Arnold's "Thyr-
sis" and Browning's late poem, "La Saisiaz." Both are elegies
for lost friends, Browning's being occasioned by the shock-
ingly sudden death of Miss Egerton Smith on the very morning
on which she and the poet had planned to climb the Salève.
Both poems nostalgically retrace the steps of the pairs of friends
on previous walks in the area; but whereas Arnold's "Thyrsis"
lovingly recreates every detail of the Cumner hills, and has
very little to say about Clough, Browning's poem touches only
briefly on the beauties of the landscape, and deals at length

with the question of the soul's immortality. "La Saisiaz" has 618 lines, of which no more than 40 contain any scenic description; in "Thyrsis," there are only some 70 lines out of 240 that do not contain scenic description. Indeed, Arnold refused to send the poem to Mrs. Clough because he was aware that it did not contain much about his friend.

Five days after the death of Miss Smith, Browning made the ascent of the Salève on his own:

> Dared and done: at last I stand upon the summit,
>   Dear and True!
> Singly dared and done; the climbing both of us
>   were bound to do.
> Petty feat and yet prodigious: every side my glance was
>   bent
> O'er the grandeur and the beauty lavished through
>   the whole ascent.
> Ledge by ledge, out broke new marvels, now
>   minute and now immense:
> Earth's most exquisite disclosure, heaven's own
>   God in evidence!
> And no berry in its hiding, no blue space in its
>   outspread,
> Pleaded to escape my footstep, challenged my
>   emerging head,
> (As I climbed or paused from climbing, now
>   o'erbranched by shrub and tree,
> Now built round by rock and boulder, now at
>   Just a turn set free,
> Stationed face to face with—Nature? rather with
>   Infinitude)
> —No revealment of them all, as singly I my path
>   pursued,
> But a bitter touched its sweetness, for the thought
>   stung "Even so
> Both of us had loved and wondered just the same,
>   five days ago!"
>                               (BW, IX, 117-18)

The beauties of the landscape are acknowledged, but they are not felt with the tender intensity of Arnold's "blue-bells trembling by the forest-ways, / And scent of hay new-mown" (AW, 542); his "Red loosestrife and blond meadow-sweet" are loved for themselves rather than for any meaning that arises from them. Browning notes the beauty of the mountains, but sees them as "heaven's own God in evidence," and as symbols of "Infinitude." This naturally leads on to the debate he has with himself about the possibility of immortality. Man, and what concerns man, is primary for Browning.

This preference for the human over the natural landscape is clearly shown in a much earlier poem, "Pippa Passes." Browning does not even imagine that his little factory worker, Pippa, might seek a rural retreat on her precious annual holiday. Instead, he makes her share his own passionate interest in people. Like the "chameleon poet," Pippa wishes to enter into the lives of various characters, to become each of them in fantasy. At the same time, Pippa herself is constantly associated with the natural world. The poem opens with her description of a splendid sunrise, and the songs she sings during the day are filled with images of natural beauty. Eleanor Cook, indeed, sees Pippa as a kind of personification of nature "coming alive to speak to just this person in just this situation. . . . The implication, when this happens, is that nature usually pursues her own course under laws given to her, but that these laws include the occasional witnessing to man; then a veil is removed and the natural world becomes animated and purposeful."[3] This is an attractive interpretation, but it implies that Pippa, and nature through her, acts with a greater degree of conscious wisdom and purposeful knowledge than is in fact the case. At the end of the poem Pippa is quite unaware of the extent to which her presence has influenced the lives of those she passed, and her songs of pastoral innocence take on a ghastly irony in the context of the sordid acts of those who hear them. All is, quite plainly, *not* "right with the world."

Ramona Merchant is surely right in suggesting that whereas

[3] Cook, *Browning's Lyrics*, p. 54.

Pippa sings of a "prelapsarian garden," Ottima and Sebald "meet in a shrubhouse, and the imagery of this section suggests a parody of the Garden of Eden."[4] There is something slightly obscene about the "tall / Naked geraniums" that "straggle" outside the window of the shrubhouse, and Sebald questions whether it can really be morning outside:

> It seems to me a night with a sun added.
> Where's dew, where's freshness? That bruised
>     plant, I bruised
> In getting through the lattice yestereve,
> Droops as it did.
>     (BW, II, 107)

The guilty lovers shut out the morning light in which Pippa so delights. Her songs only serve to emphasize the gap between man and nature. They do influence those who hear them, but Browning stresses the power of her goodness rather than the healing properties of nature. It is significant that, in spite of her pastoral songs, she is an urban worker who has no particular contact with the natural world.

In the Wordsworthian tradition, as represented by Arnold, the individual toiling in the grime of the city would need to retreat from time to time to some rural solitude to gain spiritual sustenance for the struggle. This is not so in Browning. His innocent heroines, such as Pippa and Pompilia, have an absolute goodness that does not need the restorative power of lakes, mountains, or the forest glade. Indeed, it is made clear that it is the human heart that brings to nature whatever properties are to be found there. We have already seen how Sebald found neither freshness nor dew in the morning, whereas Pippa sings of the hill-side "dew-pearled" (BW, II, 114). When Ottima and Sebald met in the woods, their guilt made of the lightning bolt an instrument of divine wrath:

---

[4] Merchant, "Pippa's Garden," *Studies in Browning and His Circle*, 2, No. 2 (1974), 12, 11.

Buried in woods we lay, you recollect;
Swift ran the searching tempest overhead;
And ever and anon some bright white shaft
Burned thro' the pine-tree roof, here burned and there,
As if God's messenger thro' the close wood screen
Plunged and replunged his weapon at a venture,
Feeling for guilty thee and me: then broke
The thunder like a whole sea overhead—
                    (BW, II, 113)

But for Pippa the woods are paradisal, innocent, and familiar:

Overhead the tree-tops meet,
Flowers and grass spring 'neath one's feet;
There was nought above me, nought below,
My childhood had not learned to know:
For, what are the voices of birds
—Ay, and of beasts,—but words, our words,
Only so much more sweet?
                    (BW, II, 153)

The woods may also provide a meeting place for innocent lovers, as in "By the Fire-Side." Musing by the fire, the speaker remembers how he and his "perfect wife" once walked along a woodland path, and how friendship turned to love:

The forests had done it; there they stood;
    We caught for a moment the powers at play:
They had mingled us so, for once and good,
    Their work was done—we might go or stay,
They relapsed to their ancient mood.
                    (BW, III, 210)

Lawrence Poston has analyzed the effect of this landscape on the lovers, pointing out that "The poem does seem to echo Wordsworth's idea of the educative force in 'one impulse from a vernal wood,' but in 'By the Fireside,' Nature is not a perpetual teacher, only a momentary contributor to the lovers' union, and sharply separated from them."[5] Although the woods are benevolent in this instance, one suspects that the "ancient mood" into which they relapse is one of indifference, if not hostility.

Often in Browning's work the powers invested in the natural world seem to be sinister, and in general he is not a lover of the forests. In "Iván Ivànovitch," for example, the forests are the realm of primitive brutality, much as they were for Tennyson in the *Idylls*, and civilization is a bright "spot of life" wrested from the darkness:

> In the drop of our land, 't is said, a village
>    from out the woods
> Emerged on the great main-road 'twixt two great
>    solitudes.
> Through forestry right and left, black verst
>    and verst of pine,
> From village to village runs the road's long
>    wide bare line.
> Clearance and clearance break the else-unconquered
>    growth
> Of pine and all that breeds and broods there,
>    leaving loth
> Man's inch of masterdom,—spot of life, spirit
>    of fire,—
> To star the dark and dread, lest right and rule
>    expire
> Throughout the monstrous wild, a-hungered to
>    resume
> Its ancient sway, suck back the world into
>    its womb.
>                                       (*BW*, IX, 235)

The wilderness here provides the grim background for the story of a mother's unnatural (or perhaps all too natural)

---

[5] Poston, "Browning and the Altered Romantic Landscape," in *Nature and the Victorian Imagination*, p. 431.

action: she has thrown her children to the wolves in order to preserve her own life. The final image of the "monstrous wild" sucking the world back into its womb perhaps gives a clue to a somewhat strange passage in Browning's first published poem, *Pauline.*

In this poem, the forest glade is given an ambiguous value. The protagonist invites Pauline to fly with him to an imaginary world, and conducts her to a wild landscape of "rocks and valleys and old woods," where, like birds, they live "on high boughs / That swing in the wind" (*BW*, I, 25). From this exposed position they retreat into the woods:

> Shall we stay here
> With the wild hawks? No, ere the hot noon come,
> Dive we down—safe! See this our new retreat
> Walled in with a sloped mound of matted shrubs,
> Dark, tangled, old and green, still sloping down
> To a small pool whose waters lie asleep
> Amid the trailing boughs turned water-plants:
> And tall trees overarch to keep us in,
> Breaking the sunbeams into emerald shafts,
> And in the dreamy water one small group
> Of two or three strange trees are got together
> Wondering at all around, as strange beasts herd
> Together far from their own land: all wildness,
> No turf nor moss, for boughs and plants pave all,
> And tongues of bank go shelving in the lymph,
> Where the pale-throated snake reclines his head,
> And old grey stones lie making eddies there,
> The wild-mice cross them dry-shod. Deeper in!
> Shut thy soft eyes—now look—still deeper in!
> This is the very heart of the woods all round
> Mountain-like heaped above us; yet even here
> One pond of water gleams; far off the river
> Sweeps like a sea, barred out from land; but one—
> One thin clear sheet has overleaped and wound
> Into this silent depth, which gained, it lies

Still, as but let by sufferance; the trees bend
O'er it as wild men watch a sleeping girl,
And through their roots long creeping plants outstretch
Their twined hair, steeped and sparkling; farther on,
Tall rushes and thick flag-knots have combined
To narrow it; so, at length, a silver thread,
It winds, all noiselessly through the deep wood
Till thro' a cleft-way, thro' the moss and stone,
It joins its parent-river with a shout.
                    (BW, I, 25-26)

An interesting shift in attitude seems to take place during the course of this description. At first the speaker sees the glade as a "retreat" into which they dive down, "safe." A few lines later there is a disturbing hint that it may have become a trap over which "tall trees overarch to keep us in." Gradually the landscape, like that of "Childe Roland," becomes anthropomorphized: the bank has "tongues," and the trees bend over the pond "as wild men watch a sleeping girl"; creeping plants stretch out "their twined hair," and rushes and flag-knots "have combined" to narrow the pond, as if in some conspiracy. When the water, escaping from this confinement, finds its way out of the wood, it "joins its parent-river with a shout." The poet seems to share the relief of escape. In the next line he exults: "Up for the glowing day, leave the old woods!" and, as if he had been drowning in the forest depths, he gasps for "Air, air, fresh life-blood, thin and searching air" (BW, I, 26).

This curious passage is rich with suggestions of subconscious significance. Like Rossetti's orchard-pit, to be discussed later, Browning's deep hollow may have sexual connotations; it is at first desired ("Deeper in! / Shut thy soft eyes.") and then feared and rejected.[6] It may also represent a journey into

6 This Freudian interpretation would receive support from Betty Miller's biography of Browning. She points out that until he met Elizabeth Barrett, Browning associated only with older, somewhat spinsterish women. "It was only, it seems, under the guarantee of sexual neutrality that he felt free to accept the privileges of a feminine friendship." *Robert Browning: A Portrait*, p. 63.

the depths of the poet's own psyche, from which he emerges
with relief into the thinner, but freer, atmosphere of objectiv-
ity. The bird soaring above the forest has the freedom to view
other lives from a safe distance. But the speaker does not even
remain floating on the air for long. He now invites Pauline to
descend with him to another landscape, this time one popu-
lated by country folk. They gaze out over the plain:

> At the muleteers who whistle on their way,
> To the merry chime of morning bells, past all
> The little smoking cots, mid fields and banks
> And copses bright in the sun. My spirit wanders:
> Hedgerows for me—those living hedgerows where
> The bushes close and clasp above and keep
> Thought in—I am concentrated—I feel;
> But my soul saddens when it looks beyond:
> I cannot be immortal, taste all joy.
>                     (BW, I, 27)

The delight in the ordinary activities of human beings is un-
mistakable, and the speaker chooses the humanized landscape
of hedgerows rather than the wild forest glade. However, he
remains somewhat confused, subject to conflicting desires. He
still feels the need for some safe refuge, so now the hedgerows
must "close and clasp above and keep / Thought in." Later,
Browning was to transform himself so successfully into the
"chameleon poet," entering and losing himself in the lives of
other characters, that he had no need of the landscape of
refuge.

It may have been partly Browning's influence that effected
a somewhat similar transformation in the poetry of his wife,
Elizabeth Barrett. In her early poems, as has been pointed out,
she delighted in the kind of hidden nook into which a child
may creep. "The Lost Bower" describes such a place, a wood-
land bower that has some affinities with the forest glade in
*Pauline*, except that for her the place is not sinister

> But the wood, all close and clenching
> Bough in bough and root in root,—

No more sky (for overbranching)
At your head than at your foot,
Oh, the wood drew me within it by a
        glamour past dispute![7]

As with her other favorite nooks, not even the sheep can
penetrate the thorny thickets through which she breaks into
a "bower of beauty," paved with moss and bluebells. The
bower is like a tiny room richly decorated with eglantine and
columbine, and fitted with cushions of moss. It has "Arch of
door and window-mullion," and is fitted "Leaf to leaf, the
dark-green ivy, to the summit from the base," like a Victorian
drawing room covered with Morris wallpaper. It is an en-
chanted place which she only finds once, and its loss is her
first great loss. Now on her couch, the invalid tries to imagine
the lost bower, and perhaps even to recreate it in her sickroom,
sealed off from the world. Robert Browning was to rescue
her from that sickroom, and the landscapes of her later poetry
are much more open, and, like his, crowded with human
figures.

In *Pauline*, Browning had acknowledged his debt to Shelley,
and also, to some extent, declared his independence of the
great Romantic poet. In his "Essay on Shelley," Browning
differentiates between "objective" and "subjective" poets; the
former "chooses to deal with the doings of men," while the
latter "whose study has been himself, appealing through him-
self to the absolute Divine mind, prefers to dwell upon those
eternal scenic appearances which strike out most abundantly
and uninterruptedly his inner light and power, selects that
silence of the earth and sea in which he can best hear the
beating of his individual heart."[8] Shelley remains for Browning
a supreme example of the subjective poet; he himself was to
become "objective," but he sees the dangers inherent in each
approach, and he describes those dangers in terms of land-
scape. Whereas the subjective artist, concentrating on sublime

[7] Elizabeth Barrett Browning, *Works*, p. 150.
[8] Browning, "Essay on Shelley," in *Victorian Poetry and Poetics*, p. 337.

effects of scenery, may become like that "race of landscape-painters whose 'figures' disturb the perfection of their earth and sky," the objective artist, whose men and women fill "the foreground with consummate mastery" may find that "his occasional illustrations from scenic nature are introduced as in the earlier works of the originative painters." Elsewhere, however, Browning expresses some admiration for those early painters, for whom landscape was subsidiary to the human figure. His interest in Renaissance Italy makes him closer to them in spirit than to later artists like Salvator and Turner. He admires the clarity of early Italian portraits, uncluttered by distracting background:

> If one could have had that little head of hers
> Painted upon a background of pale gold,
> Such as the Tuscan's early art prefers!
> ("A Face," BW, IV, 311)

Browning's Fra Lippo Lippi, however, is made to strike a balance between the two extremes. He includes landscape, but sees it mainly as a frame for the human figure:

> Do you feel thankful, ay or no,
> For this fair town's face, yonder river's line,
> The mountain round it and the sky above,
> Much more the figures of man, woman, child,
> These are the frame to?
> (BW, IV, 112-13)

Many of Browning's dramatic monologues resemble Renaissance portraits in their complete lack of scenic background, although it must be said that he is not aiming at the kind of limpid clarity of the early portrait. His characters do not "sit" for us. They gesture, talk, argue endlessly, and sometimes they act. But the probing of their motives and psychology is done largely by exploring their restless minds. Like Henry James, Browning tends to put all the action inside. He does not explore the psychology of a character by describing in minute detail the surroundings of that character, as Tennyson does in "Mariana." In general, after such early poems as *Pauline*, and with the possible exception of "Childe Roland," to be discussed later, it may be said that Browning does not perceive landscape as externalized personality, and since his chief interest is in personality, he tends to ignore landscape. The demands of the dramatic monologue also led to the exclusion of lengthy scenic description; as he himself points out, "description, as suggesting a describer," must be dispensed with in the dramatic form.[9]

Nevertheless, Browning does often manage to introduce vivid touches of natural scenery that provide a "frame" for his figures. In "My Last Duchess," for example, the fleeting mention of the bough of cherries, the orchard, and the terrace, evokes the setting of a stately house and its extensive grounds. Landscape may also be used to make a dramatic point: Porphyria glides in from a stormy setting that serves to heighten the tension of the scene that follows; Karshish meets Lazarus after crossing "a ridge of short sharp broken hills / Like an old lion's cheek teeth" (*BW*, IV, 97). In "A Grammarian's Funeral" the landscape is more extensive, but the barren mountains up which the pallbearers climb exist not for their own sake, but as symbols of the lofty and somewhat arid life's work of the scholar. The "tall mountain, citied to the top, / Crowded with culture!" (*BW*, III, 375), bears some resemblance to Tennyson's Camelot. It is a country in which man's thought is "rarer, intenser," and it might also be compared with the mountaintop monastery of the Grande Chartreuse. But, unlike the Grande Chartreuse, this mountaintop does not serve as a retreat for the poet or his persona. Browning's attitude to life in such a rarefied atmosphere is not, of course, openly stated, but even the grammarian's enthusiastic pallbearers admit that he sacrificed Life to Knowledge, and that he was "Dead from the waist down" (*BW*, III, 379).

*The Ring and the Book* may be regarded as a collection of dramatic monologues, but it also tells a story, and there must

9 Ibid.

be very few narrative poems of such a length which contain as little scenic description. We are given one or two brief glimpses of landscape in which the effects of light create a dramatic setting. In Book I, the poet imagines the wayside inn at Castelnuovo:

> By Castelnuovo's few mean hut-like homes
> Huddled together on the hill-foot bleak,
> Bare, broken only by that tree or two
> Against the sudden bloody spendour poured
> Cursewise in day's departure by the sun
> O'er the low house-roof of that squalid inn.
> (BW, V, 18)

An even more dramatic sky is described by the Pope, musing on the fate of Guido's soul:

> I stood at Naples once, a night so dark
> I could have scarce conjectured there was earth
> Anywhere, sky or sea or world at all:
> But the night's black was burst through by a blaze—
> Thunder struck blow on blow, earth groaned and bore,
> Through her whole length of mountain visible:
> There lay the city thick and plain with spires,
> And, like a ghost disshrouded, white the sea.
> So may the truth be flashed out by one blow,
> And Guido see, one instant, and be saved.
> (BW, VI, 222)

In both instances, the landscape embodies some manifestation of divine wrath or intervention, comparable to the lightning which, in "Pippa Passes," seems "to search for the guilty lovers, Sebald and Ottima, like the bared sword of divine justice."[10] But, in general, Browning is more interested in the workings of the human mind than in such dramatic scenic effects, and even where he could have introduced descriptions

---

[10] W. Raymond, *The Infinite Moment and Other Essays in Robert Browning*, p. 14.

of landscape, as in the journey of Pompilia and Caponsacchi
to Rome, he does not do so. Nor does he make much use of
the potential symbolism in landscape. The bleakness of Gui-
do's soul is perhaps briefly suggested through his "absurd wild
villa in the waste / O' the hillside" (*BW*, V, 102), and Pompilia
is equally briefly associated with the Garden of Eden. She is
a "branchlet slipt from bole / Of some tongue-leaved eye-fig-
ured Eden tree" (*BW*, V, 100), brought by the elderly couple
to their garden plot to cheer their solitude. Later, the Pope
uses a similar image of her:

> Just the one prize vouchsafed unworthy me,
> Seven years a gardener of the untoward ground,
> I till,—this earth, my sweat and blood manure
> All the long day that barrenly grows dusk:
> At least one blossom makes me proud at eve
> Born 'mid the briers of my enclosure!
> (*BW*, VI, 190)

Like Pippa, she is a natural flower of goodness that has blos-
somed in surroundings that are, for the most part, remote
from natural scenery.

The lyric, as a more subjective form than the dramatic mon-
ologue, allows for greater use of landscape description to evoke
mood. In "Meeting at Night," in fact, the speaker's mood is
evoked almost entirely through such a description:

> The grey sea and the long black land;
> And the yellow half-moon large and low;
> And the startled little waves that leap
> In fiery ringlets from their sleep,
> As I gain the cove with pushing prow,
> And quench its speed i' the slushy sand.
>
> Then a mile of warm sea-scented beach;
> Three fields to cross till a farm appears;
> A tap at the pane, the quick sharp scratch
> And blue spurt of a lighted match,

And a voice less loud, thro' its joys and fears,
Than the two hearts beating each to each!
(*BW*, III, 139)

Grammatically, this lyric is somewhat extraordinary in that it consists of two sentences without a single main verb. The syntax thus echoes the mood of anticipation: sea, land, moon, the gaining of the cove and crossing of the beach and three fields, are all sights and events to be breathlessly endured before the lovers can meet. This meeting, foreshadowed by the lighted match, the voice, and the beating hearts, takes place only after the poem has ended, but it is an event on which the whole poem depends; it is the missing main verb. The landscape, seemingly so important, is thus confined to a series of dependent clauses. It is nevertheless extremely vividly perceived, but its concrete reality serves to highlight the state of mind of the observer rather than to establish it as an important landscape in its own right. The eager lover, in a state of heightened sensual awareness, is alive to everything around him.

The companion poem, "Parting at Morning," has, by contrast, three strong verbs in only four lines, suggesting the world of men and action to which the lover must return:

Round the cape of a sudden came the sea,
And the sun looked over the mountain's rim:
And straight was a path of gold for him,
And the need of a world of men for me.
(*BW*, III, 139)

Here the landscape no longer serves to make us aware of the man's heightened sensibility. There is an absence of fine detail in the scene, which has been reduced to a symbolic pathway back to the world of men.

Landscape plays a more important role in "Two in the Campagna" (*BW*, III, 218), in which two lovers sit on the grass surrounded by

117

The champaign with its endless fleece
O feathery grasses everywhere!
Silence and passion, joy and peace,
    An everlasting wash of air—
Rome's ghost since her decease.

The "everlasting wash of air" suggests something of the lu-
minous quality of a painting by Claude, although the poem
also has the kind of close detail usually associated with the
Pre-Raphaelites. Indeed, the hushed moment of passion re-
minds one of Rossetti's "Silent Noon." However, the rela-
tionship between Browning's lovers is not as harmonious as
that described in Rossetti's sonnet. Browning's speaker catches
at a troubling thought that, like a spider thread thrown mock-
ingly across their path, seems to float tantalizingly through
the otherwise perfect day. It is the thought that his love for
her is not as complete as either of them would wish: "I would
that you were all to me, / You that are just so much, no more."
The link between his feelings and the surrounding landscape
seems to be contained in stanzas 6 and 7:

Such life here, through such lengths of hours,
    Such miracles performed in play,
Such primal naked forms of flowers,
    Such letting nature have her way
While heaven looks from its towers!

How say you? Let us, O my dove,
    Let us be unashamed of soul,
As earth lies bare to heaven above!
    How is it under our control
To love or not to love?

One senses his resentment of the pressures she brings to bear
on him. The flowers, with naked, primal innocence, perform
miracles, but casually and naturally, as if performed "in play."
Victorian lovers of the Elizabeth Barrett Browning type were
apt to be a little soulfully earnest in their demands for a total
and passionate commitment.

The landscape in "Two in the Campagna" does contribute more strongly to the poet's thought than is often the case in Browning. But it is still entirely subordinate to that thought. Indeed, it is the thread of thought that he traces through the landscape that seems to link one object to another:

> First it left
> The yellowing fennel, run to seed
> There, branching from the brickwork's cleft,
> Some old tomb's ruin: yonder weed
> Took up the floating weft,
>
> Where one small orange cup amassed
> Five beetles,—blind and green they grope
> Among the honey-meal: and last,
> Everywhere on the grassy slope
> I traced it. Hold it fast!

The links are casual, like chance associations of the mind. In spite of the suggestion of Claude, commented on earlier, there is no attempt to compose the scene so that it would resemble a landscape painting with foregrounds, distances, side-screens, and perspectives.

In another lyric, "Love among the Ruins" (*BW*, III, 146-48), Browning depicts what seems to be a tranquil pastoral scene. However, his interest lies not in the pastoral landscape, but in what it conceals. The "solitary pastures" cover the site of what was once a "city great and gay," and the leveling grass "o'erspreads / And embeds / Every vestige of the city." The poem is really in the *ubi sunt* tradition, a lament for "the multitude of men" who "breathed joy and woe / Long ago," a lament for their glory and their folly. The landscape that triumphs over them, although peaceful, lacks all distinction: "the country does not even boast a tree," and the sheep that wander home, "Half asleep," are no substitute for the lost grandeur of "the domed and daring palace" that "shot its spires / Up like fires." Isobel Armstrong makes the point that Browning "exploits with deliberate awkwardness the friction

of two modes, the pastoral and the heroic."[11] It might be
added that he is also contrasting two landscapes, one of which
is masculine, the other feminine. Throughout the poem the
past is associated with soaring vertical forms: spires, towers,
turrets, "mountains topped with temples," and "a brazen pil-
lar high / As the sky." The landscape of the present is hori-
zontal, consisting of pastures, creeping plants, "slopes of ver-
dure," grassy carpets, and rills. The feminine landscape has
won over the centuries, covering the pathetic remnants of a
heroic, masculine civilization with verdant growth, and rein-
forcing the trite little moral that ends the poem: "Love is best."
The reader is nevertheless left with an overwhelming impres-
sion of the vitality of the past. The passionate regret expressed
in "Oh heart! Oh blood that freezes, blood that burns!" re-
mains the strongest emotion in the poem, even overshadowing
the passion promised in the embrace of the woman who stands
in the ruined turret surrounded by "slopes and rills in undis-
tinguished grey" to greet her lover with "eager eyes."

   In "Love among the Ruins" the landscape of the present is
dull and quiet; it is fertile, but it lacks exuberance. In "The
Englishman in Italy," however, Browning was to invest a fer-
tile landscape with zest and energy. Italian landscapes had
provided the raw material of the picturesque, but this land-
scape does not have the static, framed quality of the pictur-
esque vista. It bustles with the activities of the countryside:
men harvesting grapes, boys treading them, the fishermen with
great baskets of quivering sea-fruit, young girls gathering snails.
The poem does contain a view from the mountains that almost
qualifies as a static landscape, but even here the mountains
and trees are infused with a strange life and energy:

   And God's own profound
   Was above me, and round me the mountains,

[11] She adds that the poem is "too short for either of these extremes to be
fully qualified by this method of dramatic juxtaposition so that the final line
cannot carry complete conviction." "Browning and the 'Grotesque' Style,"
in The Major Victorian Poets, pp. 119-20.

And under, the sea,
And within me my heart to bear witness
What was and shall be.
Oh, heaven and the terrible crystal!
No rampart excludes
Your eye from the life to be lived
In the blue solitudes.
Oh, those mountains, their infinite movement!
Still moving with you;
For, ever some new head and breast of them
Thrust into view
To observe the intruder; you see it
If quickly you turn
And, before they escape you, surprise them.
They grudge you should learn
How the soft plains they look on, lean over
And love (they pretend)
—Cower beneath them, the flat sea-pine crouches,
The wild fruit-trees bend,
E'en the myrtle-leaves curl, shrink and shut.
                              (*BW*, III, 305)

These mountains that loom into view might seem to be closely
related to the huge peak in *The Prelude* that appears to stride
after the frightened boy in his boat. However, Browning's
tone is much more frivolous than Wordsworth's, and in spite
of the use of such phrases as "God's own profound," there
is little sense of the mountains as representing "unknown
modes of being" (*Prelude* I.393). Browning endows the moun-
tains with essentially human, less mysterious, characteristics.
He enjoys seeing them as grumpy giants, playing a ponderous
game of hide-and-seek with the intruder. Their life is really a
reflection of his own vitality.

Often the energy that seems to animate all Browning's land-
scapes, even the most solitary, exists at the microcosmic level.
In "By the Fire-Side" the protagonist remembers or imagines
a climb through picturesque Italian scenery:

On our other side is the straight-up rock;
   And a path is kept 'twixt the gorge and it
By boulder-stones where lichens mock
   The marks on a moth, and small ferns fit
Their teeth to the polished block.
                     (*BW*, III, 203)

Here the smallest forms of life, the lichens and the ferns, seem to be actively scheming for their place in the world. Later on the climber comes upon a place "Where a freaked fawn-coloured flaky crew / Of toadstools peep indulged," and he observes "how the lichens fret / And the roots of the ivy strike!"

Several critics have commented on Browning's tendency to animate the landscape. Carol Christ, for example, says of "The Englishman in Italy" that it "euphorically celebrates the vitalistic harmony of nature by animating each element of the landscape."[12] Hillis Miller writes that Browning's "anthropomorphizing of the landscape is not achieved by a strenuous act of the imagination which transfers bodily processes to mountains or rivers. Everything in the world is already humanized for Browning, as soon as he sees it, and can be experienced as intimately as if it were his own body."[13] Both these critics relate this characteristic in Browning's poetry to the poet's concept of God and God's relation to the world, although they arrive at somewhat differing conclusions. Browning's humanized landscapes may indeed tell us something about his relation to God; they certainly tell us much about his relation to man. Whereas many poets have sought out the most isolated and inhuman landscapes in order to experience the sublime, Browning animates his apparently lonely landscapes with human feelings, peoples them with crowds of toadstools or fretting lichens. Such landscapes are essentially social, even when only one human figure is present.

Caliban, a less than human figure, meditates in solitude, but "feels about his spine small eft-things course," and the

---

[12] Christ, *The Finer Optic*, p. 72.
[13] Hillis Miller, *The Disappearance of God*, p. 122.

pumpkin plant "Creeps down to touch and tickle hair and beard" (BW, IV, 292). As Isobel Armstrong has pointed out, "the verbs endow the world with emphatically anthropomorphic characteristics."[14] The island in "Caliban upon Setebos," crowded with life forms that struggle and spawn, might be seen as the Darwinian paradigm for many of Browning's landscapes, although the poem is really more concerned with "natural theology" and Calvinism than with Darwin's theories. "Evidence of Darwin's view," write Irvine and Honan, "the luxuriant, ticklish multitudinous life that climbs through the mire, the snapshot impressions of exotic animals hunting exotic prey—is but the psychological data by which Browning lovingly depicted a subhuman monster and his world from the inside."[15] Moreover, we have seen that this "luxuriant, ticklish multitudinous life" was already a characteristic of Browning's landscapes in poems such as "By the Fire-Side" and "The Englishman in Italy," both written well before Darwin's publication of The Origin of Species. No doubt Darwin's theories enhanced what was clearly Browning's natural tendency, and perhaps contributed to the sense of hierarchy of life forms on the island. Caliban is all powerful "compared to yonder crabs / That march now from the mountain to the sea" (BW, IV, 295); he keeps a lumpish sea beast "In a hole o' the rock and calls him Caliban," (p. 297) in mocking imitation of his superior, Prospero. Setebos exercises authoritarian power over "Trees and the fowls here, beast and creeping thing" (p. 293), but must himself recognize the authority of the Quiet. Caliban views this hierarchy as more or less fixed, rather than evolving, although he does allow for the possibility of a metamorphosis in Setebos:

Conceiveth all things will continue thus,
And we shall have to live in fear of Him
So long as He lives, keeps His strength: no change,
If He have done His best, make no new world

[14] Armstrong, "Browning and the 'Grotesque' Style," p. 112.
[15] Irvine and Honan, The Book, the Ring, and the Poet, p. 371.

To please Him more, so leave off watching this,—
If He surprise not even the Quiet's self
Some strange day,—or, suppose, grow into it
As grubs grow butterflies: else here are we,
And there is He, and nowhere help at all.
                              (*BW*, IV, 299)

At no point does Caliban lift his gaze from the struggle for life around him in order to describe the landscape in more picturesque terms. His island is in sharp contrast to Tennyson's island paradise in "The Lotos-Eaters," where we are given a clear picture of the remotely beautiful mountain peaks and waterfalls. Caliban is part of the busy life that he describes.

The same busy life is to be found in Browning's gardens. Paracelsus, about to go out into the world, likes to think of his companions in a safe, secluded garden, "shut in so well / From all rude chances like to be my lot" (*BW*, I, 41). But instead of the usual *hortus conclusus* in which time and the life processes seem to be suspended, this "Sequestered nest" is a microcosm of the great world in which various life forms jostle for position, as on Darwin's tangled bank:

             this kingdom, limited
Alone by one old populous green wall
Tenanted by the ever-busy flies,
Grey crickets and shy lizards and quick spiders,
Each family of the silver-threaded moss—
Which, look through near, this way, and it appears
A stubble-field or a cane-brake, a marsh
Of bulrush whitening in the sun: laugh now!
Fancy the crickets, each one in his house,
Looking out, wondering at the world—or best,
Yon painted snail with his gay shell of dew,
Travelling to see the glossy balls high up
Hung by the caterpillar, like gold lamps.
                              (*BW*, I, 40)

Nature's teeming millions are described with even greater comic exuberance in "Sibrandus Schafnaburgensis," in which the riotous vitality of life in process is set against the achieved stasis of one of life's monuments, a scholarly book. The book, dumped in a hollow tree in the garden in a moment of irritation, is later rescued:

How did he like it when the live creatures
  Tickled and toused and browsed him all over,
And worm, slug, eft, with serious features,
  Came in, each one, for his right of trover?
—When the water-beetle with great blind deaf face
  Made of her eggs the stately deposit,
And the newt borrowed just so much of the preface
  As tiled in the top of his black wife's closet?

All that life and fun and romping,
  All that frisking and twisting and coupling,
While slowly our poor friend's leaves were swamping
  And clasps were cracking and covers suppling!
                    (*BW*, III, 123)

These gardens deliberately assault the myth of the paradisal garden in which there is neither change nor decay. In the medieval *hortus conclusus* it is always spring, and there are no earwigs, caterpillars, or slugs. Most of Browning's gardens look back, not to the medieval or biblical garden, but to a more basic struggle for life amongst creatures "frisking and twisting and coupling" in the primeval swamps, although, unlike Tennyson, he does not see this struggle as cruel and vicious. He delights in its wild energy.

Occasionally, however, Browning does draw on the more traditional associations of the garden. In "Women and Roses," for example, the garden-of-love setting is implied in the poem, but there is no direct landscape description. Instead, the poet concentrates on the single focal point of the rose tree and the women, past, present, and future, who "circle their rose on my rose tree" (*BW*, III, 240). This is really a garden of the

mind in the form of the traditional medieval *hortus conclusus*.
The speaker is to some extent modeled on the medieval courtly
lover, for whom the desired rose is unattainable, but he breaks
with tradition in his inability to decide "which of its roses
three / Is the dearest rose to me?" The poem also breaks with
tradition in its emphasis on time and change. The women of
the past are represented by a rose whose "leaf hangs loose
and bleached," and new roses will spring from "the dust where
our flesh moulders." A pattern of cyclical change is also set
up by the circling movement of the women, and the recurrent
verse forms of the poem. This emphasis on change brings the
shadowy dream garden of "Women and Roses" closer to those
other gardens of Browning's poetry to which it bears so little
superficial resemblance.

The garden of "The Flower's Name" is more conventional.
An enclosed rose garden, it is sacred to the memory of the
woman who walked there with the speaker, who now tries
to retrace their steps. He is also concerned with time and
change; he would like to transform this garden into a static,
paradisal garden that will forever preserve the traces of her
passage through it:

> Flower, you Spaniard, look that you grow not,
> Stay as you are and be loved for ever!
> Bud, if I kiss you 't is that you blow not:
> Mind, the shut pink mouth opens never!
> For while it pouts, her fingers wrestle,
> Twinkling the audacious leaves between,
> Till round they turn and down they nestle—
> Is not the dear mark still to be seen?
> (*BW*, III, 120)

But in spite of the tranquil and idealized nature of this
garden, there are reminders that it harbors a vigorous society
of small creatures. The speaker remembers how "she laid the
poor snail, my chance foot spurned, / To feed and forget it
the leaves among," and also how "she paused in her gracious
talk / To point me a moth on the milk-white phlox." The snail

is shown in the act of feeding, and the moth implies a caterpillar; the lady herself has pointed to some of the agents of change and decay in the garden, and indeed, her own fingers wrestled to open the tightly folded rosebud.

The speaker's desire to preserve this garden from change springs from the fact that for him it has no value except as a record of her presence. "Where I find her not, beauties vanish," he says, and finally exclaims, "Roses, you are not so fair after all," because they seem oblivious of her. As a landscape to be valued in and for itself, it simply does not exist. Like most of Browning's landscapes, it is seen through the consciousness of a dramatic character; it is impossible to detach such landscapes from the human viewer, or, as one should rather say, experiencer, since Browning's characters tend to experience landscape instead of viewing it from a distance.

While the garden of "The Flower's Name" seems to remain neutral toward the speaker, the garden in "A Serenade at the Villa" (*BW*, III, 222-24) appears to be actively hostile. The speaker, having serenaded his lady, fears that his song was unfavorably received:

Oh how dark your villa was,
   Windows fast and obdurate!
How the garden grudged me grass
   Where I stood—the iron gate
Ground its teeth to let me pass!

This is a variation on the intruder-in-the-garden theme, but Browning does not, like Tennyson, give any information about the social status of the lady or her lover. The garden is not given social significance, partly because we only experience it through the consciousness of the speaker. For him, it is a hostile landscape because it reflects his lady's indifference. As with the garden of "The Flower's Name," it has no existence for the lover apart from the emotional meaning that it derives from the woman. To give it a social significance would be to dignify it with an independent existence.

The speaker's awareness extends to the natural world out-

side the garden, and in the general dearth of light and noise
his own song is made to sound like a jarring and impudent
intrusion:

> That was I, you heard last night,
>     When there rose no moon at all,
> Nor, to pierce the strained and tight
> Tent of heaven, a planet small:
> Life was dead and so was light.

> Not a twinkle from the fly,
>     Not a glimmer from the worm;
> When the crickets stopped their cry,
>     When the owls forbore a term,
> You heard music; that was I.

> Earth turned in her sleep with pain,
>     Sultrily suspired for proof:
> In at heaven and out again,
>     Lightning!—where it broke the roof,
> Bloodlike, some few drops of rain.

The string of negatives in the first two stanzas evokes a scene
without light, life, sound, or movement, and it is this negation
of energy that a man of Browning's temperament feels as more
terrible than anything else. A garden inhabited by vigorous
monsters would have been preferable.

The same negation renders the landscape of "Childe Ro-
land" particularly horrible:

> So, on I went. I think I never saw
>     Such starved ignoble nature; nothing throve:
>     For flowers—as well expect a cedar grove!
> But cockle, spurge, according to their law
> Might propagate their kind, with none to awe,
>     You'd think; a burr had been a treasure-trove.

> No! penury, inertness and grimace,
>     In some strange sort, were the land's portion. "See
>     "Or shut your eyes," said Nature peevishly,

"It nothing skills; I cannot help my case:
" 'T is the Last Judgement's fire must cure this place,
"Calcine its clods and set my prisoners free."
(*BW*, III, 407)

Browning could delight in life in any form, even the most grotesque. He would probably have accepted Blake's aphorisms from *The Marriage of Heaven and Hell*: "Energy is eternal delight"; "Exuberance is beauty," and "For everything that lives is holy."[16] What he could not accept was the sterile nothingness of this wasteland. The peevish Nature that speaks of her own inability to bring life to the scene is an unusual personification in Browning, a parody of Wordsworth's Nature. This point has been made by Lawrence Poston, who writes: "the speaker of 'Childe Roland' seems to testify to a natural order that is both a horrifying and a grimly comic inversion of the Wordsworthian view."[17]

The landscape is also a grim inversion of Browning's own view of nature. Gradually it too becomes animated, like so many of his landscapes, but with a negative and destructive energy that is a reversal of the spawning life that he perceives elsewhere: "If there pushed any ragged thistle-stalk / Above its mates, the head was chopped; the bents / Were jealous else" (*BW*, III, 408).

In an important article, DeVane comments on the debt probably owed by Browning to Gerard de Lairesse's *The Art of Painting in All Its Branches*, and in particular to his chapter on the horrible in landscape. Harold Golder had already linked "Childe Roland" to the chivalric romances and fairy tales that were available to Browning in his father's library.[18] Valuable as this research has been, it is as well to be reminded by Ian Jack that "it is clear that the poem has a much greater psy-

---

[16] *The Poems of William Blake*, ed. Stevenson and Erdman, pp. 106, 110, 124.

[17] Poston, "Browning and the Altered Romantic Landscape," p. 433.

[18] DeVane, "The Landscape of *Childe Roland*," *PMLA*, 40 (1925), 426-32; Golder, "Browning's *Childe Roland*," *PMLA*, 39 (1924), 963-78.

chological depth than the stories which helped to inspire it."[19]
Browning's own comment that the poem "came upon me as
a kind of dream. I had to write it, then and there, and I finished
it the same day," would seem to support this view.[20] More-
over, although the parallels between "Childe Roland" and
Lairesse are striking, none of the horrible landscapes quoted
from Lairesse by DeVane contain the anthropomorphic fea-
tures found in Browning.

It is this anthropomorphizing tendency that invests the land-
scape with a surrealistic horror. The little river that crosses
Childe Roland's path is seen as "petty yet so spiteful"; its
energy is perverted and infernal, and the trees on its banks
have flung themselves "headlong in a fit / Of mute despair, a
suicidal throng" (BW, III, 410). This must be seen as an ex-
treme example of the pathetic fallacy. Any normal observer
would see the river as the life-source of the trees; the speaker,
seeing in the distorted shapes of the trees his own despair,
attributes a destructive menace to the river, but his inability
to specify the nature of that menace points to its origin in his
own mind.

In the same way, he imagines horrors that have no real
existence, fearing to "set my foot upon a dead man's cheek"
as he crosses the river, or to feel his spear "tangled in his hair
or beard!" The water rat that he spears "sounded like a baby's
shriek," another horror proceeding from his own over-
wrought brain. When he reaches the other bank and sees the
trampled mud, his mind produces "Toads in a poisoned tank, /
Or wild cats in a red-hot iron cage," and the mountains that
appear from nowhere are "like giants at a hunting," waiting,

[19] Jack, Browning's Major Poetry, p. 186. Compare this view with the
conclusion reached by Wendell V. Harris, that "the landscape is imagined as
a symbol of an idea, rather than the idea having been summoned by an actual
landscape, and the inspiration is learned legend, not the pressure of immediate
experience." "Where Late the Sweet Birds Sang: Looking Back at the Vic-
torians Looking Back at the Romantics Looking Back . . ." Victorian Poetry,
16 (1978), 168.
[20] Quoted by DeVane, A Browning Handbook, p. 229.

"Chin upon hand, to see the game at bay." The poem is full of phrases that suggest the protagonist's own awareness of the imaginary nature of these horrors: "whate'er that was"; "it may have been"; "must so have seemed"; "it would seem," and "in a bad dream perhaps."

More horrible yet is the way in which he perceives the earth itself as a diseased body:

As for the grass, it grew as scant as hair
    In leprosy; thin dry blades pricked the mud
    Which underneath looked kneaded up with blood.

And later:

Now blotches rankling, coloured gay and grim,
    Now patches where some leanness of the soil's
    Broke into moss or substances like boils;
Then came some palsied oak, a cleft in him
Like a distorted mouth that splits its rim
    Gaping at death, and dies while it recoils.
                    (*BW*, III, 408, 411)

It is impossible to separate this landscape from the mind that perceives it, creating what it perceives. Harold Bloom writes that the "greatest power of Browning's romance inheres not in its landscape . . . but in the extraordinary, negative intensity of Childe Roland's consciousness."[21] But the point, surely, is that it is Childe Roland's consciousness that creates the landscape, and it is only through that landscape that we become aware of the quality of his consciousness. Curtis Dahl also separates the landscape from the protagonist when he states that the horrors that Childe Roland perceives "are merely trials to test his strength," and that he finally triumphs over the wasteland.[22] John Willoughby, on the other hand, suggests that "the action may be internal," and "the speaker himself

[21] Bloom, *Ringers in the Tower*, p. 162.
[22] Dahl, "The Victorian Wasteland," in *Victorian Literature*, ed. Wright, p. 35.

the purposeless creator of the landscape."[23] A similar position is taken by Roma King: "Childe Roland travels a road that has no earthly destination; his visual and emotional experiences have no material counterpart. His journey is within; the horrors he experiences, described in the poem as though they were externally real, are objective approximations of his inner life."[24]

"Childe Roland," therefore, is not as much of an exception in the Browning canon as it might at first appear to be. Its wasteland might be compared with the disturbing forest landscape in *Pauline*, which was also a sinister projection of the human consciousness. In "Childe Roland" Browning has shrouded his persona in layers of mysterious disguises, but the poem is really no more "objective" than *Pauline* was. Nor does the landscape have an objective reality in either poem. These are landscapes of the psyche, in which an apparently antisocial, dehumanized wilderness is really part of the human mind.

The landscape component in Browning's poetry is, as we have seen, sharply reduced in the more truly objective, dramatic poems. In such poems, where it exists at all, it tends to be viewed through the consciousness of the dramatic character. In any case, there is in Browning a complete break with the picturesque tradition. Landscape is never seen as a static "view," or as something "out there." It is always entirely subsidiary to the human figure, and it is essentially social, populated by men and women, or by the specters of the imagination, or teeming with life at the subhuman level.

[23] Willoughby, "Browning's 'Childe Roland to the Dark Tower Came,' " *Victorian Poetry*, 1 (1963), 296, 295.
[24] King, *The Focusing Artifice*, p. 91.

# CHAPTER V

# ROSSETTI: THE EMBOWERED CONSCIOUSNESS

Dante Gabriel Rossetti grew, over the years, increasingly re-
clusive, gloomy, and withdrawn. As a young man, however,
he had been extremely gregarious. His boisterous high spirits
had attracted a band of young followers, and the walls of the
Oxford Union were painted, somewhat inexpertly, "amid shouts
of laughter and the popping and fizzing of soda-water bot-
tles."[1] It is not too difficult to understand why this Rossetti
should have admired the poetry of Browning, and although
he was not as interested in the human scene as the older poet,
Rossetti could become the "objective" poet in his ballads. His
dramatic monologues, such as "Jenny" and "A Last Confes-
sion," also owe much to Browning. However, in his most
important work, *The House of Life*, and in many other poems,
he is a subjective poet for whom the good place is an antisocial
landscape of refuge and retreat. In this respect he is closer to
the early Tennyson, whom he also admired, than to Browning.
He is closer still, in terms of his chosen landscape at least, to
Matthew Arnold, although it must be stressed that Rossetti's
enclosed woodland bowers do not have the innocent serenity
of Arnold's forest glades. Moreover, Rossetti's landscapes de-
rive from Keats rather than from Arnold, for whom he seems
to have felt no great admiration.

A useful starting point for any study of Rossetti's poetic
landscapes might be a brief consideration of some of the paint-
ings and drawings of the Pre-Raphaelite artists, including Ros-
setti himself. Generalizations are risky, since the term "Pre-
Raphaelite" is often loosely used to cover all the works pro-

[1] Henderson, *William Morris: His Life, Work and Friends*, p. 43.

duced both by the original Brotherhood, formed in 1848,[2] and by the group that formed later round Rossetti. Moreover, Rossetti was always too much of an individualist to follow easily where others led, and his peculiar vision found expression in a style that was very different from that of Hunt or Millais. Nevertheless, some general statements are possible.

"The quintessential Pre-Raphaelite composition," writes Allen Staley, "consists of a single figure or a simple group of figures before an ivy-covered wall or a foliate background."[3] One thinks immediately of such paintings as Hughes's *The Long Engagement*, or Millais's *Ophelia* (Fig. 5), paintings in which there "is no spatial depth; the background is entirely filled with foliage pressing upon the figures, and the bright colours bring each detail forward to the surface."[4] Rossetti's paintings also lack spatial depth, although in general he did not have the patience required for rendering the minutely accurate detail to be found in Millais's work. Carol Christ has discussed the Victorian penchant for such detail at some length; she states that they came "to perceive nature as a collection of disparate particular forms with nothing to offer but the experience of their own sensations."[5] Although it may be true that the Victorians had lost the Romantic sense of transcendence of particular objects, Christ's statement ignores the fact that for many Victorians particular objects were not merely the source of sensations, but were primarily of symbolic significance.[6] The lilies in Rossetti's painting of the annunciation, *Ecce Ancilla Domini*, are a case in point, although the spare

[2] This consisted primarily of Rossetti, Hunt, and Millais, although Ford Madox Brown, an older man, was sympathetic to the group. Other members were Thomas Woolner, James Collinson, Frederic George Stephens, and the industrious William Rossetti as secretary.

[3] Staley, *The Pre-Raphaelite Landscape*, p. 82.

[4] Ibid., p. 85.

[5] Christ, *The Finer Optic*, p. 13.

[6] It should be pointed out that Christ recognizes this when she states that "the conscious elaboration of detail in Pre-Raphaelite art reveals just such a symbol-making effort" (p. 61).

134

austerity of this early painting makes it somewhat atypical both of Rossetti and of the Brotherhood in general.

A more typical Pre-Raphaelite painting might be Holman Hunt's *The Hireling Shepherd* (Fig. 6), in which almost every detail is charged with symbolic meaning. Hunt's painting also depicts one of the most clear, open, and sunny landscapes to be found among the Pre-Raphaelites, but as Staley points out, "we need only to recall the spaciousness of pictures by Claude or Constable to see how, in contrast, everything in Hunt's picture crowds towards the surface."[7] This effect of surface crowding is partly achieved by lifting the horizon so as to diminish the area of sky in the picture and emphasize foreground rather than distance. The focal point becomes the group of figures and not the landscape, which merely surrounds them, or contributes to the didactic narrative. Indeed, there are very few pure landscapes to be found in the work of the Pre-Raphaelites; one might cite Holman Hunt's *Strayed Sheep* as pure landscape, but again, the painting was, for Hunt, primarily didactic. Painted in 1852, shortly after the appointment of Cardinal Wiseman, the canvas depicts the unguarded cliffs of Protestant England, on which the sheep are already straying from the Established Church.

Other lesser figures who were for a time linked with the Pre-Raphaelites did produce some pure landscapes. John William Inchbold and John Brett both visited the Alps, and Brett's panoramic landscape, *Val d'Aosta* (1858), was praised by Ruskin for its detailed accuracy. However, Ruskin also complained that it lacked emotion, and that it revealed "no awe of the mountains."[8] Staley comments that it "is not a picture of romantic scenery or towering mountains, but of a valley with its peaceful agricultural life, which is enclosed by mountains."[9] This would seem to echo the movement toward a social landscape that we have seen in Tennyson. However, the Pre-Raphaelite painters were also responding to Ruskin's

[7] Staley, *The Pre-Raphaelite Landscape*, p. 26.
[8] Ruskin, *Works*, XIV, 234.
[9] Staley, *The Pre-Raphaelite Landscape*, p. 130.

demand for truth of rendering, and it is, paradoxically, the attempt to satisfy that demand that robs John Brett's mountains of their awesome, romantic power. As W. F. Axton writes:

> But by about 1840 English landscape painting, as a genre, began to break apart, foundering on a reef of theoretical irreconcilables. The Romantic creed, which accorded to the imagination the supremely creative or "poetic" power, also insisted that that power be founded on fact, on accurate and detailed observation and description. That is why Wordsworth made so much of endeavoring "always to look steadily at my object." The tensions generated by the contrary pull of imaginative invention and accurate transcription at the core of the Romantic aesthetic, which proved so fruitful for literature, were disastrous for the graphic arts.[10]

Furthermore, the attention to minute detail sometimes destroyed the very "naturalism" that the Pre-Raphaelites were attempting to create. The hard, bright surface of Millais's *Ophelia*, for example, seems less "natural" than a sketch by Constable, and it is to the watercolorists that one should turn for a continuation of the "naturalistic" school of British landscape painting.[11]

At the same time, the strong literary, moralistic, and symbolic elements in the work of the Pre-Raphaelite painters made them a natural choice as illustrators for the Moxon *Tennyson* of 1857. Holman Hunt and Millais had already found inspiration in the early Tennyson, and both had been drawn to the "trapped maiden" theme. But Hunt's illustration for "The Lady of Shalott" (Fig. 7) and Millais's for "Mariana" are considerably more claustrophobic than the poems that inspired them. In Hunt's picture, the spectator is trapped in the

[10] Axton, "Victorian Landscape Painting: A Change in Outlook," in *Nature and the Victorian Imagination*, p. 288.
[11] For a fuller discussion of this see Leslie Parris, *Landscape in Britain*.

tower with the Lady. The only glimpse of the outside world permitted is the bright fragment in the mirror behind her. Moreover, every detail contributes to the feeling of enclosure: the circular frame of the loom surrounds the Lady like a spider's web, the threads of which wind round her legs; circular motifs are repeated in the shapes of the mirror, wall paintings, gothic arches, and windows. The same swirling rhythms occur in the patterning of the stout, brass legs that bolt the frame of the loom to the floor, and in the mass of hair that floats above the Lady's head like a second web. Hunt's painting of the same subject, executed later but based on the same design, is even more cluttered and oppressive.

In Tennyson's poem, on the other hand, the point of view moves constantly back and forth from the tower to the freedom of the busy world without. Indeed, the predominant impression gained from the poem is one of light, freshness, movement, and human activity, surrounding the gloomy focal point of the tower. Tennyson gives many lines to descriptions of the world outside the tower, where "Willows whiten, aspens quiver, / Little breezes dusk and shiver" (*TW*, 355); there is practically no description of the interior of the tower. A painter, of course, has less freedom than a poet, since he must choose to illustrate only one moment in time, and the predicament of the Lady at the critical moment when the mirror cracks is obviously at the center of the poem. But even so, a vast gulf separates Tennyson's vision from Hunt's:

> She left the web, she left the loom,
> She made three paces through the room,
> She saw the water-lily bloom,
> She saw the helmet and the plume,
>     She looked down to Camelot.
> Out flew the web and floated wide;
> The mirror cracked from side to side;
>     'The curse is come upon me,' cried
>         The Lady of Shalott.
>             (*TW*, 359)

The succession of strong, active verbs in the first five lines gives a freedom of movement and strength of decision to the Lady which Hunt has denied to his trapped, entwined creature. In spite of her cry of despair, and the doom that follows, Tennyson's Lady has seized her freedom even at the price of death. There is a sense of release in "Out flew the web and floated wide," whereas Hunt's web remains for the most part heavily weighted.

A similar contrast between poem and painting may be drawn between Tennyson's "Mariana" and the painting of the same subject by Millais. In this poem Tennyson does focus more exclusively on the psychological state of the trapped maiden, and there is no relief to be gained from the outside world. Beyond the neglected garden stretches a dreary wasteland, and Mariana's situation turns everything, even the "thick-moted sunbeam" (TW, 190), to desolation. However, Millais's painting intensifies this claustrophobic atmosphere, and further diminishes the effect of outside landscape. His Mariana stands by a window, but her gaze is blocked by stained glass, and the fragmentary landscape glimpsed does not stretch out as level waste. Instead, a wall of vegetation provides a second barrier to vision. In the illustration that Millais did for the Moxon *Tennyson*, Mariana does not even gaze out of the window, but sinks down in an attitude of despair.

Rossetti's illustrations for the Moxon *Tennyson* do not take as their theme the image of the trapped lady or soul. This is somewhat surprising, since as David Sonstroem writes, "Most of his paintings show enclosed spaces with oppressive atmospheres that confine the figures."[12] A stanza such as the following from "The Palace of Art" could almost have been written for a Rossetti painting:

> Shut up as in a crumbling tomb, girt round
>     With blackness as a solid wall,
> Far off she seemed to hear the dully sound
>     Of human footsteps fall.
>         (TW, 417)

[12] Sonstroem, *Rossetti and the Fair Lady*, p. 11.

But Rossetti may have felt that such an explicit scene limited his own invention too drastically; he preferred something "where one can allegorize on one's own hook on the subject of the poem, without killing, for oneself and everyone, a distinct idea of the poet's."[13] All the scenes that he chose to illustrate are set in the open air, although there is little sense of space or fresh air in the way in which he handles them. His *Lady of Shalott* shows the lady in her boat, with Lancelot bending over her; the perspective is shallow, and most of the surface is filled by the foreshortened figure of Lancelot.

The two stanzas that Rossetti chose from "The Palace of Art" depict imaginary scenes that decorate the Palace rooms:

> Or in a clear-walled city on the sea,
>   Near gilded organ-pipes, her hair
> Wound with white roses, slept St Cecily;
>   An angel looked at her.
>             (*TW*, 406)

and:

> Or mythic Uther's deeply-wounded son
>   In some fair space of sloping greens
> Lay, dozing in the vale of Avalon,
>   And watched by weeping queens.
>             (*TW*, 407)

Both stanzas are strikingly visual, almost "painterly," but both are transformed by Rossetti into something quite different from the original. He has filled the background of the St. Cecilia drawing with a mass of ships, buildings, and soldiers (Fig. 8), so that the sense of distance in Tennyson's "clear-walled city on the sea" is quite lost. As in so many Pre-Raphaelite paintings, the effect is of two-dimensional patterning. An even more startling transformation is made in the line "an angel looked at her"; Rossetti's angel clasps St. Cecilia and bends closely over her.

[13] Letter to William Allingham, January 1855, in *Letters of Dante Gabriel Rossetti*, ed. Doughty and Wahl, I, 239.

So also, in the design for *Arthur and the Weeping Queens* (Fig. 9), the crowded mass of queens in the foreground almost completely blocks out the surrounding landscape. Gone is Tennyson's "fair space of sloping greens"; as for Arthur, he is almost lost to sight in a bower of queens. Even when Rossetti chooses to illustrate scenes that are set in the open, he somehow contrives to surround and enclose his figures, and to rob the background of its distance. He has what one might call the "embowering consciousness."

This consciousness may be demonstrated by paging through any volume of Rossetti's paintings; in one illustration after another, single figures or small tightly-knit groups are set against a closely patterned background, which encloses them and allows almost no sense of spatial depth. The same "embowering consciousness" is also, though less obviously, a characteristic of his poetry. In many of his poems the human figures are placed in an enclosed space, often a bower set in a garden or in a woodland glade.

Most often, as one might expect, the bower is a safe haven for lovers, but it is not always or simply that. It can also take on the qualities of a shrine, and sometimes, as with Tennyson's gardens, its privacy turns into privation. But Rossetti does not, like Tennyson, make his retreat into a symbol of the poetic consciousness, or a "garden of the mind." It is not a place for solitary contemplation, but is almost always associated with the presence of the Beloved. Unlike Arnold's forest glade, which it superficially resembles, it is not a presexual paradise. Indeed, in its most positive form, it is a bower of sexual bliss, an erotic space that is cut off from society and the world of men, laws, and action. No hint of the social, economic, or marital status of the lovers is allowed to penetrate the enclosure.

For his bower of bliss, Rossetti could have drawn on two powerful traditions in English poetry. Spenser's "Bowre of blis" in *The Faerie Queene*, although outwardly beautiful, is a place of currupt sensuality dominated by an evil enchantress who turns men into beasts. Its groves and arbors must be broken down "with rigour pitilesse" by Sir Guyon.[14] Rossetti has no equivalent of Sir Guyon, and does not see sensual love as corrupt, but some of his women, as will be shown later, do have the qualities of the *femme fatale*.

Another famous bower of bliss is to be found in *Paradise Lost*, and as the title of Rossetti's poem, "Eden Bower," suggests, this lost paradisal bower is an important mythic prototype. Milton's bower is the seat of innocent sexual love, unlike Spenser's, and his description of Adam and Eve's nuptial couch, so secluded and richly decorative, has the quality of a painting by Rossetti:

the roof
Of thickest covert was inwoven shade
Laurel and myrtle, and what higher grew
Of firm and fragrant leaf; on either side
Acanthus, and each odorous bushy shrub
Fenced up the verdant wall; each beauteous flower,
Iris all hues, roses, and jessamine
Reared high their flourished heads between,
        and wrought
Mosaic.[15]

Rossetti lacks Milton's stern theology and moral purpose, of course, but in "The Blessed Damozel" (see Fig. 12) he imagines a paradise that is essentially a recovery of the nuptial bower of Adam and Eve. Rossetti's lovers, looking forward to a physical reunion in heaven, are not, after all, so different from Milton's Edenic lovers, "Imparadised in one another's arms" (IV.506).

The paradisal bower of Christian mythology also has its pagan counterpart. In Rossetti's "Love Enthroned" the bower is the imaginary dwelling place of the god of Love:

[14] Spenser, *The Faerie Queene*, II.xii.83.
[15] Milton, *Paradise Lost*, IV, 692-700.

Love's throne was not with these; but far above
All passionate wind of welcome and farewell
He sat in breathless bowers they dream not of.[16]

In this context "breathless" is not meant to suggest the oppressive and stifling atmosphere that one feels in so many of Rossetti's paintings; it is meant to suggest only that Love's bowers are unearthly and above the turmoil and uncertainty of passion, like Keat's "All breathing human passion far above," in the "Ode on a Grecian Urn" (Keats, p. 535). This striving for the imperishable ideal is also to be found in "Love's Lovers," where there is a "bower of unimagined flower and tree" (RW, 77).

The earthly bower cannot guarantee such perfection. In a hostile world, its main function is to provide a safe and secret retreat for the lovers, but even within its protective enclosure absolute bliss can only rarely be attained. Precisely because it excludes the world, the bower can only be a temporary haven. The lovers' brief moment of unity is constantly threatened by outside forces, natural change, and, above all, by the passage of time:

A little while a little love
    The scattering autumn hoards for us
    Whose bower is not yet ruinous
Nor quite unleaved our songless grove.
            ("A Little While," RW, 206)

Human love seems to depend entirely on the seasonal pattern, so that "songless" applies not only to the absence of birds in the grove, but also to a certain autumnal joylessness in their love, which will be scattered like the last leaves. "Nor quite unleaved" links summer's rich and abundant growth with fulfilled love, and also suggests the lovers' need for protection, cover, and concealment. Similarly, in "Sleepless Dreams" (RW, 87), the night that brings dreams of love is "deep-leaved,"

[16] Dante Gabriel Rossetti, Works, ed. William Michael Rossetti, p. 74. Hereafter cited as RW with page numbers.

and in "Winged Hours" (*RW*, 83), the speaker looks forward despairingly to that hour when they will be separated, and he will be "wandering round my life unleaved."

Even worse is the desolation and emptiness of "A New Year's Burden," in which the lovers do meet, but without love:

> Along the grass sweet airs are blown
> Our way this day in Spring.
> Of all the songs that we have known
> Now which one shall we sing?
> Not that, my love, ah no!—
> Not this, my love? why, so!—
> Yet both were ours, but hours will come and go.
>
> The grove is all a pale frail mist,
> The new year sucks the sun.
> Of all the kisses that we kissed
> Now which shall be the one?
> Not that my love, ah no!—
> Not this, my love?—heigh-ho
> For all the sweets that all the winds can blow!
>
> The branches cross above our eyes,
> The skies are in a net:
> And what's the thing beneath the skies
> We two would most forget?
> Not birth, my love, no, no,—
> Not death, my love, no, no,—
> The love once ours, but ours long hours ago.
>
> (*RW*, 207)

Human love may decline with the seasons, but spring does not necessarily bring renewal. Rossetti's use of a bleak and wintry landscape as an objective correlative for dead love looks forward to Thomas Hardy's "Neutral Tones." The balladlike refrain also suggests Hardy, as does the ironic, despairing tone of the poem. The branches that once protected the lovers are now leafless and form a net, as if old love and

ROSSETTI

its bower have become a trap of dead memories from which
the lovers cannot escape.

Sometimes the bower even acts to exclude the lover himself,
as well as the hostile world. In "The Song of the Bower" the
speaker yearns for the beloved: "What were my prize, could
I enter thy bower, / This day, to-morrow, at eve or at morn?"
(*RW*, 207). The keynote of Rossetti's love poetry is, in general,
desire, or regret for what is past, rather than fulfillment.

However, in a small group of the sonnets in *The House of
Life* he does celebrate a fulfilled love. These poems, almost
certainly inspired by Jane Morris, have unusually sunny and
bright backgrounds. In "The Lovers' Walk" the setting is by
a woodland stream on a June day:

> Sweet twining hedgeflowers wind-stirred in no wise
>   On this June day; and hand that clings to hand:—
>   Still glades; and meeting faces scarcely fann'd:—
> An osier-odoured stream that draws the skies
> Deep to its heart; and mirrored eyes in eyes:—
>   Fresh hourly wonder o'er the Summer land
>   Of light and cloud; and two souls softly spann'd
> With one o'erarching heaven of smiles and sighs:—
> Even such their path, whose bodies lean unto
>   Each other's visible sweetness amorously,—
>   Whose passionate hearts lean by Love's high decree
> Together on his heart for ever true
> As the cloud-foaming firmamental blue
>   Rests on the blue line of a foamless sea.
>                                      (*RW*, 78)

There is no sense of confinement to a secret bower here, and
the lovers seem to be open to all the beauties of "the Summer
land," although a protective note is given by the "twining
hedgeflowers," the "still glades," and the complete lack of
threatening or intrusive wind. It is as though for one rare
moment the whole earth has become love's bower, "With one
o'erarching heaven of smiles and sighs." Even the sea is robbed
of its customary threat, and is used here as an image of calm

144

and loving unity. It is "foamless," which once again suggests lack of wind, and gives the scene something of the quality of the "breathless bowers" of "Love Enthroned" (*RW*, 74).

In "Youth's Spring-Tribute" (*RW*, 79) the setting is again by a woodland stream, and the lovers lie "On this sweet bank." It is early spring, and a hint of menace is still present from the wind: "Spring's foot half falters," and "through her bowers the wind's way is still clear." But on this day at least, "April's sun strikes down the glades," and the lovers can relax.

Wind is consistently seen as an enemy to love; for Rossetti, unlike Shelley, it does not suggest freedom and exhilaration, only the desolation and destruction of winter. It is an agent of change: it strips away the protective covering over the lovers, "and when flown / All joys, and through dark forest-boughs in flight / The wind swoops onward brandishing the light" ("Ardour and Memory," *RW*, 96). Light is here brandished like a sword, and is in general also regarded as an enemy, except where the source of light is the Beloved. Her face may be "like a governing star," which "Gathers and garners from all things that are / Their silent penetrative loveliness" ("Gracious Moonlight," *RW*, 81), or her glance may be "like water brimming with the sky / Or hyacinth-light where forest-shadows fall" ("Her Gifts," *RW*, 85). On rare occasions and in conditions of perfect stillness, the full light of summer can be used to celebrate the perfect union of the lovers; this is achieved in "Silent Noon":

Your hands lie open in the long fresh grass,—
    The finger-points look through the rosy blooms:
    Your eyes smile peace. The pasture gleams and glooms
'Neath billowing skies that scatter and amass.
All round our nest, far as the eye can pass,
    Are golden kingcup-fields with silver edge
    Where the cow-parsley skirts the hawthorn-hedge.
'Tis visible silence, still as the hour-glass.

Deep in the sun-searched growths the dragon-fly
Hangs like a blue thread loosened from the sky:—

So this wing'd hour is dropt to us from above.
Oh! clasp we to our hearts, for deathless dower,
This close-companioned inarticulate hour
When twofold silence was the song of love.
                                        (RW, 81)

This is perhaps the most open setting ever depicted by Rossetti as a meeting-place of happy lovers, and even here the lovers are protected by "the long fresh grass" which forms a "nest" for them. Their security is further enhanced by the absence of wind, which creates the illusion that at this noon hour, time itself has stopped: everything is "still as the hour-glass." However, as Stephen Spector has pointed out, the "attempt to construct a sanctuary must ultimately fail," and the choice of noon as the perfect moment underlines the precarious nature of the happiness achieved by the lovers.[17] Noon is literally a moment, gone almost before it is perceived, and even in this poem there is a suggestion of change: "The pasture gleams and glooms / 'Neath billowing skies that scatter and amass." The skies are beautiful, and carry no immediate threat, but they are a reminder of what may come. The modulation from "gleams" to "glooms" is significant, and "scatter" brings in a note of destruction. The lovers in their grassy nest are safe from the wind for the moment, but its effects are still visible in the clouds above them.

Just as love needs to be enclosed and hidden, so the most perfect and beautiful things are hidden from vulgar eyes:

                    Heaven's own screen
Hides her soul's purest depth and loveliest glow;
    Closely withheld, as all things most unseen,—
    The wave-bowered pearl,—the heart-shaped seal of
        green
That flecks the snowdrop underneath the snow.
            ("True Woman: Herself," RW, 93)

[17] Spector, "Rossetti's Self-Destroying 'Moment's Monument': 'Silent Noon,' " Victorian Poetry, 14 (1976), 54.

1. John Martin, *Manfred on the Jungfrau*

2. Thomas Rowlandson, *Doctor Syntax Tumbling into the Water*

3. A Victorian "wild" garden

4. A Victorian garden with formal elements

5. John Millais, *Ophelia*

6. William Holman Hunt, *The Hireling Shepherd*

7. William Holman Hunt,
*The Lady of Shalott*

8. Dante Gabriel Rossetti, *St. Cecilia*

9. Dante Gabriel Rossetti, *King Arthur and
the Weeping Queens*

10. Dante Gabriel Rossetti, *The Day Dreams*

11. Dante Gabriel Rossetti, *How They Met Themselves*

12. Dante Gabriel Rossetti, *The Blessed Damozel 1871-1877*

13. (*above*) George Robert Lewis, *Hereford, Dynedor and the Malvern Hills, from the Haywood Lodge, Harvest Scene, Afternoon*
14. (*middle*) Thomas Hardy, *Her Death and After*
15. (*below*) Thomas Hardy, *She, to Him*

Man can only know the perfect woman as a "sacred secret" (*RW*, 93), and for such a woman the bower becomes a shrine which encloses her perfection and places the lover at a respectful distance. A particularly beautiful example of this may be found in "The Day Dream," written for the painting of the same title (Fig. 10):

The thronged boughs of the shadowy sycamore
　　Still bear young leaflets half the summer through;
　　From when the robin 'gainst the unhidden blue
Perched dark, till now, deep in the leafy core,
The embowered throstle's urgent wood-notes soar
　　Through summer silence. Still the leaves come new;
　　Yet never rosy-sheathed as those which drew
Their spiral tongues from spring-buds heretofore.

Within the branching shade of Reverie
Dreams even may spring till autumn; yet none be
　　Like woman's budding day-dream spirit-fann'd.
Lo! tow'rd deep skies, not deeper than her look,
She dreams; till now on her forgotten book
　　Drops the forgotten blossom from her hand.
　　　　　　　　　　　　　　　(*RW*, 231)

Here the woman is protected by the "thronged boughs," but there is no sense of her being trapped, and the atmosphere is not oppressive. Rossetti maintains a delicate balance between the rich fullness of summer foliage and the "young leaflets" which continue to act as a reminder of spring and new life. But the throstle's song is "urgent," and even the new leaves are not "rosy-sheathed" like those of spring. The woman is to some extent free from the seasonal tyranny, since her "budding day-dream" is "spirit-fann'd." Moreover, she gazes "tow'rd deep skies," not with the frustrated longing of a Mariana by her window, but in hopeful reverie; her "Dreams even may spring till autumn," and her gaze is deeper than the sky.

It has been claimed that the "phenomena of Nature are admitted by [Rossetti] only on condition that they enter his verse with a very personal significance, reduced to symbols."[18] This may be largely true, but "reduced" has a pejorative tone. Rossetti's spring buds certainly carry a symbolic significance, but the lines that describe them are rich with accurately observed detail. The man who saw the "spiral tongues" of new leaves thrusting from their rosy sheaths, or the robin "Perched dark" in silhouette against the "unhidden blue" of the winter sky, is not merely dealing in arid symbols. In fact, Rossetti uses a wealth of natural imagery in *The House of Life* sonnets; this was recognized in a perceptive article by Henri Talon, although Talon went too far when he suggested that Rossetti's "vision et son sentiment de la nature . . . sont l'âme de son esthétique."[19]

Rossetti's shrine-like bowers are seldom as serene as in "The Day-Dream," however. In "The Portrait," for example, the atmosphere is charged and heavy:

In painting her I shrined her face
'Mid mystic trees, where light falls in
Hardly at all; a covert place.
(*RW*, 169)

George Ford has commented on the "way in which Keats's rendering of landscape anticipated the Victorians,"[20] and one might quote the woodland glade of "embalmèd darkness" in the "Ode to a Nightingale" as anticipating Rossetti's "covert place." And, as in Keats's "Ode," there is a balance between attraction and revulsion in the poet's attitude to this dim, mystic bower. After the reverent tone of the opening lines, the stanza takes an unexpected turn, and the "covert place" becomes strangely noisy and populated:

Where you might think to find a din
Of doubtful talk, and a live flame

[18] Welby, *The Victorian Romantics 1850-1870*, p. 33.
[19] Talon, "Dante Gabriel Rossetti, peintre-poète dans *La Maison de Vie*," *Études anglaises*, 19 (1966), 5.
[20] Ford, *Keats and the Victorians*, p. 138.

Wandering, and many a shape whose name
Not itself knoweth, and old dew,
And your own footsteps meeting you,
And all things going as they came.
(*RW*, 169)

The sacred grove is haunted by strange voices and ghostly shapes; it is the shrine of memory. What Rossetti is really describing is the artistic process whereby the poem or painting ("The Portrait") becomes the repository of the past, a place where you encounter "old dew." The work of art is a means of cheating both time and the laws of nature, "As though mine image in the glass / Should tarry when myself am gone," but, as these lines suggest, the process of cheating time involves introspection and a turning back upon oneself that may result in meeting "your own footsteps meeting you." Rossetti's self-enclosed bowers are, in the end, solipsistic, and one even begins to doubt the existence of the Beloved. In this dim world, where no light must penetrate, is she not merely an artifact, an image in the glass of the poet's imagination?

Such an interpretation receives some support from the "Willowwood" sonnets. In the first of these the lover sits by a woodside well with Love beside him, gazing into the waters. His passionate longing transforms the reflection of Love into the image of the Beloved. But the logic of the poem demands that we recognize, in the end, that both Love and the Beloved are nothing more than reflections of the poet himself. What he must kiss when he leans down to greet "her own lips rising there" (*RW*, 90) are his own lips reflected in the water.

Rossetti was haunted by the idea of meeting his own image, and made it the subject of a dramatic and somewhat disturbing painting, *How They Met Themselves* (Fig. 11), in which a couple "encounter their visual doubles, whose sight (according to the assumed superstition) brings death."[21] In the painting the two couples meet in just such a deep, dim wood as that described in "The Portrait." The bower, meeting place

---

[21] Sonstroem, *Rossetti and the Fair Lady*, p. 32.

of lovers, is therefore also closely associated with death. Indeed, it might be said that the very qualities that make the bower a perfect trysting place (its secrecy and remoteness from the concerns of the world) are also the qualities of the grave.

In "The Portrait" Rossetti moves between two remembered worlds, one of which, the hushed, shrinelike bower in the woods, is included in both poem and painting. The other, a more realistic world containing a house, enters only the poem. Its exclusion from the painting implies that poem and painting had different functions for Rossetti. The painting is a kind of icon, an object of worship bearing little relation to reality. It is also a static monument to a possibly imaginary moment in time. The poem, on the other hand, moves through time. It describes how the lovers met in the woods, but were driven into the house by a real thunderstorm. That evening in the house he spoke his soul to her again, and Rossetti uses one of his vivid flashes of landscape to convey a sense of impending doom:

> That eve I spoke those words again
> Beside the pelted window pane;
>   And there she hearkened what I said,
>   With under-glances that surveyed
> The empty pastures blind with rain.
>             (*RW*, 169)

The real woman that he remembers in the poem, who takes shelter from the rain, stands by the window, and directs her glance to the bleak reality outside, is a very different creature from the goddess enshrined forever " 'Mid mystic trees" in his poem/painting. If she had lived, her keen perception of the outside world, and, one suspects, her divided attention (she listens to his lovemaking while watching the rain outside), might have come between her and her ardent lover. Because she died, he can safely enshrine her in his painting, giving her the immortality of art. In his poem he takes more risks, remembering the complex human being.

The woodland groves where the lovers meet can also become the ghostly landscape described by Love in "Willow-wood: 3" (*RW* 91), which is haunted by lovers separated through death. They cannot rest in love's bower, but must "walk with hollow faces burning white." They have achieved the immortality that normally eludes Rossetti's lovers, but such an immortality is pure torment: "Better all life forget her than this thing / That Willowwood should hold her wandering!" Willowwood is a landscape of the mind, dominated by memory. It exists only in Love's song, and, as we have seen, Love and the poet are one. Moreover, this song is sung while the poet is kissing the reflection in the well, so that the poet is directing the advice to "forget her" against himself at the very moment that memory has recreated her face and the illusion of a kiss. When both song and kiss end in "Willow-wood: 4" (*RW*, 91), her face falls back drowned. In this last sonnet of the series, the wind again plays a role as an agent of destruction. The lovers are compared to two roses who "Together cling through the wind's well-away," but who "drop loosened" at the end of the day. The difference between the wind here and in other poems, however, is that it is seen in this poem as performing a necessary, if somewhat painful, function. By the end of the sequence, the poet may not be completely free from the sterility of death, but for a while, at least, he has drowned his obsession.

The dual nature of the bower as a place of both love and death is explored further in the poem "Fiammetta," and in "The Orchard Pit." "Fiammetta" is another of Rossetti's sonnets written for a companion painting, and the poem has a strikingly visual quality:

Behold Fiammetta, shown in Vision here.
    Gloom-girt 'mid Spring-flushed apple-growth she
        stands;
    And as she sways the branches with her hands,
Along her arm the sundered bloom falls sheer,
In separate petals shed, each like a tear;
    While from the quivering bough the bird expands

His wings. And lo! thy spirit understands
Life shaken and shower'd and flown, and Death drawn
near.

All stirs with change. Her garments beat the air:
The angel circling round her aureole
Shimmers in flight against the tree's grey bole:
While she, with reassuring eyes most fair,
A presage and a promise stands; as 'twere
On Death's dark storm the rainbow of the Soul.

(*RW*, 220)

The "Spring-flushed apple-growth" that provides a beautiful
frame for the lady would seem to symbolize new life and hope,
but the apple is usually associated by Rossetti with temptation
and the Fall, as in "Eden Bower."[22] Moreover, another kind
of "fall" is involved here as the shaken bough sheds its blooms,
presaging death. The lady herself is as ambiguous as her bower.
She is "gloom-girt," and her action causes the blossoms to
fall and the bird to fly. Yet she has "reassuring eyes most
fair." A symbol of death and change, she represents an attempt
on Rossetti's part to come to terms with those powerful and
threatening forces. Whereas in "Silent Noon" Rossetti had
attempted to enshrine the static moment, here he is strongly
attracted to mutability. Fiammetta is associated with move-
ment throughout: things around her sway and quiver, shake
and shimmer. No wind is mentioned, but her "garments beat
the air" as if she were the wind herself. Through her, the poet
is brought to understand "Life shaken and shower'd and flown,
and Death drawn near." In some respects a dark poem, this
represents a movement away from sterile self-absorption, or
the equally sterile worship of a self-created image of the Be-
loved.

More sinister than Fiammetta, the lady of "The Orchard

[22] See also Rossetti's design for the Oxford Union, *Launcelot at the Shrine
of the Sanc Grael* (Surtees, *Paintings and Drawings*, Pl. no. 118), in which
Guenevere stands gazing at Launcelot with her arms stretched out on the
branches of an apple tree. The symbolism in this painting, however, is strangely
ambiguous, since Guenevere seems to be both temptress and Christ-figure.

152

Pit" gives no reassurances, and her bower amid the apple trees screens the hidden pit of death:

In the soft dell, among the apple trees,
    High up above the hidden pit she stands,
And there forever sings, who gave to these,
That lie below, her magic hour of ease,
    And those her apples holden in their hands.
                                        (*RW*, 240)

In this ultimate nightmare, the "soft dell" that should be a refuge for happy lovers is transformed into a grave. But in spite of the horrors of the pit, death is offered by the lady as a gift, a "magic hour of ease" to be desired almost as much as love.

In the prose version of "The Orchard Pit," a story that has strong echoes of Keats's "La Belle Dame Sans Merci," the knight dreams that he follows the siren's song "down the slope through the thick wall of bough and fruit and blossom" (*RW*, 609). She sings first of Love, then of Life, finally of the sweetness of Death:

And then my path was cleared; and she stood over against me in the fork of the tree I knew so well, blazing now like a lamp beneath the moon. And one kiss I had of her mouth, as I took the apple from her hand. But while I bit it, my brain whirled and my foot stumbled; and I felt my crashing fall through the tangled boughs beneath her feet, and saw the dead white faces that welcomed me in the pit.

It is interesting to note that in this version the knight does bite the apple, thus lending support to the reading of the poem preferred by Oswald Doughty in his 1957 edition of Rossetti's *Poems*. Where most editors, including William Rossetti, have "bitter apples" in line 2, Doughty has "bitten apples."[23] This

---

[23] Rossetti, *Poems*, ed. Doughty, p. 307. See also George Ford's note on the poem in *The Norton Anthology of English Literature*, 4th ed., New York: Norton, 1979, II, 1,519.

reading identifies the lady more strongly with the Tempter in the Garden, and the bite is followed by a literal Fall into death.

As I have already suggested, there is a strong resemblance between Rossetti's soft but treacherous orchard pit, and the deep, woodland pool in Browning's *Pauline*. In Rossetti, the pit is more obviously symbolic of the female sexual organ, and indeed, it is very tempting to see all Rossetti's bowers as tending toward such symbolism. Unlike Browning, however, Rossetti is very strongly drawn to the bower or pit, even when it holds out the promise of death.

The association between sexuality and death, so strong in "The Orchard Pit," is only present when the woman is seen as a *femme fatale*. In poems celebrating a less dangerous love the bower is not sinister, though it may still be described in sexually suggestive language, as in "Sleepless Dreams," where the speaker imagines "Some shadowy palpitating grove" (*RW*, 87). If the lady is neither a *femme fatale* nor the Beloved, she may be a fallen woman for whom the bower becomes a place of alienation rather than the setting for bliss or dangerous seduction.

Such a bower may be found in "The Bride's Prelude," where a contrast is drawn between the innocent sister who stands by the window "With eyes that sought the sun," and the guilty sister who shrinks back into the gloom:

> But where the walls in long brocade
> Were screened, as one who is afraid
> Sat Aloÿse within the shade.
>
> And even in shade was gleam enough
>     To shut out full repose
> From the bride's tiring-chamber, which
> Was like the inner altar-niche
> Whose dimness worship has made rich.
>                         (*RW*, 17)

The last two lines are heavily ironic, since no one now worships Aloÿse; her chamber is a shrine only for her own troubled thoughts, which hang on the air like incense. The glimpses of the outside world that are gained from the window of this chamber only serve to make the atmosphere within more oppressive:

Some minutes since, two rooks had toiled
  Home to the nests that crowned
Ancestral ash-trees. Through the glare
Beating again, they seemed to tear
With that thick caw the woof o' the air.
(RW, 22)

One is reminded of the "Birds in the high Hall-garden" that call "Maud, Maud" (TW, 1061), but although their cry seemed sinister, at least it came to Maud and her lover in the open air. Everything in Rossetti's poem is more stifling. Even though his rooks seem to be toiling home in the full light of day instead of at twilight, there is no relief to be gained from the sun, which is merely a "glare." Indeed, the air has a thick, palpable quality that enables the caw of the rooks to rip through it as if it were fabric.[24] The sound filters into the chamber, but neither sister sees the landscape; even Amelotte has her face buried, and feels "Between her hands in narrow space / Her own hot breath upon her face" (RW, 23).

In Rossetti's paintings, as indicated earlier, there are very few landscapes that are not enclosed and bowerlike. Indeed, Ruskin complained that Rossetti refused the "aid of pure landscape and sky," and that "his foliage looked generally fit for nothing but a fire-screen, and his landscape distances like the furniture of a Noah's Ark from the nearest toyshop."[25] In his poems, however, there are many vivid glimpses of landscape, although, as Mégroz has pointed out, the "forces and scenes of non-human nature . . . are made to serve as metaphysical imagery by Rossetti much more than as pictorial description

[24] There is perhaps an echo here of Shakespeare's "Light thickens, and the crow / Makes wing to the rooky wood" (Macbeth, III.ll.50-51).
[25] Ruskin, Works, XXXIII, 271-72.

for its own sake."[26] This is true of "The Bride's Prelude," in which the heat and stillness of the chamber are set against the desolate landscape evoked by Aloÿse as she tells her story. When she and her family fled the ravages of war they were exposed to the elements; wind and wave assumed terrifying shapes and stalked across the bleak wasteland:

> At dawn the sea was there
> And the sea-wind: afar
> The ravening surge was hoarse and loud
> And underneath the dim dawn-cloud
> Each stalking wave shook like a shroud.
> (*RW*, 29)

And later, when they took shelter, the threatening sea wind battered their refuge:

> Through the gaunt windows the great gales
> Bore in the tattered clumps
> Of waif-weed and the tamarisk-boughs;
> And sea-mews, 'mid the storm's carouse,
> Were flung, wild clamouring, in the house.
> (*RW*, 31)

Like Tennyson, Arnold, and, as we shall see, Swinburne, Rossetti often associated the sea with death. As Florence Boos writes, he "admired the sensations peculiar to enclosed and baroquely decorated places, so it is natural that the enveloping and expansive sea should suggest to him chiefly images of rupture and loss."[27] One might go further and say that any open landscape suggested "rupture and loss" to Rossetti. We have already noted his antipathy to the wind, associated with unprotected landscapes, and we have seen how in "The Portrait" the "empty pastures blind with rain" are set against the sanctuary of the "deep dim wood." In the same poem the

---

[26] Mégroz, *Dante Gabriel Rossetti: Painter Poet of Heaven in Earth*, p. 186.

[27] Boos, *The Poetry of Dante G. Rossetti: A Critical Reading and Source Study*, p.68.

speaker describes a world emptied of her presence in terms of open heath, exposed to the skies:

For now doth daylight disavow
  Those days—nought left to see or hear.
Only in solemn whispers now
  At night-time these things reach mine ear;
When the leaf-shadows at a breath
Shrink in the road, and all the heath,
  Forest and water, far and wide,
  In limpid starlight glorified,
Lie like the mystery of death.
                    (*RW*, 170)

He cannot sleep, and wanders at night through the "glades where once she walked with me" to the "desolate verge of light" where "Yearned loud the iron-bosomed sea" (*RW*, 170).

In the ballads and narrative poems almost all open land-scapes, and, in particular, seascapes, are associated with disaster. One might quote "The King's Tragedy," "A Last Confession," and "Sister Helen" as examples. A partial exception is open grassland, which can be treated as pastoral rather than wasteland, and is therefore associated with innocence. In "A Last Confession," for example, the speaker tells how he first met the woman who has betrayed him. She was then a child:

                    when first I found her
Alone upon the hill-side; and her curls
Shook down in the warm grass as she looked up
Out of her curls in my eyes bent to hers.
                    (*RW*, 45)

The setting serves to underline the child's vulnerability and her need for his, at this stage, fatherly protection. The "warm grass" transforms the bleakness somewhat, and provides a nest for her over which he bends, creating a scene very much like that in "Silent Noon." However, the meeting on the exposed hillside may also give some hint of the role that the

157

child will play when she becomes a woman. Possibly one is meant to catch an echo of Keats's "cold hill's side" here, and of the meeting between the knight and La Belle Dame: "I met a lady in the meads / Full beautiful, a fairy's child" (*Keats*, p. 503). Rossetti's lady is no elfin queen, but she is equally without mercy. When he meets her for the last time, after her betrayal of him, it is on the sand with the sound of the sea in his ears. No warm grass offers protection on this occasion, and he stabs her against the lurid background of a reddened sea and sky.

"The Woodspurge" is yet another example of an open landscape used to convey loss:

The wind flapped loose, the wind was still,
Shaken out dead from tree and hill:
I had walked on at the wind's will,—
I sat now, for the wind was still.

Between my knees my forehead was,—
My lips, drawn in, said not Alas!
My hair was over in the grass,
My naked ears heard the day pass.

My eyes, wide open, had the run
Of some ten weeds to fix upon;
Among those few, out of the sun,
The woodspurge flowered, three cups in one.

From perfect grief there need not be
Wisdom or even memory:
One thing then learnt remains to me,—
The woodspurge has a cup of three.

                                        (RW, 205)

The setting is in some respects similar to that in "Silent Noon," with the main figure crouched in the grass. But the insistence on the presence of the wind makes it plain that this grass does not provide a secure "nest." The speaker tries to create his own shelter by burying his forehead between his knees, but still the exposed "naked ears heard the day pass." In this posture his landscape is reduced to "some ten weeds," and like the hero of *Maud* with the seashell, he concentrates in his misery on the structure of this small and seemingly insignificant object.

The use of bleak, open spaces to convey loss or alienation is a technique that is peculiar to Rossetti's poetry, and does not occur in his painting. It is interesting in this connection to compare the poem "The Blessed Damozel" with its companion painting (Fig. 12). In the poem Rossetti creates effects of vast distances and emptiness, a cosmic landscape of space:

> Her gaze still strove
>   Within the gulf to pierce
> Its path; and now she spoke as when
>   The stars sang in their spheres.
>
> The sun was gone now; the curled moon
>   Was like a little feather
> Fluttering far down the gulf.
> (*RW*, 4)

In the painting the gulf between the lady and her lover on earth is conveyed only by the line of the picture frame separating the two sections, and by the damozel's gaze, down toward some point out of the picture. Behind her are the groves of paradise and a protective circle of lovers embowered in each other's arms, that ultimate haven. It must be left to art critics to determine whether the difference between poem and painting is owing to Rossetti's technical limitations as a painter, or to a deliberate view of the art of painting as concerned with a two-dimensional surface. Whatever the answer, it is certain that he was able or willing to exploit certain effects in his poetry that were excluded from his painting.

One such effect is the impressionistic description of a fleeting landscape as seen from a speeding train, which Rossetti wrote in the form of a verse letter or diary of his travels in 1849. It is the most sustained piece of landscape description

that he ever produced, and the effects that he achieves are
masterly:

A constant keeping-past of shaken trees,
And a bewildered glitter of loose road;
Banks of bright growth, with single blades atop
Against white sky; and wires—a constant chain—
That seem to draw the clouds along with them
(Things which one stoops against the light to see
Through the low window; shaking by at rest,
Or fierce like water as the swiftness grows);
And, seen through fences or a bridge far off,
Trees that in moving keep their intervals
Still one 'twixt bar and bar; and then at times
Long reaches of green level, where one cow
Feeding among her fellows that feed on,
Lifts her slow neck, and gazes for the sound.

(RW, 176)

Richard Stein compares this poem to Turner's Rain, Steam, and Speed, but in fact no painting, not even the most impressionistic, can give the kind of effect that Rossetti achieves here.[28] This liberation from the fixed viewpoint had to wait in the visual arts for the movie camera. A more valid comparison might be drawn between Rossetti's poem and some of Dickens's descriptions of railway or coach journeys. In the prose piece, "A Flight" (in Reprinted Pieces) Dickens achieves visual effects similar to those of Rossetti. In his novels, he exploits the power and speed of the iron monster, often giving the train a symbolic significance that is lacking in Rossetti's poem.[29] For Rossetti, the train journey created novel visual effects, but his poem suggests that he was not involved at a very deep emotional level; indeed, it has something of the tone

[28] Stein, The Ritual of Interpretation, p. 209.
[29] For example, in Dombey and Son, the train becomes a symbol of Death: "Louder and louder yet, it shrieks and cries as it comes tearing on resistless to the goal: and now its way, still like the way of Death, is strewn with ashes thickly." Dombey and Son, ed. Garrod, p. 281.

160

of an exercise to beguile "the sore torments of the route" (*RW*, 185). Among the torments that he lists are "toothache, and headache," and "heavy well-kept landscape." The clue to his disgust may be found in that "well-kept." After describing the "Fields mown in ridges; and close garden-crops," the poet "did not scribble more . . . but yawned, and read" (*RW*, 177). It is obvious that the humanized, social, and pastoral landscapes did not speak to his imagination, which craved the more romantic and isolated settings of woodland glades and bowers.

However, the romantic sublime of mountains and lakes left him equally untouched, according to Hall Caine, who accompanied him on a visit to Cumberland.[30] The closest that Rossetti seems to have come to a Wordsworthian appreciation of scenic beauty is in the sonnet "The Hill Summit":

This feast-day of the sun, his altar there
  In the broad west has blazed for vesper-song;
  And I have loitered in the vale too long
And gaze now a belated worshipper.
Yet may I not forget that I was 'ware,
  So journeying, of his face at intervals
  Transfigured where the fringed horizon falls,—
A fiery bush with coruscating hair.

And now that I have climbed and won this height,
  I must tread downward through the sloping shade
And travel the bewildered tracks till night.
  Yet for this hour I still may here be stayed
  And see the gold air and the silver fade
And the last bird fly into the last light.
                  (*RW*, 98)

Rossetti himself did not rate the poem very highly. In a letter to Allingham he wrote: "Here's one which I remember writing in great glory on the top of a hill I reached one afternoon in

[30] See Mégroz, *Dante Gabriel Rossetti*, p. 204.

Warwickshire last year. I'm afraid, though, it isn't much good."[31]
Moreover, William Rossetti is probably right in ascribing a
symbolic meaning to the poem: "that of a career which, having
reached its shining culmination, has thereafter to decline into
the shade, and close in the night of the tomb" (RW, 655n.).
This is crudely reductive as a paraphrase, and very "Victorian"
in its insistence on a moral. In other poems, however, the poet
himself deliberately and more obviously supplies the symbolic
interpretation of a natural description. "The Sea-Limits," for
example, makes the symbolic significance of the sea clear, and
in "Sunset Wings" an impressionistic description of starlings
flying home to roost is given a moral twist: "Even thus Hope's
hours, in ever-eddying flight, / To many a refuge tend" (RW,
220). Like Holman Hunt, Rossetti tended to find "in Nature
a typology for the things of the spirit."[32]

What he does not find is the kind of spiritual sustenance
that Arnold had found. He shares Arnold's taste for land-
scapes of refuge, but he has no desire to be alone with nature;
he wishes his retreat to be shared by "the one necessary per-
son."[33] His ideal landscape is therefore less solitary than Ar-
nold's; it takes no account of social laws and it excludes the
crowded scene, but it contains the perfect society of two lov-
ers. However, it is perhaps inevitable that the man whose
"felicitous space"[34] is an enclosed bower should sometimes
end up feeling trapped or threatened by his surroundings. The
drive toward a refuge that is completely safe and cut off from
the world is basically paranoiac, and that paranoia may feed
the terrible fear that the refuge itself conceals the most extreme

[31] Quoted by Baum in his edition of The House of Life, p. 172.
[32] Meisel, " 'Half Sick of Shadows': The Aesthetic Dialogue in Pre-Raph-
aelite Painting," in Nature and the Victorian Imagination, p. 328.
[33] "By the end of September 1872 Rossetti was back at Kelmscott. 'But
all, I now find by experience,' he wrote to his brother, 'depends primarily
on my not being deprived of the prospect of the society of the one necessary
person.' " Henderson, William Morris, p. 132.
[34] I have borrowed this happy phrase from the title of George Ford's essay
in Nature and the Victorian Imagination.

danger. Tennyson had discovered the perils of solipsism in his antisocial landscapes of withdrawal. Rossetti made the same discovery, and added the perilous attractions of the *femme fatale*; but unlike Tennyson, he did not move out of his enclosed bowers toward a social landscape.

CHAPTER VI

# MORRIS:
# THE FIELD FULL OF FOLK

In many respects no two poets could be more dissimilar than
Rossetti and William Morris, although both have been la-
belled "Pre-Raphaelite." In most of Morris's poetry we seem
to emerge from the dim, shadowy recesses beloved by Rossetti
into a world that C. S. Lewis describes as "at first very pale
and cold, but also very fresh and spacious."[1] Moreover, Mor-
ris's spacious world is likely to be much more highly populated
than Rossetti's. Instead of the closed society of two, Morris,
like William Langland, looks forward to the pastoral or georgic
ideal of a "fair feld ful of folk," such as that depicted by
George Robert Lewis in his *Harvest Scene* (Fig. 13).[2]

Morris's preference for the social landscape should throw
some light on whether he was really an escapist who sought
"to evade life rather than to express it," as many critics have
claimed.[3] More recently, critics have defended him against
such a charge. For example, John Hollow sees this "idle singer
of an empty day" as someone who is vitally concerned with

[1] Lewis, "William Morris," in *Rehabilitations and Other Essays*, p. 40.
[2] This painting is undoubtedly an idealized depiction of the dignity of labor,
but I cannot agree with Barrell's assertion that such paintings serve the ide-
ology of the ruling classes. He states that "the picture is entirely directed to
confirming the liberty of the poorest of England's subjects, and not to chal-
lenging their servitude" (*The Dark Side*, p. 117). Is it possible to confirm
liberty without challenging servitude? Whatever the intentions of the artist
may have been, the painting has a life of its own, and it remains subtly
subversive. To suggest that laborers do have dignity, worth, and freedom is
at least to suggest that they ought to have those qualities.
[3] Hoare, *The Work of Morris and Yeats in Relation to Early Saga Liter-
ature*, p. 140.

164

the problem of immortality in a world empty of God.[4] Marxist critics, such as Jessie Kocmanová, have also stressed the realistic element in Morris's poetry, and his "narrative power, organizing intellect, materialistic thought and concern for humanity, which led to the latest flowering in his socialist poetry."[5] Some of us might be prepared to grant the validity of much of Kocmanová's criticism without necessarily sharing her high opinion of Morris's socialist verse. Certainly, if Morris had simply been an escapist, one would expect him to have favored landscapes of refuge and retreat, such as those chosen by Rossetti and Arnold. Instead he turns, like the mature Tennyson, to the social landscape, although, as we shall see, he projects it very differently. On the other hand, those critics who see Morris purely through Marxist spectacles may sometimes ignore that aspect of his work which was most Pre-Raphaelite. Morris looked forward to a socialist utopia, but he also looked back, like many Victorians, to a preindustrial age. His love of the Middle Ages and of medieval literature made the enclosed garden a place of special significance to him, and I shall deal with his use of this type of setting first.

Such a setting is almost always seen by Morris as a meeting place for lovers. Guenevere remembers meeting Launcelot in "a quiet garden walled round every way," and in "King Arthur's Tomb" Launcelot thinks of his past happiness with the Queen as "the old garden life."[6] Blue Calhoun has made the point that Morris is deliberately using the Edenic theme in such poems, emphasized by "the introduction of Launcelot in biblical rhetoric: 'In that garden fair came Launcelot walking.'"[7] "The Defence of Guenevere" is, of course, a dramatic

[4] Hollow, "Singer of an Empty Day: William Morris and the Desire for Immortality."

[5] Kocmanová, "The Poetic Maturing of William Morris," *Brno Studies in English*, 5 (1964), 208.

[6] *The Collected Works of William Morris*, ed. May Morris, I, 4, 11. Hereafter cited as *MW* with volume and page numbers.

[7] Calhoun, *The Pastoral Vision of William Morris*, p. 44.

monologue, and Morris rigorously excludes authorial judg-
ment from the poem, but as we hear Guenevere talking we
cannot but be aware that even in those happy garden days,
hers was not the consciousness of pristine innocence:

"I was right joyful of that wall of stone,
That shut the flowers and trees up with the sky,
And trebled all the beauty: to the bone,

"Yea right through to my heart, grown very shy
With weary thoughts, it pierced, and made me glad;
Exceedingly glad, and I knew verily,

"A little thing just then had made me mad."
(MW, I, 4)

The aestheticism of "trebled all the beauty," the "weary
thoughts," and the self-awareness all make Guenevere the
product of a more conscious world than that depicted in *Gen-
esis*, or even in Malory. The myth of Eden works here to
provide an ironic contrast to the lady who protests somewhat
too much:

"Nevertheless you, O Sir Gauwaine, lie,
Whatever happened on through all those years,
God knows I speak truth, saying that you lie."
(MW, I, 5)

John Hollow has pointed out that "the problem with these
lines has always been that they seem both to admit and to
deny guilt."[8] Such ironic overtones make the garden a less
than innocent place, and indeed, as with Tennyson, most of
the gardens in Morris's poems have a touch of ambiguity. "A
Garden by the Sea," for example, opens with an idyllic de-
scription:

I know a little garden-close,
Set thick with lily and red rose,

[8] Hollow, "William Morris and the Judgment of God," *PMLA*, 86 (1971),
447.

Where I would wander if I might
From dewy morn to dewy night,
And have one with me wandering.
(*MW*, IX, 149)

This is charming, but the next stanza introduces a disturbing note of sterility:

And though within it no birds sing,
And though no pillared house is there,
And though the apple-boughs are bare
Of fruit and blossom, would to God
Her feet upon the green grass trod,
And I beheld them as before.

As George Ford has noted, the phrase "no birds sing" seems to have been borrowed from Keats's "La Belle Dame Sans Merci."[9] Morris's poem is, in general, very different, but it also contains a deserted lover, "alone and palely loitering." Keats's lover wanders through a bleak landscape, remembering the flowery meadows and magic grot associated with the lady. In Morris's poem, on the other hand, it is the enchanted garden itself which is an unfruitful and birdless landscape, and as the poem unfolds the garden becomes the symbol of a wasted life, the very opposite of the happy fulfillment so cosily suggested in the opening stanza. It is a desolate place:

For which I cry both day and night,
For which I let slip all delight,
Whereby I grow both deaf and blind,
Careless to win, unskilled to find,
And quick to lose what all men seek.

The Edenic garden also turns sour in "Golden Wings," where "Fair Jehane du Castel beau" lives "Midways of a wallèd garden, / In the happy popular land" (*MW*, I, 116). At first glance this garden is a fruitful paradise, untouched by violence:

[9] Ford, *Keats and the Victorians*, p. 155.

On the bricks the green moss grew,
  Yellow lichen on the stone,
  Over which red apples shone;
Little war that castle knew.

The garden is secure, with its moat and painted drawbridge, but there is no sense of being confined or trapped. The "fresh west wind" blows across the water, the drawbridge is regularly raised and lowered "with gilded chains," and the moat seems to serve a decorative rather than a military function. The lords and ladies sit in the bridge house, feeding cakes to the swans, or wander through the gardens hand in hand. The one discordant note is the lonely Jehane du Castel beau, who waits for "Golden Wings" to come. The description of the unhappy maiden in the castle tower is reminiscent of Tennyson's "Mariana":

I sit on a purple bed,
Outside the wall is red,
Thereby the apple hangs,
And the wasp, caught by the fangs,

Dies in the autumn night,
And the bat flits till light,
And the love-crazed knight

Kisses the long wet grass:
The weary days pass,—
Gold wings across the sea!
          (MW, I, 120)

Both wall and apples have been mentioned earlier in a happier context. Here, the red coloring seems to prefigure the blood that will be shed, and the dying wasp is both predator and victim. Unlike Mariana, Jehane takes some decisive action that results in death and destruction for the castle and its inhabitants. The poem ends with a vivid description of the garden that has now become a dreary and sinister wasteland:

The apples now grow green and sour
　Upon the mouldering castle-wall,
　Before they ripen there they fall:
There are no banners on the tower.

The draggled swans most eagerly eat
　The green weeds trailing in the moat;
　Inside the rotting leaky boat
You see a slain man's stiffen'd feet.
(*MW*, I, 123)

A particularly beautiful garden, without sinister attributes, is used as the setting for love fulfilled in "Thunder in the Garden":

Earth's fragrance went with her, as in the wet grass
Her feet little hidden were set;
She bent down her head, 'neath the roses to pass,
And her arm with the lily was wet.
(*MW*, IX, 156)

But although the moment of fulfillment is richly evoked, the poem as a whole is suffused with the feeling that this happiness, like the sudden thunderstorm, is but a fleeting moment of relief in the normal drought of the speaker's life. He remembers the "ending of wrong," when she "Changed all with the change of her smile"; he is so unaccustomed to her kindness that "I to myself was grown nought but a wonder"; his lips "had craved her so often" and his hand "had trembled to touch," and he marvels at the tears that fill those "eyes I had hoped not to soften." The woman who has such power over him can transform the garden into a paradise or a wasteland at will. The garden itself has no power to confer happiness.

We may suspect that "Thunder in the Garden" was rooted in Morris's personal experience, and that the garden it celebrates was based on that of Kelmscott Manor. Most of the poems in which lovers meet in a garden are, like the Arthurian poems, less recognizably personal. In the tale, "The Man Born

to Be King" (*MW*, III, 107-67) from *The Earthly Paradise,*
the base-born hero, Michael, is sent to the Castle of the Rose
bearing a letter from the King with the command that he
should be killed. He falls asleep in the Queen's walled garden,
and is found there by the King's only daughter, who reads
the letter and replaces it with instructions that he should be
wed to her immediately. This is a variation on the intruder-
in-the-garden theme so often used by Tennyson. Here too, the
maiden is socially superior to her suitor, but in Morris's ver-
sion of the story all the action belongs to the maiden. There
is no question of the hero attempting to challenge the social
system, like the hero of *Maud*; Michael is a passive instrument
of Fate, and it is in keeping with his passive role that he should
be sleeping peacefully while the Princess falls in love with him
and writes the letter that saves his life. Although the tale ends
happily with an epithalamium, it is only chance that trans-
forms what should have been the garden of death into the
garden of love. The essential ambiguity of the garden is main-
tained.

A somewhat different version of the same theme may be
found in "The Story of Cupid and Psyche," where Love finds
Psyche asleep in the garden:

> Withal at last amidst a fair green close,
> Hedged round about with woodbine and red rose,
> Within the flicker of a white-thorn shade
> In gentle sleep he found the maiden laid.
> (*MW*, IV, 14)

This is the garden of innocent maidenhood: a kind of Eden,
certainly, but Psyche lives a lonely and unfulfilled life in it
because her beauty is too great to win her an earthly lover.
Her immortal lover, Cupid, takes her to his garden paradise
where she becomes his bride. This garden is a place of artifice
rather than of natural beauty:

> Void of mankind, fairer than words can say,
> Wherein did joyous harmless creatures play

After their kind, and all amidst the trees
Were strange-wrought founts and wondrous images;
And glimmering 'twixt the boughs could she behold
A house made beautiful with beaten gold,
Whose open doors in the bright sun did gleam;
Lonely, but not deserted did it seem.
(*MW*, IV, 18)

Yet in spite of its beauty it is in many ways not a happy place for Psyche. Her nights are filled with bliss, but during the lonely days time hangs heavily on her hands and she yearns for the companionship of father and sisters. The garden that excludes all human society is not in the end a "good place."

When she is turned out of the garden for breaking the injunction not to look upon her lover, Psyche wanders in misery across the land until she arrives at the garden of Venus. The beauty of the place does not prevent her from feeling a "pang of deadly fear" as she stands in the gateway gazing at "small flowers as red as blood . . . amid the soft green grass" (*MW*, IV, 48). However, she enters and comes to a "rose-hedged garden" with beautiful minstrel girls dancing round a fountain before the throne of Venus. Here she is made to undertake various seemingly impossible tasks for the implacable goddess, one of which involves a journey to the underworld. Entering the dark cavern that leads to the underworld, she comes upon the gardens of Proserpine:

The shadowy meads which that wide way run through,
Under a seeming sky 'twixt grey and blue;
No wind blew there, there was no bird or tree
Or beast, and dim grey flowers she did but see
That never faded in that changeless place,
And if she had but seen a living face
Most strange and bright she would have thought it there.
(*MW*, IV, 64)

Morris shows none of the fascination for the realms of Proserpine that was to characterize Swinburne's poetry, and later,

Lawrence's. Psyche yearns for the bright normality of a "living face" rather than for any Laurentian "splendour of torches of darkness."[10]

All the gardens in "The Story of Cupid and Psyche" exclude human society and the normal activities of life. Psyche, as a mortal beloved by one of the gods, is trapped between earth and heaven, and it is her fate to be lonely. Excluded from the joyous company that surrounds Venus, she cannot return to her earthly life either, and she wanders through the world like an exiled spirit:

> Like a thin dream she passed the clattering town;
> On the thronged quays she watched the ships come in
> Patient, amid the strange outlandish din;
> Unscared she saw the sacked towns' miseries,
> And marching armies passed before her eyes.
>
> (MW, IV, 43)

After a long period of trial and suffering she is rewarded by recognition as the bride of Love, and is granted immortality. Happiness comes not in retiring once more to the private but lonely world of Love's garden, but in being received into the company of gods and goddesses. Although she accepts the gift of immortality, however, Psyche does not do so without a touch of regret for the mortal world she leaves behind:

> Then pale as privet, took she heart to drink,
> And therewithal most strange new thoughts did think,
> And unknown feelings seized her, and there came
> Sudden remembrance, vivid as a flame,
> Of everything that she had done on earth,
> Although it all seemed changed in weight and worth,
> Small things becoming great and great things small;
> And godlike pity touched her therewithal
> For her old self, for sons of men that die;
> And that sweet new-born immortality
> Now with full love her rested spirit fed.
>
> (MW, IV, 73)

[10] Lawrence, "Bavarian Gentians," in Poems, III, 140.

It is important that the tale ends on this note rather than on union with the beloved in a paradisal garden. Paradoxically, in losing her mortality, Psyche in a sense returns to the concerns of the "sons of men that die." The garden, and the love that it enshrines, is never quite enough for Morris. His ideal is the earthly paradise, not Rossetti's "breathless bowers" set "above / All passionate wind of welcome and farewell" (RW, 74).

The refusal to accept a static, antisocial paradise as the ultimate good partly accounts for the actions of the knight in "The Hill of Venus." He leaves the "tree-set garden, that no weed, / Nor winter, or decay had ever known" (MW, VI, 292), not because Venus has tired of him, but because pleasure itself dies in a world that knows no change. He asks Venus:

> "How do I better thee,
> Who never knew'st a sorrow or a pain?
> Folk on the earth fear they may love in vain,
> Ere first they see the love in answering eyes,
> And still from day to day fresh fear doth rise."
> (MW, VI, 298)

The "fresh fear" that is a condition of earthly love is also the guarantee of fresh pleasure in that love. In the changeless garden paradise the delicate balance between fear and reassurance is lost. Venus cannot fear loss because, being perfect, she has no real needs. She allows the knight to depart with calm indifference, and he reproaches her, demanding some passionate human reaction from her. He flees neither pain nor suffering, but the terrible prospect of eternal, changeless bliss:

> "But now I flee, lest God should leave us twain
> Forgotten here when earth has passed away,
> Nor think us worthy of more hell or pain
> Than such a never-ending, hopeless day!—"
> (MW, VI, 302)

Death would be preferable to such immortality, although Morris's knight does not yearn for death with the same passionate, erotic intensity as does the knight in Swinburne's "Laus Veneris."

Morris ultimately rejects the enclosed garden as the *locus amoenus* because it is too remote from the real world, and too lonely and isolated. For the same reason he also rejects the wilderness. This may seem to be a surprising statement to make about a man who was fascinated by Iceland, and who traveled extensively through that country on two occasions. If one examines the quality of his response to and interest in Iceland, however, it becomes apparent that Morris was no romantic primitivist who idealized unspoilt nature. In his *Journals of Travel in Iceland* Morris describes his first glimpse of the country: "and beyond that we saw the mainland, a terrible shore indeed: a great mass of dark grey mountains worked into pyramids and shelves, looking as if they had been built and half-ruined" (*MW*, VIII, 19).

In his attitude to mountains Morris is closer to Thomas Burnet than to his acknowledged master, Ruskin, for whom mountains were the objects "where chiefly the beauty of God's working was manifested to man."[11] Burnet, on the other hand, had seen the postdiluvial earth with its mountains as "the image or picture of a great Ruine . . . the true aspect of a World lying in its rubbish."[12] Morris is awed by the crags of Iceland, but he does not find them beautiful; consistently, he sees the lava slopes and mountains as dreary wastes, and joyfully greets the sight of a grassy valley: "to the west nothing but an awful dead grey waste of lava, but to the east are grey green pastures with the emerald green patches of home-meads" (*MW*, VIII, 33). And again he writes: "On our right is a mass of jagged bare mountains, all beset with clouds, that, drifting away now and then show dreadful inaccessible ravines and closed up valleys with no trace of grass about them among the toothed peaks and rent walls; I think it was the most

[11] Ruskin, *Works*, VI, 414.
[12] Burnet, *The Sacred Theory of the Earth*, p. 91.

horrible sight of mountains I had the whole journey long"
(*MW*, VII, 77).

What impressed Morris in Iceland was the human story
that he read in the terrible landscape, the heroism of the men
who had settled this inhospitable wasteland. Of Herdholt he
writes: "Yes it is an awful place . . . a piece of turf under your
feet, and the sky overhead, that's all; whatever solace your
life is to have here must come out of yourself or these old
stories" (*MW*, VIII, 108).

The stoicism of the early settlers appealed to him, and it
has been pointed out that at the time of his visits to Iceland
Morris himself had need of the greatest stoicism, since this
was the period of Rossetti's sojourn at Kelmscott with Jane
Morris. Morris wrote to Aglaia Coronio that "it was no idle
whim that drew me there, but a true instinct for what I needed,"
and the "tragic, but beautiful land with its well remembered
stories of brave men, killed all querulous feeling in me, and
have [sic] made all the dear faces of wife and children, and
love, and friends dearer than ever to me."[13]

In his poem, "Iceland First Seen," Morris again stresses the
essentially human interest that drew him to undertake the
journey:

> Ah! what came we forth for to see that our hearts
>     are so hot with desire?
> Is it enough for our rest, the sight of this
>     desolate strand,
> And the mountain-waste voiceless as death but for
>     winds that may sleep not nor tire?
> Why do we long to wend forth through the length
>     and breadth of a land,
> Dreadful with grinding of ice, and record of
>     scarce hidden fire,
> But that there 'mid the grey grassy dales sore
>     scarred by the running streams

[13] *The Letters of William Morris to His Family and Friends*, ed. Henderson,
pp. 58-59.

Lives the tale of the Northland of old and the
undying glory of dreams?
(*MW*, IX, 125)

Heroism, human endurance, and stoicism are also the qual-
ities that Morris celebrates in his Northern epics, such as
*Sigurd the Volsung*, and, indeed, one reads this late poem
chiefly as a record of Morris's values. This point has been
made by R. C. Ellison, who sees the epic as expressing a
"vision of the possibility of true human greatness, of social
justice, of the freedom and value of the individual; the socialist
vision, in fact, which was just beginning to become dominant
in his mind."[14] Morris's interest in expressing or exploring
such values allows little room for passages of pure landscape
description. In the whole of Book I, which recounts the life
and death of Sigmund, and which covers sixty pages of text,
there is nothing more than the most fleeting reference to the
type of landscape setting in which the action takes place. In
Book II, landscape does play a more important role, but only
because the narrative demands it: Sigurd and Regin ride up
through the mountains and into the desert in order to find
and kill Fafnir. It is assumed throughout that the wilderness
is a barren place where monsters dwell, and that a man will
only go there under dire necessity. The mountains are not
sublime; they are waste places, and after Sigurd has killed
Fafnir he rides on through the desert and "longs for the dwell-
ings of men-folk, and the kingly people's speech" (*MW*, XII,
119).

At one point Morris does seem to be preparing the reader
for a picturesque scenic view, when Sigurd and Brynhild climb
Hindfell to gaze out over the world:

So they climb the burg of Hindfell, and hand in hand
they fare,
Till all about and above them is nought but the
sunlit air,

[14] Ellison, " 'The Undying Glory of Dreams,' " in *Victorian Poetry*, ed.
Bradbury and Palmer, p. 169.

And there close they cling together rejoicing in
    their mirth;
For far away beneath them lie the kingdoms of the
    earth,
And the garths of men-folk's dwellings and the
    streams that water them,
And the rich and plenteous acres, and the silver
    ocean's hem,
And the woodland wastes and the mountains, and
    all that holdeth all;
The house and the ship and the island, the loom and
    the mine and the stall,
The beds of bane and healing, the crafts that
    slay and save,
The temple of God and the Doom-ring, the
    cradle and the grave.
          (*MW*, XII, 129)

It is significant that what we are given is a description of the
dwellings of men, rather than of jagged peaks and purple
distances. Morris even focuses on things that they could not
possibly have seen from the mountain, such as "the loom and
the mine and the stall," because these are the means by which
man has humanized the landscape.

Morris's interest in and admiration for the arts and crafts
of the men who build in the wilderness comes out in one
passage after another:

And the three wend on through the wild-wood till
    they come to a grassy plain
Beneath the untrodden mountains; and lo a noble
    house,
And a hall with great craft fashioned, and made
    full glorious;
But night on the earth was falling; so scantily
    might they see
The wealth of its smooth-wrought stonework and
    its world of imagery.
          (*MW*, XII, 78)

More real than Camelot, such dwellings are nevertheless just as much an achievement of art set against the surrounding wilderness. Morris does not take a romantic delight in picturesque tumble-down cottages, or crude, rustic stonework; he has a thoroughly practical and craftsmanlike eye for the "smooth-wrought stonework" and skilful decoration. In this respect, he might be compared to the speaker in Browning's "Up at a Villa," whose delight in the clean regularity of the houses in the city square has already been noted.

From early childhood Morris was familiar with another type of wilderness, the forest. Mackail writes of him, "He never ceased to love Epping Forest, and to uphold the scenery of his native country as beautifully and characteristically English. The dense hornbeam thickets, which even in bright weather have something of solemnity and mystery in their deep shade . . . reappear again and again in his poetry and his prose romances."[15] The forest did indeed fascinate Morris, but he does not share Arnold's desire to withdraw into the forest glade. His forests are peopled by his medievalizing imagination with knights, dragons, and wolves, or they may be seen as the setting for joyful hunting parties of lords and ladies, as in this passage from *Sigurd*:

> There oft with horns triumphant their rout by the
>    lone tree turns,
> When over the bison's lea-land the last of the sunset
>    burns;
> Or by night and cloud all eager with shaft on string
>    they fare,
> When the wind from the elk-mead setteth, or the
>    wood-boar's tangled lair:
> For the wood is their barn and their storehouse,
>    and their bower and feasting-hall,
> And many an one of their warriors in the woodland
>    war shall fall.
>                                             (*MW*, XII, 140)

[15] Mackail, *The Life of William Morris*, p. 7.

Arnold's protagonist had glimpsed just such a hunting party from his retreat by the abbey wall in "Stanzas from the Grande Chartreuse," but he remained solitary and withdrawn; in "Thyrsis" too, he flees from the jovial troop of Oxford hunters. Morris, on the other hand, seems to identify with the hunters. He transforms the forest from a solitary into a social landscape, and, in addition, he shows that it serves man's needs by supplying both pleasure and provender. He seldom approves of a landscape that does not combine beauty with utility.

Sometimes the forest can provide a refuge for desperate men. After all his brothers have been devoured by wolves, Sigmund frees himself from his bonds and lives in a cave like a wild man, planning his revenge on King Siggeir. Another variation on the Robin Hood theme may be found in "The Hall and the Wood." In this poem, the hero, Rafe, discovers that his ancestral Hall has been destroyed, but his men appear from the surrounding forest and invite him to dwell with them:

In the fair green-wood where lurks no fear,
Where the King's writ runneth not,
There dwell they, friends and fellows dear,
While summer days are hot.
(MW, IX, 114)

The forest may offer a refuge to the displaced hero, but nature is also shown as being indifferent to man; indeed, it thrives on human disaster, and the ruined Hall becomes the domain of wild plants and animals:

There turned the cheeping chaffinch now
And feared no birding child;
Through the shot-window thrust a bough
Of garden-rose run wild.
(MW, IX, 111)

More typically, Morris, like Tennyson, sees the forest as a place where evil is encountered rather than as a refuge. The hero of "Goldilocks and Goldilocks" rides off from his pas-

toral home into a dark and sinister wood where he meets the
heroine, enslaved by a wicked witch. He saves her from the
witch, and after many perilous adventures they emerge from
the woods and return to his village in the "land of Wheaten
Shocks" (*WM*, IX, 248).

The indifference or hostility of wild nature to man is brought
out strongly in the Prologue to *The Earthly Paradise*. This
tells of the basic romantic quest of those who commit them-
selves to a "strange desperate voyage o'er the sea" (*MW*, III,
12) in search of the earthly paradise, where they will achieve
immortality. The voyagers encounter a variety of landscapes
and societies, and consistently they praise orderly, settled pas-
toral communities rather than primitive savages. Their first
sight of land already contains a sharp contrast between de-
sirable and hostile landscapes: they arrive at the "flowery
shore, the dragon-guarded wood" (*MW*, III, 30), and find it
impossible to penetrate the forest. Finally they find a path,
and come to a settlement of simple, gentle people, "So simple
folk and virtuous, / So happy midst their dreary forest bow-
ers" (*MW*, III, 37). The voyagers, however, do not find hap-
piness in these "dreary forest bowers," and continue their
voyage. They climb a mountain barrier and find "A savage
land, a land untilled again," (*MW*, III, 48), inhabited by can-
nibals. After many brutal experiences they turn back, and
come to more civilized communities:

> And as we went the land seemed fair enough,
> Though sometimes did we pass through forests rough,
> Deserts and fens, yet for the most, the way
> Through ordered villages and tilled land lay,
> Which after all the squalid miseries
> We had beheld, seemed heaven unto our eyes.
> (*MW*, III, 54)

Even better than the "ordered villages" is a "city fair enow /
That spread out o'er the well-tilled vale below" (*MW*, III, 54).
It is, needless to say, a preindustrial city with its green gardens
and richly dressed folk. The voyagers think they have reached

180

the Earthly Paradise at last, and agree to stay a while. They are tired of "sea and sky, / Or untilled lands and people void of bliss" (MW, III, 56). Happiness is measured in terms of the civilizing skills practiced by the people: wilderness and savages rank lowest, pastoral simplicity next, but the truly beautiful city is highest:

> But entering now that town, what huge delight
> We had therein, how lovely to our sight
> Was the well-ordered life of people there.
> (MW, III, 56)

> Think then, if we, late driven up and down
> Upon the uncertain sea, or struggling sore
> With barbarous man upon an untilled shore,
> Or at the best, midst people ignorant
> Of arts and letters, fighting against want
> Of very food—think if we now were glad
> From day to day, and as folk crazed and mad
> Deemed our old selves, the wanderers on the sea.
> (MW, III, 57)

The white-walled city that the voyagers find so attractive is also the fourteenth-century London of Morris's imagination, a London "small and white and clean, / The clear Thames bordered by its gardens green" (MW, III, 3). London had now become a smoke-belching monster, but the English countryside, wherever it remained unspoilt, still approached Morris's pastoral ideal: "This land is a little land; too much shut up within the narrow seas, as it seems, to have much space for swelling into hugeness; there are no great wastes overwhelming in their dreariness, no great solitudes of forests, no terrible untrodden mountain-walls: all is measured, mingled, varied, gliding easily one thing into another . . . neither prison nor palace, but a decent home."[16]

Morris seems to be rejecting the romantic extremes of terror and splendor, and to be settling for the quiet pastoralism of

---

[16] Quoted ibid., p. 13.

"a decent home." Such homeliness was not perhaps the best thing for his poetry, but it is easy to understand how Morris would have relished the pastoral countryside as a relief from the grime and horror of industrial London. May Morris describes how whenever her father came down to Kelmscott, the family would meet him on the road: "He would get out and walk down with us, and oh the quiet of those golden August evenings along the white road, with warm breaths of meadow-sweet from the wide, bright-flowered ditches; and how he would look round and take it all in with satisfaction— like a man come out of prison" (*MW*, XII, xv).

In many of his poems, however, particularly the early ones, Morris surprises us by using this rural setting as a backdrop to acts of violence and treachery. In "The Haystack in the Floods," for example, the tragedy takes place in a pastoral landscape, although some hint of disaster is suggested through the "old soaked hay" (*MW*, I, 124) that has been ruined for use. Perhaps, as Charlotte Oberg suggests, "the sodden haystacks amid the watery waste suggest a soured and rancid fertility corresponding to the aborted love of Jehane and Sir Robert."[17] But Morris is usually careful to avoid any suggestion of such an emotional and symbolic correspondence between man and the landscape. Often, he deliberately contrasts a happy and indifferent nature with man's tragic folly. For example, "Riding Together" has a refrain that tells of the "sunny weather" or "clear fresh weather," and that seems to mock the human action:

They bound my blood-stained hands together,
They bound his corpse to nod by my side:
Then on we rode, in the bright March weather,
    With clash of cymbals did we ride.
            (*MW*, I, 135-36)

A similar contrast between nature and man is shown in "The Folk-Mote by the River," in which a war council is held in the corn fields:

[17] Oberg, *A Pagan Prophet: William Morris*, p. 132.

182

So when the bread was done away
We looked along the new shorn hay,

And heard the voice of the gathering-horn
Come over the garden and the corn;

For the wind was in the blossoming wheat
And drave the bees in the lime-boughs sweet.
                    (*MW*, IX, 170)

The "gathering-horn" summons the men who have been reaping to put away their scythes and take up their swords, but the lime-boughs are no less sweet for this fact. Human tragedy is placed in an overall context of vigorous and uncaring natural life; Morris is that poet for whom "the primrose is for ever nothing else than itself—a little flower apprehended in the very plain and leafy fact of it, whatever and how many soever the associations and passions may be that crowd around it."[18]

Even where Morris does use the landscape in a manner to suggest a touch of the pathetic fallacy, he is careful to point out the lack of true empathy between man and nature. "Error and Loss" (*MW*, IX, 108) is a mournful lyric about a hopeless love triangle, and the landscape suggests the mood of the speaker: "The misty hills dreamed, and the silent wood / Seemed listening to the sorrow of my mood"; but he follows this immediately with a disclaimer: "I know not if the earth with me did grieve, / Or if it mocked my grief that bitter eve."

In other poems Morris shows man alienated from nature in a more subtle manner. In "The Half of Life Gone" the speaker is watching an idyllic pastoral scene, but he is cut off from the happy activities he observes: "They are busy winning the hay, and the life and the picture they make, / If I were as once I was, I should deem it made for my sake" (*MW*, IX, 197). Like Coleridge in the "Dejection Ode," Morris sees the beauty but does not feel it, "and for me there is void and dearth / That I cannot name or measure" (*MW*, IX, 198). It

[18] Ruskin, *Works*, V, 209.

is made clear that it is only the speaker who is out of tune; the landscape is sunny, bright, and useful.

This is not so in the sonnet "Summer Dawn," in which the predawn landscape seems to reflect his mood of frustrated longing and waiting:

> Pray but one prayer for me 'twixt thy closed lips,
> Think but one thought of me up in the stars.
> The summer night waneth, the morning light slips,
> Faint and grey 'twixt the leaves of the aspen, betwixt the
>     cloud-bars,
> That are patiently waiting there for the dawn:
> Patient and colourless, though Heaven's gold
> Waits to float through them along with the sun.
> Far out in the meadows, above the young corn,
>     The heavy elms wait, and restless and cold
> The uneasy wind rises; the roses are dun;
> Through the long twilight they pray for the dawn.
> Round the lone house in the midst of the corn,
>     Speak but one word to me over the corn,
>     Over the tender, bow'd locks of the corn.
>
> (*MW*, I, 144)

Here Morris allows himself a far greater degree of romantic subjectivity than in most of his poetry. The adjectives "patient," "restless," and "uneasy," give human attributes to the clouds, trees, and wind; the roses "pray," and the corn has "tender, bow'd locks." In spite of this anthropomorphism, however, the poem is really remarkably free of subjective distortion. The speaker seizes the moment when the colorless landscape, stirred by a predawn wind, happens to correspond to his mood. But the elm trees would in fact be "heavy" with dew, which would also account for the "bow'd locks" of the corn. At the same time the speaker is fully aware that "Heaven's gold / Waits to float through them," and then the dreary landscape will be transformed into a rich, pastoral scene, while the speaker will, presumably, remain lonely, frustrated, and alienated.

A pastoral setting is used once more in the enigmatic poem

"Spell-Bound," in which the speaker, a sort of masculine Mariana, is imprisoned by a wizard:

He bound me round with silken chains
I could not break; he set me here
Above the golden-waving plains,
Where never reaper cometh near.
(*MW*, I, 106)

Nature remains bounteous and beautiful; the "golden land is like a bride," but the note of frustration is given in the failure of the reaper, like Mariana's suitor, to come. It is important that the failure is at the human level. Man is out of harmony with nature when he is out of harmony with himself, or when his own institutions breed violence and distrust. Morris did not share Arnold's belief in the power of natural influences to soothe and rejuvenate, but he did share Arnold's love of the English countryside. Even though a gap between man and nature has opened up, the pastoral landscape remains a "good place" for Morris. The task is to make man fit to inhabit that place.

Blue Calhoun has discussed Morris's "preference for humanized nature" at length; she concludes that "He believed in civilization—its necessity and value. The romantic quest moves away from society and into the enchanted wilderness. His Wanderers of *The Earthly Paradise* tried to be romantic and failed. . . . More and more after *The Defence of Guenevere* the characteristic pattern of Morris's journeys would be not away from but toward society."[19] The suggestion is that Morris was in many respects more "classical" than "romantic" in his attitudes. It is a suggestion that was made earlier by C. S. Lewis, who wrote that "in one sense Morris is as classical as Johnson."[20]

In fact, Morris combined romantic and classical qualities. His love of pastoral landscapes and small, white-walled towns

[19] Calhoun, *The Pastoral Vision*, pp. 80, 31.
[20] Lewis, "William Morris," p. 39.

is a love of what Pater terms "that quality of order in beauty" which he sees as the essential element of classicism.[21] Pater defines romanticism as "the addition of strangeness to beauty," and adds that the romantic spirit "seeks the Middle Age, because in that overcharged atmosphere of the Middle Age, there are unworked sources of romantic effect, of a strange beauty, to be won, by strong imagination, out of things unlikely or remote."[22] Morris creates a pastoral, classical landscape, and in many of his poems, places the violent and romantic events of medieval legend against this background. Even in his love of the English countryside, however, one might detect a romantic element. It is not a love of the sublime or the picturesque, but it is characterized by a certain excess. It is a love of exuberant, natural fertility that breaks the bounds of order. He writes of the Kelmscott Manor garden and its surroundings: "How I love the earth, and the seasons, and the weather and all things that deal with it, and all that grows out of it—as this has done! The earth and the growth of it and the life of it!"[23]

In his designs for wallpapers and tapestries, Morris took this exuberant natural growth and stylized it into orderly, geometric patterns. In his poetry he delights in the fertility of nature, but he prefers that fertility to be ordered by man and to be useful to him. Perhaps Morris might have been a greater poet if he had taken a less rational and utilitarian view, but he himself would have judged his role as a poet as less important than his role as a man and a socialist. Nevertheless, he does not see nature as existing simply to serve man and his moods. In particular, his rejection of the pathetic fallacy and of romantic subjectivism shows that for Morris nature has a life of its own that often runs counter to man's needs. Harmony between man and nature can only be achieved when both are at their best. For this, nature must be fertile, and man must be a skilled cultivator of the soil, with an orderly

[21] Pater, *Appreciations: With an Essay on Style*, p. 245.
[22] Ibid., pp. 246, 248.
[23] Quoted by Mackail, *The Life of William Morris*, p. 227.

186

and equitable social system, and a love of beauty. When this happens, then Morris's utopia, the small, white-walled city surrounded by pastoral countryside, might be achieved.

It is just such a utopia that Morris describes in *News from Nowhere*, the landscape of which is chiefly pastoral, but includes elements of garden and wilderness. England has become a "garden, where nothing is wasted and nothing is spoilt, with the necessary dwellings, sheds, and workshops scattered up and down the country, all trim and neat and pretty" (*MW*, XVI, 72). It should be noted that this "garden" has nothing in common with the socially exclusive aristocratic preserves attached to great houses, nor with the walled gardens that provided lovers with private retreats. Nor is it like the moated castle garden in "Golden Wings," which is shown to be an illusory paradise, subject to violent attack from outside. In *News from Nowhere* the whole country has become a garden for the use of everyone: "the fields were everywhere treated as a garden made for the pleasure as well as the livelihood of all" (*MW*, XVI, 191). There is some resemblance between this garden and the garden of England described at the end of Tennyson's *Princess*, except that Morris's version is truly democratic, a socialist paradise.

The romantic element in this landscape persists, but is part of the total plan. Certain portions of England have been deliberately left as wilderness areas: they are there because the people "like these pieces of wild nature, and can afford them" (*MW*, XVI, 74), and in addition, they are useful as a source of timber. The wilderness, like everything else in Morris's utopia, performs a social function and is essentially under control. It is not a source of terrible, inhuman "otherness," nor, in this perfectly happy society, can it be a refuge for outcasts or for evil forces. One is reminded of the fragment of "wilderness" in Pope's garden at Twickenham.

Jack Lindsay writes of Morris that his basic motivation was "his constant attachment to the garden and forest of his childhood, which held for him the imagery of beauty and of freedom."[24] There is much truth in this, but it makes Morris's ideal sound less mature and more romantic than it really was. Moreover, Lindsay has omitted the two most important elements in Morris's ideal landscape: the green field and the small community. The central image of a happy and fruitful life in *News from Nowhere* is not provided by either the forest or the garden, but by the hayfields where men and women of all occupations—laborers, scholars, and scientists—gather to work in a joyous community of purpose. It is indeed a "fair feld ful of folk," remarkably similar to Langland's fourteenth-century ideal. Forest and garden have traditionally been places where one escapes from society; Morris is concerned with perfecting society rather than with escaping from it. "Suppose people lived," he writes, "in little communities among gardens and green fields, so that you could be in the country in five minutes' walk, and had few wants . . . then I think one might hope civilization had really begun."[25]

The ideal is essentially rural, but Morris includes the city in his utopia. In *News from Nowhere*, London is a noble and beautiful city of fine buildings and spacious gardens. Moreover, it is made clear that the old divisions between the town and country have largely disappeared; nature has been brought into the city, and the country has been "vivified by the thought and briskness of town-bred folk which has produced that happy and leisurely but eager life" exhibited for our admiration (*MW*, XVI, 72).

In striving to unite the best of the country and the city, Morris achieved a wholeness of vision that goes far beyond the kind of sentimental pastoralism defined by Leo Marx:

What is attractive in pastoralism is the felicity represented by an image of a natural landscape, a terrain either unspoiled or, if cultivated, rural. Movement toward such a symbolic landscape also may be understood as movement away from an "artificial" world, a world identified with

[24] Lindsay, *William Morris: His Life and Work*, p. 377.
[25] Letter to Louis Baldwin, March 1874, *Letters*, p. 62.

"art," using this word in its broadest sense to mean the disciplined habits of mind or arts developed by organized communities. In other words, this impulse gives rise to a symbolic motion away from centers of civilization toward their opposite, nature, away from sophistication toward simplicity, or, to introduce the cardinal metaphor of the literary mode, away from the city toward the country. When this impulse is unchecked, the result is a simple-minded wishfulness, a romantic perversion of thought and feeling.[26]

Morris certainly desired a simpler, more rural life. But his particular type of pastoralism is not a movement away from "disciplined habits of mind or arts developed by organized communities." Nor is it a rejection of the city. His ideal landscape is basically rural and pastoral, but it includes elements from town, garden, and wilderness. In order to blend these diverse elements he cleanses the town of its dirt and violent hurry, rids the forest of its terror, and robs the garden of its social exclusiveness. Such a vision may be utopian, but it is too inclusive to be called escapist. Moreover, Morris's utopian ideal has much in common with that essentially practical Victorian enterprise, the attempt to bring nature into the urban wasteland by building city parks and garden suburbs. Walter Creese's comment on the ideal behind the garden suburb might be applied, without much change, to Morris:

> Though more often honored in the breach than in the observance, the idea of the garden suburb maintained its hold on the Victorian imagination. The idea was shaped by two very different impulses—the one, emotional and esthetic, retained the Romantic wish to flee into woodland alleys and places of nestling green; the other, communal in emphasis, stressed the values of social cohesion and interdependence.[27]

[26] Marx, *The Machine in the Garden*, pp. 9-10.
[27] Creese, "Imagination in the Suburb," in *Nature and the Victorian Imagination*, p. 52.

The only correction one would have to make in this passage for it to apply to Morris would be to shift the emphasis from the landscapes of retreat suggested in "places of nestling green" to the more communal landscape of the hayfield. This makes it possible for Morris to achieve a more unified ideal than the planners of the garden suburb.

CHAPTER VII

# SWINBURNE:
# THE SUBLIME RECOVERED

Swinburne, with his rebellious nature, strange appearance, and even stranger behavior, was the enfant terrible of the Victorian poetic scene during the sixties and seventies. Although he found much to admire in the work of Tennyson, Browning, and Arnold, he reacted against them as Establishment figures of the older generation, and, in particular, he rejected Tennyson's increasing concern for social and moral values. As a young man he had enthusiastically allied himself with the Pre-Raphaelites, but his poetry bears little resemblance to that of either Rossetti or Morris. He had little taste for Rossetti's hushed, enclosed bowers, and even less for Morris's socially useful landscapes. His own landscapes clearly reflect his rejection of society.

However, too much attention has perhaps been paid in the past to Swinburne as a mere rebel and iconoclast, and recent commentators, such as Rosenberg, McGann, and Riede, have stressed the more positive aspects of his genius.[1] David Riede is surely right in suggesting that Swinburne is a great romantic mythmaker, and nowhere is his mythmaking more apparent than in his treatment of landscape. His love of wild and solitary settings springs not merely from his rejection of society, but from the most profound and passionate depths of his nature. His feeling for the more sublime aspects of nature, and particularly for the sea, has an intensity that is probably unsurpassed in English poetry. He should be remembered not only for the shocking crime of introducing Dolores to the

[1] Rosenberg, "Swinburne," *Victorian Studies*, 11 (1967), 131-52; McGann, *Swinburne: An Experiment in Criticism*; Riede, *Swinburne: A Study of Romantic Mythmaking*.

191

SWINBURNE

Young Person, but for throwing open the Victorian drawing room and exposing its inmates to the elemental clash of wind and waves, and to the stark beauties of a landscape untouched by man.

It was perhaps necessary to break some windows before people would take notice of what lay outside the drawing room, and Swinburne performed this task with relish. For one thing, he subverted the traditional associations of the garden, transforming it from a symbol of paradisal innocence into something disturbingly different. Even when he exploits the conventional associations, as in "The Two Dreams," which is based on Boccaccio and contains an enclosed rose garden, he introduces a subversive note. Much of the poem is disarmingly traditional, being written in pseudo-Chaucerian English. The heroine is straight out of a medieval romance:

Her face was white, and thereto she was tall;
In no wise lacked there any praise at all
To her most perfect and pure maidenhood.[2]

And when the hero dies he sounds remarkably like Chaucer's Troilus;[3] "O help me, sweet, I am but dead" (*SW*, II, 27). The rose garden is introduced in similarly conventional terms: "There grew a rose-garden in Florence land / More fair than many" (*SW*, II, 16). However, in the detailed description of the garden, Chaucer and Boccaccio give way to pure Swinburne:

Even this green place the summer caught them in
Seemed half deflowered and sick with beaten leaves
In their strayed eyes; these gold flower-fumèd eves
Burnt out to make the sun's love-offering,
The midnoon's prayer, the rose's thanksgiving,

[2] *The Complete Works of Algernon Charles Swinburne*, II, ed. Gosse and Wise, 17-18. Hereafter cited as *SW* with volume and page numbers.
[3] Compare Troilus: "I n'am but ded." *Troilus and Criseyde* V.1246, in *The Works of Geoffrey Chaucer*, ed. F. N. Robinson, 2nd ed. (London: Oxford University Press, 1957).

192

The trees' weight burdening the strengthless air,
The shape of her stilled eyes, her coloured hair,
Her body's balance from the moving feet—
All this, found fair, lacked yet one grain of sweet
It had some warm weeks back: so perisheth
On May's new lip the tender April breath;
So those same walks the wind sowed lilies in
All April through, and all their latter kin
Of languid leaves whereon Autumn blows—
The dead red raiment of the last year's rose—
The last year's laurel, and the last year's love,
Fade, and grow things that death grows weary of.

(SW, II, 19)

The idyllic spring freshness of the medieval garden has been replaced by a garden in the full and oppressive heat of summer, presaging the further change of winter in its "half deflowered" blooms and "beaten leaves." Like Browning, Swinburne sees the garden not as a static paradise, but as embodying the change and decay that its rich growth implies. Moreover, the seasonal change mirrors the decaying passion of the lovers, now in the summertime of their satiety. It is the intense quality of their passion and of life in the garden that forces both toward extinction. The flowers do not merely perfume the air; they burn themselves out in an extravagant love-offering to the sun. The trees produce such an abundance of foliage that they burden "the strengthless air." The lovers have lived at the same intensity, but they are condemned to watch their passion fade slowly. At least last year's rose dies and is the sweeter for producing new blossoms. Human lovers cannot hope for such a renewal. She, sensing the decay of passion in him, revives their love with an embrace so violent that he dies. Like the speaker in Browning's "Porphyria's Lover," she prefers the eternal possession of death to the hazards of a life that is subject to the flux of time.

The garden of "The Two Dreams" is not only subject to time; its idyllic quality is also subverted by the evil nature of the dreams recounted by the lovers. She tells how she saw "a live thing flaked with black / Specks of brute slime and leper-coloured scale" (*SW*, II, 22), crawling from his mouth and then devouring him. He, after enjoying the "tender little thorn-prick of her pain," describes his own dream, in which he received a kiss that wounded him. Cruelty has entered the garden, and it operates at a more disturbing level than that of the cruel mistress of the courtly love tradition. The woman of "The Two Dreams," whose kiss is death, is first cousin to a long line of fatal women that includes Keats's "La Belle Dame Sans Merci," and Rossetti's somber ladies. They reach their most extreme development in Swinburne's Dolores, Our Lady of Pain.

"Dolores" also represents a more extreme subversion of the garden. The Lady of Pain is herself a "garden where all men may dwell," which is "lit with live torches" (*SW*, I, 284, 291), and drenched with blood and tears. Such a garden is not merely antisocial; it is a deliberate affront to society. Tennyson's early gardens had been antisocial places of solitary withdrawal, but they had always represented an attempt to recover the innocence of Eden. Swinburne's gardens, far from being Edenic, are often not even Gardens of Earthly Delights; they are more likely to be Gardens of Infernal Pleasures, presided over by sinister women or implacable goddesses.

Lucrezia Borgia is one such fatal woman, addressed by the poet in "A Ballad of Life," but her sinister qualities are played down in the poem, and she emerges as something of a "stunner" in a Pre-Raphaelite setting:

I found in dreams a place of wind and flowers,
   Full of sweet trees and colour of glad grass,
     In midst whereof there was
A lady clothed like summer with sweet hours.
   Her beauty, fervent as a fiery moon,
     Made my blood burn and swoon
       Like a flame rained upon.
Sorrow had filled her shaken eyelids' blue,

And her mouth's sad red heavy rose all through
Seemed sad with glad things gone.

(*SW*, I, 139)

This could have been written for one of Rossetti's paintings;
it has a static, pictorial, brooding quality unusual in Swin-
burne, and the flowers, trees, and grass suggest the kind of
woodland bower beloved of Rossetti. One word, however,
marks it as belonging to Swinburne, and that is "wind." It
has already been noted that Rossetti almost always finds the
wind a hostile element, whereas Swinburne delighted in it,
and even imports it, somewhat incongruously, into this other-
wise hushed, Pre-Raphaelite landscape.

In fact, it may not be too much of an exaggeration to say
that Rossetti's heaven, the enclosed, protected space, was
Swinburne's hell. In "Laus Veneris" the horror of the knight's
fate is conveyed most powerfully through the feeling of claus-
trophobia within the Venusberg:

Inside the Horsel here the air is hot;
Right little peace one hath for it, God wot;
The scented dusty daylight burns the air,
And my heart chokes me till I hear it not.

(*SW*, I, 147)

The prisoner of Venus longs for death, so that he might merge
with the free, elemental forces outside the gloomy cavern:

Ah yet would God this flesh of mine might be
Where air might wash and long leaves cover me,
Where tides of grass break into foam of flowers,
Or where the wind's feet shine along the sea.

(*SW*, I, 148)

This yearning for freedom from lust through union with
the great cosmic forces is one of the most enduring themes in
Swinburne's poetry, but there is a part of him that also saw
subjection to a beautiful, ruthless woman as a kind of para-
dise. He has to explore that paradise of lust in order to discover

195

what a hell it really represents, and the knight of Venus who is "damned to joyless pleasure,"[4] is nevertheless damned because he has gained his pleasure too well. It is significant that Morris, in his version of the legend, imagines the pleasures that tempt the knight very differently. His Venus inhabits a kind of utopian pastoral landscape, a natural paradise, which palls through its unchanging perfection. In Swinburne's "Laus Veneris" there is practically no landscape within the mountain. The landscape is all outside, and represents the freedom the knight has lost. The natural world is now the yearned-for paradise, just as Venus was the once yearned-for love. The two represent the basic dualism of Swinburne's nature: the desire for freedom set against the desire for subjugation, or, as Harold Nicolson expresses it, "the impulse towards revolt and the impulse towards submission."[5] In "Laus Veneris" the subjugation to lust is shown as destructive and sterile, while the elemental world represented by the "wind's wet wings" (SW, I, 149) outside the prison of love remains, as elsewhere in Swinburne, the true object of desire.

The fascination with corruption and the fatal woman persists, however, and finds expression in Swinburne's fine elegy, "Ave Atque Vale" (SW, III, 44-51). He imagines Baudelaire "at the great knees and feet / Of some pale Titan-woman," an image derived directly from Baudelaire's "La Géante." In "La Géante" the sleeping woman is compared to a mountain.[6] Swinburne seems to have developed this image, associating the Titan woman more specifically with the earth and with great natural forces: her "awful tresses . . . still keep / The savour and shade of old-world pine-forests / Where the wet hill-winds weep." She thus moves away from the Dolores type of cruel lover, closer to an earth goddess. She should perhaps be identified with Proserpine, Queen of the Underworld and

---

[4] Swinburne's own comment in Notes on Poems and Reviews (SW, XVI, 365).

[5] Nicolson, Swinburne, p. 14.

[6] Baudelaire's persona imagines himself sleeping "Comme un hameau paisible au pied d'une montagne." Les Fleurs du Mal, ed. Raynaud, p. 32.

daughter of the earth-goddess, Demeter. According to Walter
Pater, Proserpine was not, in the earliest myths, clearly sep-
arated from her mother: "Demeter—Demeter and Perseph-
one, at first, in a sort of confused union—is the earth, in the
fixed order of its annual changes, but also in all the accident
and detail of the growth and decay of its children."[7] The
emphasis in Swinburne is, of course, on "decay," and he imag-
ines that in the underworld Baudelaire will find strange, poi-
sonous flowers similar to those he created in life:

> Where all day through thine hands in barren braid
> Wove the sick flowers of secrecy and shade,
> Green buds of sorrow and sin, and remnants grey,
> Sweet-smelling, pale with poison, sanguine-hearted.

Such "fleurs du mal" are a ghastly parody of the floral tributes
traditionally offered in the classical pastoral elegy, and they
celebrate qualities that are the reverse of those usually asso-
ciated with the garden. In place of innocence, purity, and
fruitfulness, this anti-garden produces sin, secrecy, and bar-
renness; instead of being associated with the control of violent
passion, it is a place for the cultivation of extreme license. It
is associated with death rather than with life, and links with
what Swinburne sees as Baudelaire's desire for "sleep and no
more life." Oblivion is the chief consolation offered in this
stark elegy, and the only real immortality is to be found in
the "shut scroll" of poems, which ensures a continuing com-
munion of souls between the dead and the living. Dim inti-
mations of some afterlife in a classical Hades are recognized
as nothing more than the products of the poet's imagination,
"Yet with some fancy, yet with some desire, / Dreams pursue
death as winds a flying fire."

In an earlier poem, "The Garden of Proserpine" (SW, I,
299-302), Swinburne had allowed his dreams to pursue death
as an end to be desired for its own sake. Rejecting the pastoral

[7] Pater, "Demeter and Persephone," in *Greek Studies*, p. 92.

world of "men that sow to reap," he celebrates "fruitless fields
of corn" and the barren gardens of death:

> No growth of moor or coppice,
>     No heather-flower or vine,
> But bloomless buds of poppies,
>     Green grapes of Proserpine,
> Pale beds of blowing rushes
> Where no leaf blooms or blushes
> Save this whereout she crushes
>     For dead men deadly wine.

Proserpine offers death, but she also offers a life beyond the
turmoil of passion. To enter her garden is to enter a still,
closed world, cut off from the freshness and freedom of wind
and waves. In this respect it resembles the world of the Venus-
berg, but in this poem Swinburne's protagonist is strongly
attracted to the place "where all trouble seems / Dead winds'
and spent waves' riot." The death wish expressed in this poem
is basically negative and escapist; the speaker is "tired of tears
and laughter" and "weary of days and hours." Swinburne
was later to deal with the death wish differently and more
positively, but at this point the desire seems to be for deliv-
erance from "too much love of living."

It is significant that Swinburne's Proserpine seems to have
no desire to return from the realm of death. She "Forgets the
earth her mother, / The life of fruits and corn." This fleeting
reference to Demeter is the only mention the poet makes of
that side of Proserpine which is traditionally associated with
the seasonal renewal of life in the world. His pale goddess
owes little to the story of Demeter and Persephone as told in
the Homeric hymn; she is closer to the Persephone of Homer's
*Odyssey*, as described by Pater:

> Homer, in the Odyssey, knows Persephone also, but
> not as Kore; only as the queen of the dead . . . dreadful
> Persephone, the goddess of destruction and death, ac-
> cording to the apparent import of her name. She accom-
> plishes men's evil prayers; she is the mistress and manager

of men's shades, to which she can dispense a little more or less of life, dwelling in her mouldering palace on the steep shore of the Oceanus, with its groves of barren willows and tall poplars. But that Homer knew her as the daughter of Demeter there are no signs; and of his knowledge of the rape of Persephone there is only the faintest sign.[8]

It is this goddess of death, destruction, and above all, sleep, that Swinburne celebrates in the "Hymn to Proserpine" (*SW*, I, 200-206). The desire expressed by the speaker in this poem seems to echo the words of Tennyson's lotos-eaters:

I am sick of singing: the bays burn deep and chafe: I
 am fain
To rest a little from praise and grievous pleasure
 and pain.
. . . . . . . . . . . . . . . . . . . . . . . . . . . . .
I say to you, cease, take rest; yea, I say to you all,
 be at peace.
. . . . . . . . . . . . . . . . . . . . . . . . . . . . .
And grief is a grievous thing, and a man hath enough
 of his tears:
Why should he labour, and bring fresh grief to
 blacken his years?
. . . . . . . . . . . . . . . . . . . . . . . . . . . . .
Sleep, shall we sleep after all? for the world is not
 sweet in the end;
For the old faiths loosen and fall, the new years
 ruin and rend.

Proserpine is seen as the queen of night and darkness, presiding over a moonlit and somnolent world that is close in spirit to Tennyson's island:

In the night where thine eyes are as moons are in
 heaven, the night where thou art,

[8] Ibid., p. 94.

Where the silence is more than all tunes, where sleep
overflows from the heart,
Where the poppies are sweet as the rose in our world,
and the red rose is white,
And the wind falls faint as it blows with the fume of
the flowers of the night.
And the murmur of spirits that sleep in the shadow of
Gods from afar
Grows dim in thine ears and deep as the deep dim soul
of a star,
In the sweet low light of thy face, under heavens
untrod by the sun,
Let my soul with their souls find place, and forget
what is done and undone.

The garden of Proserpine is to Swinburne what the island
of the lotos-eaters had been to Tennyson, but with the im-
portant difference that Swinburne seems to endorse the desire
of his persona for oblivion far less ambiguously than Ten-
nyson. Nor need we dismiss Tennyson's ambiguity as a cow-
ardly compromise with Victorian respectability; the impulse
in him toward the joys of living, the ordinary joys of wife and
home and family, was at least as strong as the impulse toward
death. In Swinburne that basic desire for "the settled bliss"
(*TW*, 434) seems to have been absent, and when he moved
beyond the death wish it was toward something very different
from the quiet pleasures of the hearth.

The contrast between the two poets comes out sharply in
their differing treatments of the myth of Persephone, although
in drawing such a contrast it must be remembered that Ten-
nyson's "Demeter and Persephone" was written when he was
in his seventies, with the period of the lotos-eaters safely be-
hind him. It may, in fact, have been written, as Curtis Dahl
suggests, as a reply to Swinburne's "Hymn to Proserpine."
Dahl comments on the way in which "Tennyson's interpre-
tation of the myth meets and contradicts Swinburne's almost
point for point," and he concludes:

For both poets [Persephone] is symbolic of the basic processes of nature. Swinburne equates her with the endlessly, purposelessly swirling and destroying sea that so often stands in his poetry for the ultimate and essential reality of nature. Tennyson, however, sees in her, daughter of the Earth-Goddess, a symbol of the regenerative, resurrective force of nature that parallels and symbolizes the spiritual resurrection of Christian belief.[9]

Tennyson treats the myth almost entirely from the point of view of the Earth Goddess, although some tribute is paid to the powers of darkness when Demeter tells her daughter that "those imperial disimpassioned eyes / Awed even me at first" (*TW*, 1375). G. Robert Stange suggests that Persephone may be seen as a type of the artist, and that "one aspect of her legend conveys Tennyson's sense of the poet's penetration of the realm of the imagination, of the forbidden region of shadows which must be entered before the highest beauty or the highest meaning of experience may be perceived."[10] The awe that emanates from Persephone suggests such an interpretation, but it is not strongly developed in the poem. It was, however, as will be shown later, to become a major theme in Swinburne's poetry, although there is no hint of it in either the "Hymn to Proserpine" or "The Garden of Proserpine." In both poems the underworld is the realm of death or sleep, and neither goddess nor poet visits it in order to return, regenerated, to the world of light. In "Ave Atque Vale" (*SW*, III, 44-51) there is a suggestion that Baudelaire's knowledge of "Secrets and sorrows unbeheld of us: / Fierce loves, and lovely leaf-buds poisonous" was akin to the infernal knowledge of Proserpine. In her strange garden he, the "gardener of strange flowers," may find blossoms similar to those of his

[9] Dahl, "A Double Frame for Tennyson's Demeter?" *Victorian Studies*, 1 (1958), 360.

[10] Stange, "Tennyson's Mythology: A Study of *Demeter and Persephone*," *ELH*, 21 (1954), 74.

poetic vision, but there will be no return from the underworld for him either. Swinburne is, in this poem, absolute for death. David Riede has rightly compared this stage of Swinburne's development to "the 'centre of indifference' through which Carlyle's Teufelsdröckh had to pass to get from the 'Everlasting Nay' (corresponding to Swinburne's 'Dolores' phase) to the 'Everlasting Yea.' "[11] It might also be compared with the nihilistic state described by Birkin in Lawrence's *Women in Love*. Birkin sees modern civilization as part of "that dark river of dissolution" and Aphrodite as "the flowering mystery of the death-process"; dissolution "is a progressive process— and it ends in universal nothing—the end of the world," which also means "a new cycle of creation after—but not for us. If it is the end, then we are of the end—fleurs du mal, if you like."[12]

In his poem "A Forsaken Garden" (*SW*, III, 18-20), Swinburne describes a more realistic and earthly version of the garden of death, one that is poised at the center of indifference, in the void after the process of dissolution has been completed, but before the new life can begin. This is expressed in the ambiguous, one might say amphibious nature of the garden:

> In a coign of the cliff between lowland and highland
>     At the sea-down's edge between windward and lee,
> Walled round with rocks as an inland island,
>     The ghost of a garden fronts the sea.
> A girdle of brushwood and thorn encloses
>     The steep square slope of the blossomless bed
> Where the weeds that grew green from the graves of
>     its roses
>         Now lie dead.

It is "between lowland and highland," between "windward and lee," and, belonging to neither land nor sea, it is an "inland island." Its wall of rocks is neither quite natural, nor is it the traditional ivy-covered, man-made wall of the *hortus*

[11] Riede, *Swinburne*, pp. 60-61.
[12] Lawrence, *Women in Love*, pp. 164-65.

*conclusus.* What Rosenberg calls "this fusion of the artificial with the aboriginal"[13] is also suggested in the "square" of the abandoned bed, which has a wild girdle of "brushwood and thorn." These details are not merely decorative. In giving the garden such ambiguity, Swinburne places it in limbo between land, order, and civilization on the one hand, and sea, chaos, and wilderness on the other. It is also caught between life and eternity. Life belongs to the land and to the "meadows that blossom and wither"; its chief characteristic is that it is subject to time, change, and mortality. Eternity belongs to the sea. This point is made by the ghostly lover: "look forth from the flowers to the sea; / For the foam flowers endure when the rose-blossoms wither."

But the rose has long since withered in this forsaken garden, and now there remains "naught living to ravage and rend." What does remain will not decay:

Earth, stones and thorns of the wild ground growing,
    While the sun and the rain live, these shall be:
Till a last wind's breath upon all these blowing
    Roll the sea.

It is in this stasis, this imitation of eternity, that Swinburne recovers for his anti-garden one of the most important qualities of the traditional garden, since for most poets the ideal garden is either a static world of repose and meditation, or a place where lovers may meet for a precious moment caught and held out of the flux of time, the moment made eternal. For Swinburne, this repose is only possible in the garden of death. His forsaken garden has achieved such a perfection of barrenness that it has, paradoxically, defeated death, at least until the apocalypse:

Till the slow sea rise and the sheer cliff crumble,
    Till terrace and meadow the deep gulfs drink,
Till the strength of the waves of the high tides humble
    The fields that lessen, the rocks that shrink,

[13] Rosenberg, "Swinburne," p. 145.

Here now in his triumph where all things falter,
Stretched out on the spoils that his own hand spread,
As a god self-slain on his own strange altar,
Death lies dead.

Man can achieve a similar triumph over death, but only by
surrendering to death, as this garden has done. Such a sur-
render is envisaged in "The Triumph of Time," in which the
speaker turns from an earthly lover, who has failed him, to
the bleak margins of the sea, where he gazes on a landscape
of endurance:

But clear are these things; the grass and the sand,
Where, sure as the eyes reach, ever at hand,
With lips wide open and face burnt blind,
The strong sea-daisies feast on the sun.
(SW, I, 171)

There is stoic resignation in this barren scene with its "strong
sea-daisies," and one is reminded of the landscape in Arnold's
"Resignation," in which "solemn wastes of heathy hill / Sleep
in the July sunshine still" (AW, 94). However, Arnold's land-
scape is one that seems "to bear rather than rejoice" (AW,
100); Swinburne's goes beyond passive resignation. The wide
open lips of the daisies imply an appetite for life, or perhaps
for death. Moreover, although the faces of the daisies are
"burnt blind" by the heat, they also feast on the sun, so that
they both take and give life; the roles of victim and predator
are reciprocal. Since Swinburne usually associates the sun with
Apollo, god of song and poetry, the daisies may also be seen
as symbols of the poet himself, and of his peculiar relationship
to the source of his inspiration.

The passion of the daisies for the sun is paralleled by the
apparent desire of the landscape to merge with the sea:

The low downs lean to the sea; the stream,
One loose thin pulseless tremulous vein,
Rapid and vivid and dumb as a dream,
Works downward, sick of the sun and the rain.
(SW, I, 171)

The description of the falling stream would seem to owe something to Tennyson's streams in "The Lotos-Eaters," which, "like a downward smoke, / Slow-dropping veils of thinnest lawn, did go" (*TW*, 430), but in fact Swinburne's purposes are quite different. Tennyson is primarily concerned with a beautiful visual effect, and secondly with an emotional effect: the great delicacy and slow movement of the dropping veils enhance the languorous calm of the island paradise. Swinburne has moved further from the school of picturesque landscape description than Tennyson. In describing the stream as "One loose thin pulseless tremulous vein," he is not drawing attention to its pictorial qualities. He is making a statement about its relationship to the sea. The stream is part of the body of the sea, a "vein," but "pulseless" because it has become detached or "loose." In tremulous longing it hastens downward, "sick of the sun and the rain" because they are the agents of the cycle in which the stream is caught up, separated from, and then returned to its mother, the sea, through evaporation and precipitation. This passage of seemingly vague, diffuse Swinburnian description yields the most precise meanings. Even "The low downs lean to the sea" is a scientifically accurate account of the gradual erosion of the land by physical forces, rather than an example of the pathetic fallacy.

The scientific accuracy of the passage is, however, given emotional coloring by identification of the speaker with the stream. He too is "born of the sea":

I will go back to the great sweet mother,
  Mother and lover of men, the sea.
I will go down to her, I and none other,
  Close with her, kiss her and mix her with me;
Cling to her, strive with her, hold her fast.
                    (*SW*, I, 177)

In the sea he is able to achieve that perfect union with the beloved that he had desired of the woman he loved:

were you once sealed mine,
Mine in the blood's beat, mine in the breath,

Mixed into me as honey in wine,
Not time, that sayeth and gainsayeth,
Nor all strong things had severed us then.
(*SW*, I, 173)

Denied this immortality, he chooses to mingle with the sea, becoming, like the stream, "A pulse of the life of thy straits and bays, / A vein in the heart of the streams of the sea" (*SW*, I, 178).

The immortality offered by the sea is, however, that of eternal change. To surrender to its bitter embrace is to surrender to the principle of mutability:

I shall sleep, and move with the moving ships,
    Change as the winds change, veer in the tide;
My lips will feast on the foam of thy lips,
    I shall rise with thy rising, with thee subside.
(*SW*, I, 177)

Such a surrender implies the complete extinction of personality, but this loss is seen as a guarantee of freedom. He asks the sea to "Set free my soul as thy soul is free," and claims that, once freed from the body, "Naked and glad would I walk in thy ways, / Alive and aware of thy ways and thee."

Although the sea in "The Triumph of Time" promises freedom, it still has many of the characteristics of the cruel mistress, whose "large embraces are keen like pain" (*SW*, I, 177). In "Hesperia" the sea is associated with Our Lady of Sleep rather than with Our Lady of Pain, and the poet imagines a more peaceful and gentle surrender, resulting, however, in an even more complete loss of personality and its burdens. In "The Triumph of Time" he is still pitting his strength against the sea: he will "cling to her, strive with her, hold her fast." In "Hesperia" there is no struggle:

And my heart yearns baffled and blind, moved vainly
        toward thee, and moving
As the refluent seaweed moves in the languid
        exuberant stream,

Fair as a rose is on earth, as a rose under water
    in prison,
That stretches and swings to the slow passionate
    pulse of the sea,
Closed up from the air and the sun, but alive, as a
    ghost rearisen,
Pale as the love that revives as a ghost rearisen
    in me.

                        (*SW*, I, 304)

The loss of will and separate identity implied by this passage
represents a further stage in the death process, and is therefore,
paradoxically, closer to the possibility of new life. Trapped
in their underwater prison without sun or air, the roses of the
sea are in the realm of death, and yet, as they sway in the
saline bath of the Great Mother, they are also in the womb
of life, "alive as a ghost rearisen."

    In terms of Swinburne's personal myth, as outlined in
"Thalassius," this return to the sea and consequent resurrec-
tion can be seen as the commitment of the poet to his art. In
"Thalassius" the poet is born of the sea and the sun. Leaving
the sea, he encounters Love, who is also Sorrow and Death;
then he rides for a while in the fierce, wild train of Lust. Finally
sickened, he returns to the sea, falls into a deep sleep, and
awakens "Pure as one purged of pain that passion bore" (*SW*,
III, 301). The process of regeneration begins, and "the earth's
great comfort and the sweet sea's breath / Breathed and blew
life in where was heartless death." His poetic awakening,
which follows, is described in terms that suggest the submer-
gence of the individual soul in the great cosmic rhythms of
the sea:

Now too the soul of all his senses felt
The passionate pride of deep sea-pulses dealt
Through nerve and jubilant vein
As from the love and largess of old time,
And with his heart again
The tidal throb of all the tides keep rhyme

And charm him from his own soul's separate sense
With infinite and invasive influence
That made strength sweet in him and sweetness strong,
Being now no more a singer, but a song.
(*SW*, III, 302)

Thus, as David Riede writes, "sun and wind and sea take hold
of the poet, making him a part of the cosmic song of nature";[14]
the poet becomes part of nature, but nature is also expressed
through his song:

Have therefore in thine heart and in thy mouth
The sound of song that mingles north and south,
The song of all the winds that sing of me,
And in thy soul the sense of all the sea.
(*SW*, III, 303)

Singer and sea are one, as in Wallace Stevens's "The Idea of
Order at Key West":

It was her voice that made
The sky acutest at its vanishing.
She measured to the hour its solitude.
She was the single artificer of the world
In which she sang. And when she sang, the sea,
Whatever self it had, became the self
That was her song, for she was the maker.[15]

The whole question of the relationship between perceiver
and perceived, which lies at the heart of Romantic poetic
theory, is here settled by Stevens in favor of the perceiver.
Nature, the sea, is created by the poet as "maker." In "Tha-
lassius" the relationship is more truly reciprocal. The wind
breathes life into the poet, whose song then becomes the breath
of the wind; this links, as Richard McGhee has pointed out,

---

[14] Riede, *Swinburne*, p. 179.
[15] *The Collected Poems of Wallace Stevens*, p. 129.

with the Romantic image of "the correspondent breeze," discussed by M. H. Abrams in his classic essay.[16]

In "On the Cliffs," however, the animating source seems to come from man rather than from nature. The poem opens with a powerful description of the bleak landscape bordering the North Sea, with its "gaunt woods," "wan wild sparse flowers," and "steep green sterile fields" (SW, III, 305). This barren landscape must be brought to life by the song of the lyric poet, Sappho, here embodied in the nightingale, whose "ruling song has thrilled / The deep dark air and subtle tender sea" (SW, III, 316). Before her voice was heard, "Dumb was the field, the woodland mute, the lawn / Silent; the hill was tongueless as the vale" (SW, III, 315). Nature is so much dead matter without the life given to it by the perceiving poet. "For Wordsworth," writes David Riede, "the informing force in nature is a mysterious pantheistic deity; for Swinburne, it is poetry."[17] This, at least, emerges quite clearly from "On the Cliffs." But Swinburne was not a didactic poet. Less theoretical than Wordsworth, he is often caught in the flux of changing moods and feelings, and his various seas, like Tennyson's, speak with many voices.

In "The Garden of Cymodoce," for example, he sings a song of rapturous praise of the sea, and of that "favourite corner of all on earth known to me, the island of Sark."[18] There he states that he has loved the sea with a love "more strong / In me than very song" (SW, III, 318), which certainly implies that the sea has a reality that equals, or even surpasses, his poetry. In other poems he sings not of a beautiful and beneficent sea, but of a sea that is

[16] McGhee, " 'Thalassius': Swinburne's Poetic Myth," Victorian Poetry, 5 (1967), 127-36. And see Abrams, "The Correspondent Breeze: A Romantic Metaphor," Kenyon Review, 19 (1957), 113-30.

[17] Riede, Swinburne, p. 159. See also Riede's article, "Swinburne's 'On the Cliffs': The Evolution of a Romantic Myth," Victorian Poetry, 16 (1978), 189-203, for a full and valuable commentary on the poem.

[18] Letter to Matthew Arnold, 1880, in The Swinburne Letters, ed. Lang, IV, 142.

Wild, and woful, and pale, and grey,
A shadow of sleepless fear,
A corpse with the night for bier.
("Neap-Tide," *SW*, III, 221)

Often the sea is associated with death and destruction, as
in the very fine poem "By the North Sea," where the "waters
are haggard and yellow / And crass with the scurf of the beach"
(*SW*, IV, 326). This sea is a devourer of corpses, the mate of
Death, and it borders a land that is bleak and desolate:

A land that is lonelier than ruin;
    A sea that is stranger than death:
Far fields that a rose never blew in,
    Wan waste where the winds lack breath;
Waste endless and boundless and flowerless
    But of marsh-blossoms fruitless as free:
Where earth lies exhausted, as powerless
        To strive with the sea.
                (*SW*, IV, 325)

The poet, however, finds consolation in this bleak wasteland.
Its barren emptiness confers the peace of oblivion:

Slowly, gladly, full of peace and wonder
    Grows his heart who journeys here alone.
Earth and all its thoughts of earth sink under
    Deep as deep in water sinks a stone.
                (*SW*, IV, 331)

Emerging from this Center of Indifference, he perceives a new
beauty in the landscape, which has undergone a "sea-change":

Tall the plumage of the rush-flower tosses,
    Sharp and soft in many a curve and line
Gleam and glow the sea-coloured marsh-mosses
    Salt and splendid from the circling brine.
Streak on streak of glimmering seashine crosses
    All the land sea-saturate as with wine.
                (*SW*, IV, 331)

The sea has claimed this land for its own, saturating it with brine and rendering it useless to man; the "pastures are herd-less and sheepless" (*SW*, IV, 325). But in so doing, the sea has transformed it into a landscape of strange, gleaming beauty, like a Turner painting. The process traced in these stanzas encapsulates the movement of the poem as a whole from Death, through the Void, to a renewal of life and beauty. This renewal only comes after a total acceptance of death. Nothing, not even the graves of the dead, can stand against time and the destructive power of the sea.

Nothing, that is, save the wind, whom the sea recognizes as "her lord and her lover" (*SW*, IV, 338). The wind is pow-erful and free because he gives no hostages to time; he has no possessions or material body to lose. He therefore achieves immortality, but is doomed to seek, never to find, "but seeking rejoices / That possession can work him no wrong" (*SW*, IV, 339). The poet identifies with the wind, and can achieve a similar immortality through his song, but he must accept both "the boon and the burden / Of the sleepless unsatisfied breeze." Part of that burden entails the sacrifice of ordinary life, its goals and rewards:

> For the wind's is their doom and their blessing;
> To desire, and have always above
> A possession beyond their possessing,
> A love beyond reach of their love.
> Green earth has her sons and her daughters,
> And these have their guerdons; but we
> Are the wind's and the sun's and the water's,
> Elect of the sea.
> (*SW*, IV, 339)

Swinburne's choice of bleak landscapes and seascapes is therefore a necessary part of his vocation as a poet. Ordinary men and women may receive the reward of the rich pastoral life implied in "green earth," but they will decay with that earth. The poet will pay for his immortality by inhabiting landscapes that are "herdless and sheepless."

Sometimes the poet finds it impossible to make the sacrifice demanded of him in order to become one of the "elect of the sea." This happens in "Evening on the Broads," in which no joyful union between poet and sea or wind takes place. In this poem the sea is presented as a less than perfect lover: she rejects light and love because she has "None to reflect from the bitter and shallow response of her heart" (*SW*, IV, 306). But the poet is equally ungenerous, giving nothing of himself to the sea. He remains a detached and critical observer, "here by the sand-bank watching, with eyes on the sea-line" (*SW*, IV, 305). However, the mood of the poet fluctuates, and there is a slow rise and fall of hopefulness and despair, perhaps corresponding to the rhythm of the sea itself.

The poem opens with a solemn nocturne in which the last light of the dying sun is held in suspense for a moment, but "half repossessed by the night" (*SW*, IV, 302). Images of death and darkness are balanced against images of life and light: death descends on the deathless waters, yet death, or darkness, is itself seen as protective, fostering new life:

As a bird unfledged is the broad-winged night, whose
    winglets are callow
Yet, but soon with their plumes will she cover her
    brood from afar,
Cover the brood of her worlds that cumber the skies
    with their blossom
    Thick as the darkness of leaf-shadowed spring is
    encumbered with flowers.
                    (*SW*, IV, 302)

The sunset itself seems to mirror the poet's own mood, "being sick of division" between the conflicting desires for night and day. It is "Fearful and fain of the night," which is associated with death, but death is also new life, "begotten / Out of the womb of the tomb" (*SW*, IV, 303). Clinging to "the loves of the morning and noon," the sunset cannot die, and therefore cannot be reborn. The speaker in the opening section seems to become more and more convinced of the

"sure new birth" being nurtured in the darkness. Then sud-
denly there is a change of mood, heralded by the word "But":

> But here by the sand-bank watching, with eyes on
>     the sea-line, stranger
> Grows to me also the weight of the sea-ridge gazed
>     on of me,
> Heavily heaped up, changefully changeless, void
>     though of danger
> Void not of menace, but full of the might of the
>     dense dull sea.
>                                    (SW, IV, 305)

For the first time in the poem, the presence of the perceiver,
sharply separated from the scene, is stressed. The mention of
"eyes" and "gazed," the repetition of "me," set these lines
apart from the opening section. The night is now seen as
something sinister, not protective. In the lines that follow, the
speaker's presence is continually insisted upon, and everything
is described in direct relation to himself. The wave is "before
me," the sandbank "is behind me"; he sees the water as "the
wall of a prison" or "the wall of a grave"; "Standing still dry-
shod, I see it as higher than my head." The threatening forces
that surround him make him cling to the fact of his own
identity, his presence in the landscape as an eye and a con-
sciousness. Like the poised sunset, he is unwilling to surrender
to death and darkness. It is this fear that makes him regard
the sea purely as the agent of destruction, with "foam-lipped
horses / Whose manes are yellow as plague, and as ensigns of
pestilence hang" (SW, IV, 307).

But once again a change of mood sets in as the speaker
remembers "Shakespeare's vision" and Perdita, the new life
cast up by the sea, "bright as a dew-drop engilt of the sun on
the sedge." The hope is momentary, and the speaker remains
unable to commit himself to the darkness. As in "By the North
Sea," the wind plays an important role here, but it is a more
desolate wind, sounding a cry of triumph that is "even as the
crying of hunger that maddens / The heart of a strong man

aching in vain as the wind's heart aches" (*SW*, IV, 309). When darkness at last descends on the land, there is a sense of dread rather than of possible fulfillment:

> And the sunset at last and the twilight are dead:
> and the darkness is breathless
> With fear of the wind's breath rising that seems
> and seems not to sleep:
> But a sense of the sound of it alway, a spirit
> unsleeping and deathless,
> Ghost or God, evermore moves on the face of the
> deep.
>
> (*SW*, IV, 309)

Susan Lorsch describes this landscape as "designified," and comments: "This opaque landscape rebuffs the human imagination, allowing for 'no transparent' romantic 'rapture.' "[19] My own reading of the poem suggests that the landscape is "opaque" largely because the observer clings fearfully to his own separate identity. "Romantic rapture" can never seize the neutral observer by the throat; it comes only after the observer has ceased to observe and has given himself to what he feels are superior forces. The complete surrender of self is necessary, and "Evening on the Broads" charts the failure of such a surrender. However, the poem should not be used to diagnose a general failure of the romantic impulse in Swinburne. In many other poems the rapturous union between man and landscape is achieved, as, for example, when Tristram surrenders so joyfully to the sea.

Swinburne's version of the legend of Tristram and Iseult differs sharply from both Arnold's and Tennyson's in that it is a full and passionate celebration of human sexual love. And yet, the most perfect moment of ecstasy and fulfillment granted to Tristram comes with his embrace of an inhuman lover, the sea:

[19] Lorsch, "Algernon Charles Swinburne's 'Evening on the Broads': Unmeaning Landscape and the Language of Negation," *Victorian Poetry*, 18 (1980), 95.

214

And round him all the bright rough shuddering sea
Kindled, as though the world were even as he,
Heart-stung with exultation of desire:
And all the life that moved him seemed to aspire,
As all the sea's life toward the sun: and still
Delight within him waxed with quickening will
More smooth and strong and perfect as a flame
That springs and spreads, till each glad limb became
A note of rapture in the tune of life.
                                (SW, IV, 144)

Swinburne's description of the attitudes of both Byron and
Shelley toward nature is surely the most appropriate comment
on this passage: "Their passion is perfect, a fierce and blind
desire which exalts and impels their verse into the high places
of emotion and expression. They feed upon nature with a holy
hunger, follow her with a divine lust as of gods chasing the
daughters of men" (SW, XV, 126).

Tristram's union with the sea is the high point of a poem
in which the sea is, in many respects, the true protagonist. It
is present, not merely as a background, but as an active par-
ticipant at every important moment in the lives of the lovers.
When their love begins to blossom, the sea trembles sympa-
thetically:

And his face burned against her meeting face
Most like a lover's thrilled with great love's grace
Whose glance takes fire and gives; the quick sea shone
And shivered like spread wings of angels blown
By the sun's breath before him; and a low
Sweet gale shook all the foam-flowers of thin snow
As into rainfall of sea-roses shed
Leaf by wild leaf on that green garden-bed
Which tempests till and sea-winds turn and plough.
                                (SW, IV, 45)

This sea-garden echoes the conventional garden of love, but
it is no safe, enclosed space: it is full of movement and change,

tilled by tempests and ploughed by sea winds. Like tiny figures in a Turner canvas, the lovers are dwarfed by cosmic forces, and, as always in Swinburne, subject to time. The frail "foam-flowers of thin snow" are even more precarious than the roses of the land, and perhaps more highly valued for that reason. Swinburne's lovers, like Rossetti's, meet in an antisocial landscape, but whereas Rossetti's bowers are protective, the elemental backdrop to the illicit passion of Tristram and Iseult offers no real refuge except in death. Whereas Rossetti's protagonist tracks his own footsteps in self-absorbed misery, and kisses his own reflection, Swinburne's Tristram delights in the sublime terror of the sea. Moreover, although the sea represents freedom from social laws, it is not always sympathetic to the lovers. When Iseult of Brittany curses them, it echoes her vindictive hatred:

The sea's was like a doomsman's blasting breath
From lips afoam with ravenous lust of death.
(*SW*, IV, 124)

The sea can be all things to all men; when Iseult of Ireland prays that she might repent of her sin, her prayer is punctuated by the sound of the waves crashing against the walls of the palace, echoing her own anguish.

The sea is a vast and indifferent element which can seem to echo whatever emotions petty individuals may attribute to it. It is the "sundering sea," separating Tristram in Brittany from Iseult in Ireland; it takes them away from each other, and bears them back to each other with equal indifference. It mirrors their joy and their passion, their guilt, and the voice of God's anger. This is not simply the pathetic fallacy. Swinburne's sea is the primordial flux from which all life, all passion comes, and to which it must eventually return. It does therefore contain within itself all the emotions that the various actors in the tragedy see mirrored in its surface, or hear in the sound of its waves. Love, hate, desolation, repentance, and revenge can be separated from the matrix. It is all life, but it is also, preeminently, change and death.

This is the message of the sea to Tristram as he leaves his Queen for the last time and sails back to Brittany. After a long passage celebrating the sea's beauty, Tristram seems to hear the prophecy that he will not return alive:

And the wind mourned and triumphed, and the sea
Wailed and took heart and trembled; nor might he
Hear more of comfort in their speech, or see
More certitude in all the waste world's range
Than the only certitude of death and change.
                                     (SW, IV, 138)

Even at its most beautiful the sea is a destructive element, and it is used throughout the poem like a tragic chorus. It surrounds and threatens Mark's "wave-walled palace," which rises "Sheer from the fierce lip of the lapping foam" (SW, IV, 59). When Tristram and Iseult are reunited for a brief period of happiness at Joyous Garde, the turbulent, grey sea is there as a reminder of death and change. The lovers, recognizing that their passion will destroy them, are in love with their own destruction, "As men that shall be swallowed of the sea / Love the sea's lovely beauty" (SW, IV, 73). Finally, the sea invades the tomb in which the lovers are laid, so that they are united with it in death, a union joyfully presaged by Tristram's final swim.

Tristram and Iseult also spend an idyllic period in the shelter of a forest bower:

There was a bower beyond man's eye more fair
Than ever summer dews and sunniest air
Fed full with rest and radiance till the boughs
Had wrought a roof as for a holier house
Than aught save love might breathe in.
                                     (SW, IV, 66)

But Swinburne cannot rest content with this enclosed, Pre-Raphaelite setting. The bower is near the sea, and the lovers are exposed to the elements:

Far and fain
Somewhiles the soft rush of rejoicing rain
Solaced the darkness, and from steep to steep
Of heaven they saw the sweet sheet lightning leap
And laugh its heart out in a thousand smiles,
When the clear sea for miles on glimmering miles
Burned as though dawn were strewn abroad astray.

(SW, IV, 69)

The Pre-Raphaelite bower has dissolved into the fierce immensity of a luminous Turner. Indeed, this section of the poem culminates in the complete identification of the lovers with the elemental forces:

And with the lovely laugh of love that takes
The whole soul prisoner ere the whole sense wakes,
Her lips for love's sake bade love's will be done.
And all the sea lay subject to the sun.

(SW, IV, 72)

Swinburne's basic desire to become part of nature makes his view of the fate of Merlin in Broceliande very different from that of either Tennyson or Arnold. Tennyson's Merlin is simply lost and imprisoned: "And in the hollow oak he lay as dead, / And lost to life and use and name and fame" (TW, 1620). Arnold appreciates the beauty of the forest glade in which Vivian bewitches Merlin, but he has no vicarious desire to become part of it; his Merlin is a "prisoner till the judgement-day" (AW, 237). Swinburne sees Merlin as, if anything, fortunate in his trance. He "Takes his strange rest at heart of slumberland," but is aware of all the change and growth around himself:

He hears above him all the winds on wing
Through the blue dawn between the brightening boughs,
And on shut eyes and slumber-smitten brows
Feels ambient change in the air and strengthening sun,
And knows the soul that was his soul at one

With the ardent world's, and in the spirit of earth
His spirit of life reborn to mightier birth
And mixed with things of elder life than ours.
(SW, IV, 116)

Becoming part of nature, he hears the cosmic song, and like Tristram, becomes a "note of rapture in the tune of life" (*SW*, IV, 144). He is frankly envied by Iseult, who says: "some joy it were to be / Lost in the sun's light and the all-girdling sea, / Mixed with the winds and woodlands" (*SW*, IV, 116).

Merlin's sentient trance might be compared with the experience described in "A Nympholept," which also takes place in a woodland setting. In both cases the protagonist becomes a part of all that surrounds him, but in "A Nympholept" the experience has a violent and even terrifying intensity that is very different from Merlin's sleep. Such an experience can only be called "sublime," and it takes place not in the Alps, but at noon in a forest glade. We have seen the importance of such a setting to both Arnold and Rossetti, but for them it was, if anything, a refuge from the sublime. Swinburne takes this most Victorian and Pre-Raphaelite of landscapes and transforms it with "invasive power" that is "Creative and subtle and fierce . . . / Through darkness and cloud, from the breath of the one God, Pan" (*SW*, VI, 68).

In "Silent Noon," Rossetti had also felt the perfection of the hour, "dropped to us from above" (*RW*, 81); but his emphasis had been on its perfect peace, as of silence made visible. Swinburne's poem opens peacefully with "Summer, and noon, and a splendour of silence" (*SW*, VI, 68), but the sunbeams are shafts "from the string of the God's bow" which "cleave" the foliage. Noon is the perfect moment of fulfillment, the moment of consummation between earth and sun, when "the deep mid mystery of light and of heat seems / To clasp and pierce dark earth, and enkindle dust" (*SW*, VI, 69). The silence of the woodland is not that of peace, but of passionate anticipation and also of dread. The speaker, like the earth, prepares to receive the God:

The naked noon is upon me: the fierce dumb spell,
The fearful charm of the strong sun's imminent might,
Unmerciful, steadfast, deeper than seas that swell,
Pervades, invades, appals me with loveless light,
With harsher awe than breathes in the breath of night.
(*SW*, VI, 72)

The speaker acknowledges that the "supreme dim godhead" whose presence he senses is "Perceived of the soul and conceived of the sense of man" (*SW*, VI, 73). But this god, which is Pan, or All, is more than a mere creation of man's; he is "conceived," but also "perceived." The speaker insists on the reality of the vision that appears. The power that seizes him is divine: it is above and beyond him, and yet, paradoxically, it is also rooted in his own heart. Pan is more than the other gods, the "shadows conceived and adored of man"; he is the "dark dumb godhead innate in the fair world's life," and therefore in the life of man as well, who alone has the power to perceive him because man is that part of nature which has become self-conscious. In recognizing the power of the god that is both within himself and an outside force, man recognizes the unity of all living things. He also accepts a kind of Blakean marriage of contraries: God is "dark as the dawn is bright, / And bright as the night is dark"; he is "first and last," and "depth and height"; he unites fear and love; he is eternal, but he "has change to wife" (*SW*, VI, 76).

Freed from the limitations of self by what can only be described as a non-Christian mystical experience, the speaker asks: "My spirit or thine is it, breath of thy life or of mine, / Which fills my sense with a rapture that casts out fear?" (*SW*, VI, 80). In this poem, landscape, which implies an observer, has ceased to exist. Man and nature have achieved a triumphant union in which "nought is all, as am I, but a dream of thee" (*SW*, VI, 81).

A somewhat different kind of unity is achieved in "The Lake of Gaube" (*SW*, VI, 200-202), one of Swinburne's few poems inspired by mountain scenery. The lake celebrated in this remarkable poem is in the central Pyrenees, near Cauteretz. It is the same region that was visited by Tennyson and Hallam in 1830, and that inspired the beautiful scenic description in "Oenone." I have already shown how Tennyson was to modify the early version of this poem by softening and humanizing the picturesque landscape in the 1842 version. Swinburne does not humanize the landscape in "The Lake of Gaube"; he emphasizes its sublime and terrible qualities.

He has little interest, however, in the picturesque qualities of the scene. Even in the opening stanza, which comes closest to being pictorial, the emphasis is on the unifying power of the sun:

The lawns, the gorges, and the peaks, are one
Glad glory, thrilled with sense of unison
In strong compulsive silence of the sun.

The speaker desires to become part of this "glad glory," but in order to achieve this, he must submit to the extinction of his own separate personality by plunging into the dark, icy waters of the lake. As has been pointed out by Meredith Raymond, "The Lake of Gaube" is a death poem, but through this "death" the "spirit may experience utter freedom and self-obliviousness or a moment of annihilation preceding renewal."[20]

In "A Nympholept" the speaker bathed himself in the fiery light of noon and was granted knowledge of the God who is both darkness and light. Now he must dive into the darkness in order to arrive at unity with the sun, and he must submit to the dark not simply without fear, but with ecstasy:

As the bright salamander in fire of the noonshine
    exults and is glad of his day,
The spirit that quickens my body rejoices to pass
    from the sunlight away,
To pass from the glow of the mountainous flowerage,
    the high multitudinous bloom,

[20] Raymond," 'The Lake of Gaube': Swinburne's Dive in the Dark and the 'Indeterminate Moment,' " *Victorian Poetry*, 9 (1971), 197.

Far down through the fathomless night of the water,
the gladness of silence and gloom.
Death-dark and delicious as death in the dream
of a lover and dreamer may be,
It clasps and encompasses body and soul with
delight to be living and free.

Such a rhapsodic invocation of the realm of death looks forward to D. H. Lawrence's "Bavarian Gentians," in which oblivion is seen as a consummation, the embrace of the dark god amidst "the splendour of torches of darkness, shedding darkness on the lost bride and her groom."[21] But Swinburne's swimmer breaks out of the darkness after his moment of oblivion, and "Shoots up as a shaft from the dark depth shot, sped straight into sight of the sun." He has earned his right to join earth, air, and mountains in their "sense of unison" beneath the sovereign power of the sun, and since the sun is associated with Apollo, it becomes possible, as Kerry Mc-Sweeney suggests, to see the plunge into the lake as "a superb image for the freedom and joy of poetic creation and of man's union with nature."[22]

A useful comparison might also be drawn between this dive into the dark lake and Empedocles' leap into the volcano in Arnold's poem. For Empedocles, the leap is an act of despair leading to extinction, although he does, as has been pointed out, recover the sense of the sublime for a brief moment before death. For Swinburne, extinction is the necessary prelude to a renewed sense of life and, in particular, to the accession of poetic power. Swinburne recovers the sense of the sublime for the Victorians by exploring and accepting its terrible aspects. He is attracted to those landscapes which "excite the ideas of pain and danger," and which are, therefore, "productive of the strongest emotion which the mind is capable of feeling."[23]

[21] Lawrence, *Poems*, II, 140.
[22] McSweeney, "Swinburne's 'A Nympholept' and 'The Lake of Gaube,' "
*Victorian Poetry*, 9 (1971), 213.
[23] Burke, *The Sublime and the Beautiful*, p. 58.

The eighteenth-century sublime had degenerated into the picturesque, in which the observer is separated from the landscape, and the terrors of the scenery are turned into a checklist of set emotions for the tourist. Swinburne completely rejects the picturesque, desiring to become a part of the landscape. Arnold's Empedocles had seen that only by the leap into the volcano could a sense of primal terror be regained that would purge life of its triviality. But Arnold was too much of a pessimist, caught in the web of Victorian doubt, to believe that there could be anything after that leap. Swinburne, although rejecting Christianity and the Christian afterlife more completely than Arnold, nevertheless accepts death as part of the process whereby the soul achieves true life and freedom.

Swinburne is the great poet of paradoxes, which are basic to his philosophy that true freedom can only be achieved by the unity of such opposites as flesh and spirit, life and death, light and darkness, pain and pleasure. It is therefore fitting that his landscapes should be at once completely antisocial, and yet in a certain respect completely humanized, since in most of them the division between man and the landscape has disappeared. In a truly reciprocal relationship, man becomes part of the cosmic song, but he is also the singer of that song.

# CHAPTER VIII

# HARDY:
# THE CHASTENED SUBLIME

Thomas Hardy has often been exluded from general studies of Victorian poetry, partly because of his greater fame as a novelist, and partly because he did not publish his first book of poems until 1898. It is for precisely those reasons that I have chosen to include him; not enough attention has been paid to this very fine poet,[1] and in any case, it seems fitting that a study of this sort should end with at least one foot in the twentieth century. Moreover, Hardy is known as a "country man," and is therefore an important figure to include in any discussion on the use of landscape.

Too often, however, "Hardy the countryman" has seemed to suggest a sentimental and provincial writer. Although some of his early novels, such as *Under the Greenwood Tree*, have the quality of a pastoral idyll, Hardy was soon to move toward a darker vision of country life. As a recent study has shown,[2] he was fully aware of the grim conditions and narrow lot of the rural laborer, and in his poetry and later novels the pastoral note is, on the whole, strikingly absent. In the famous opening chapter of *The Return of the Native*, for example, he rejects landscapes of conventional beauty and fertility, and chooses the "vast tract of unenclosed wild known as Egdon Heath" as being more in harmony with the times:

> The time seems near, if it has not actually arrived, when the chastened sublimity of a moor, a sea, or a mountain

[1] However, Donald Davie has made large, and perhaps justified, claims for the influence of Hardy on modern British poetry. See *Thomas Hardy and British Poetry*.
[2] See Merryn Williams, *Thomas Hardy and Rural England*.

will be all of nature that is absolutely in keeping with the moods of the more thinking among mankind.[3]

Just as William Morris had found that the bleak wastes of Iceland, with their message of stoic endurance, satisfied some inner need, so Hardy turns to a landscape that is "slighted and enduring" (*Return*, p. 6). Indeed, Hardy may have intended a reference to Morris, since he adds that "spots like Iceland may become to the tourist what the vineyards and myrtle-gardens of South Europe are to him now" (*Return*, p. 5). This was written in 1877, some six years after Morris had become one of the first "tourists" to visit Iceland.

Any attempt to link Hardy, the pessimist, and Morris, the "happiest of poets,"[4] does at least have the charm of novelty, and it is even possible to extend the comparison. Both men had a strong feeling for the English countryside, and although Morris took greater delight in the lush and fertile aspects of nature, he also loved the "sad lowland country" that surrounded Kelmscott.[5] Moreover, in spite of their different social backgrounds, Morris and Hardy shared a sympathy for the aspirations of the humblest men and women, although Hardy lacked Morris's utopian vision, and Morris found *Tess of the D'Urbervilles* "grim."[6] In the end, it must be admitted, the differences between the two writers outweigh the similarities.

A more fruitful line of comparison might be drawn between Hardy and Swinburne, a line suggested by David Riede, who stresses their common agnosticism.[7] But in spite of a certain similarity in their philosophical positions, and in spite of the admiration that Hardy expressed for Swinburne in his elegy, "A Singer Asleep," it must be admitted that there seems to be an enormous gulf between the impassioned lyricism of

[3] *The Return of the Native*, p. 5.
[4] According to Yeats in "The Happiest of the Poets," in *Ideas of Good and Evil*, pp. 70-87.
[5] Quoted by Henderson in *William Morris*, p. 117.
[6] Ibid., p. 344.
[7] Riede, *Swinburne*, p. 218.

Swinburne, and the spare, dry simplicity of much of Hardy's poetry. The comparison is worth drawing, however, and particularly in relation to the landscapes favored by the two poets. Both of them are, in a sense, regional poets, though they both transcend regionalism. What Emily Brontë did for the Yorkshire moors, Swinburne did for the North Sea coast and the Isle of Wight, and Hardy did for "Wessex."[8] Moreover, all three poets exhibit a perverse love for the most barren and bleak landscapes, landscapes that in their rugged harshness may be called "sublime," although they have nothing in common with the stock landscapes of the eighteenth-century sublime or the picturesque. Indeed, these nineteenth-century poets show little interest in mere "scenery"; the picturesque, so often associated with Italy and the Grand Tour, has given way to a sense of place that is very English, and firmly rooted in personal experience.

But again, the resemblance between Hardy and Swinburne cannot be pushed too far. Swinburne's landscapes often suggest comparison with Turner's paintings; Hardy's are more subdued, closer sometimes to Constable, but often expressing a bleaker reality. Nor can one imagine Hardy writing about the kind of ecstatic surrender to elemental nothingness described by Swinburne in "The Lake of Gaube"; if he had written such a poem his swimmer would no doubt have caught a chill soon after his rash plunge, the natural punishment for such an act of hubris. Hardy's own phrase, "chastened sublimity," perfectly expresses his more somber, less ecstatic relation to the natural world. He sees man as being part of nature, but not as a result of an act of volition, such as the dive into the lake. Man is a part of nature whether he likes

---

[8] This fact has spawned an enormous industry in literary guided tours of the "Hardy country." Most of them have little or nothing to say about Hardy as an artist, and they tend to concentrate on "identifying" scenes from the novels. The following may stand as examples of the genre: Hopkins, *Thomas Hardy's Dorset*, and Maxwell, *The Landscape of Thomas Hardy*. Maxwell's book does at least have reproductions of some pleasant watercolors by the author of various Hardy "scenes."

it or not, subject, like other creatures, to the harsh laws of an indifferent nature.

Hardy's sense of the unity between man and nature is in part the result of a countryman's unsentimental view of things. Landscape is seldom described in his poems; it is experienced. The men and women who trudge the country roads in foul weather have little inclination for admiring a fine prospect:

> I pace along, the rain-shafts riddling me,
> Mile after mile out by the moorland way,
> And up the hill, and through the ewe-leaze gray
> Into the lane, and round the corner tree.[9]

The speaker threads his way "up . . . and through . . . / Into . . . and round," like a moving but integral part of the landscape, never rising above it for a view of the world.

Even when Hardy does give the reader a lofty view, it is soon placed in somewhat ironic juxtaposition with the lives of ordinary men and women who have other concerns than scenic beauty. "Life and Death at Sunrise" (*HW*, 730) opens with a fine landscape effect:

> The hills uncap their tops
> Of woodland, pasture, copse,
> And look on the layers of mist
>     At their foot that still persist.

A wagon creaks into the scene, which is still, at this point, pictorial, but two men meet, and the poem ends with their exchange of news. They talk of a birth and a death in such matter-of-fact, casual terms ("Oh, a coffin for old John Thinn: / We are just going to put him in") that the sunrise of the opening lines begins to look like a piece of deliberately "poetic" staginess. From the point of view of the two rustics, the sunrise is an even more prosaic occurrence than birth or death, and quite unworthy of comment.

[9] *The Complete Poems of Thomas Hardy*, ed. Gibson, p. 276. Hereafter cited as *HW* with page numbers.

In most of his poems Hardy uses the dramatic form, which
further diminishes the sense of any observed landscape. The
women who work the fields at Flintcomb-Ash are hardly aware
of their surroundings, except in terms of the direct effect of
snow and rain on their bodies: "The wet washed through us—
plash, plash, plash" (HW, 881). Hardy the novelist gives a
lengthy and memorable description of Flintcomb-Ash in *Tess
of the D'Urbervilles*, but in the poem the landscape has be-
come what the women suffer.

Such an incidental treatment of landscape as a part of hu-
man suffering rather than as something to be admired may
also be found in the traditional ballads, which Hardy knew
and loved, and which undoubtedly influenced him.[10] In other
respects too, his treatment of landscape seems to show such
an influence. The use of proper names in "A Trampwoman's
Tragedy," for example, is an authentic ballad note:

> From Wynyard's Gap the livelong day,
>     The livelong day,
> We beat afoot the northward way
>     We had travelled times before
> The sun-blaze burning on our backs,
> Our shoulders sticking to our packs,
> By fosseway, fields, and turnpike tracks
>     We skirted sad Sedge-Moor.
>                 (HW, 195)

The names not only help to create the feeling that a real
journey is being undertaken; they appeal confidently to the
audience's knowledge of local places. No description of "sad
Sedge-Moor" is needed, because its attributes are part of the
folk memory. There is a sense of place here that goes back to
a period before the creation of landscape as scenery.

In this poem the countryside is seen entirely from the point

---

[10] This has been pointed out by various critics. See, for example, Thom
Gunn, "Hardy and the Ballads," *Agenda: Thomas Hardy Special Issue*, 10,
Nos. 2 & 3 (1972), 19-46. Southworth also discusses "the strong and con-
genial ballad influence in the poems." *The Poetry of Thomas Hardy*, p. 173.

of view of the tramps as something to be traversed, but in other poems it takes on a more independent existence. In "The Homecoming," for example, landscape, wind, and rain are used in a balladlike refrain to suggest impending doom and lonely misery:

> Gruffly growled the wind on Toller downland
> > broad and bare,
> And lonesome was the house, and dark, and
> > few came there.
> > > (*HW*, 250)

The bleak landscape in this poem is almost the personification of Fate, and Hardy's tragic fatalism may also be seen as part of his inheritance from the ballads, and from an even older tradition, that of the Anglo-Saxon elegies. But in Hardy the ancient, pre-Christian belief in Fate or Chance as the final arbiter of human affairs falls on the fertile ground of modern skepticism. As a young man he had read Darwin, Huxley, Spencer, Schopenhauer, and Comte, and for him Darwinian theory was "the truth that shall make you free" (*HW*, 561). Hardy had inherited an unsentimental view of nature from his peasant forebears; this was reinforced by his own encounter with modern thought. Man sometimes imagines that nature is either a benevolent or a malevolent force; Hardy knows that it is quite indifferent to man's fate. In "Suspense" he describes a bleak, wintry scene that seems at first to reflect the unhappiness of the separated lovers, but the poem rejects this idea of nature's empathy:

> But it matters little, however we fare—
> Whether we meet, or I get not there;
> The sky will look the same thereupon,
> And the wind and the sea go groaning on.
> > (*HW*, 891)

Like Tennyson, Hardy was aware that nature was "red in tooth and claw." Hardy's "In a Wood" specifically rejects the sentimental urban view of nature as a refuge from cruelty and competitive strife:

> Heart-halt and spirit-lame,
>     City-opprest,
> Unto this wood I came
>     As to a nest;
> Dreaming that sylvan peace
> Offered the harrowed ease—
> Nature a soft release
>     From men's unrest.
>
> But, having entered in,
>     Great growths and small
> Show them to men akin—
>     Combatants all!
> Sycamore shoulders oak,
> Bines the slim sapling yoke,
> Ivy-spun halters choke
>     Elms stout and tall.
>                 (HW, 64)

The word "nest" in the first stanza suggests that the speaker's expectations are similar to those of Arnold or Rossetti, seeking a retreat in the forest glade or bower. But this is a world of "plunder and prey" like the little wood in *Maud*, or like the sinister woodland hollow in Browning's *Pauline*. Browning's protagonist escapes from the wood with relief, and Hardy turns "back to my kind," where "now and then are found / Life-loyalties." Nature is not, after all, a good teacher; indeed, it may not be too much to say that for Hardy "nature, like God, is dead."[11] Certainly, between the Nature of Wordsworth and that of Hardy falls the long shadow of Darwin. Nature is, for Hardy, "glow-forsaken, / Darkness-overtaken!" (HW, 61), although no less potent for being perceived as less benevolent.

Indeed, nature is often viewed as an adversary rather than

---

[11] Paulin, *Thomas Hardy: The Poetry of Perception*, p. 15.

a friend. Egdon Heath is an obvious example, but even in the suburban garden Hardy is aware of man's struggle for survival against encroaching natural forces:

They clear the creeping moss—
Elders and juniors—aye,
Making the pathways neat
    And the garden gay;
And they build a shady seat. . . .
    Ah, no, the years, the years;
See, the white storm-birds wing across!
    ("During Wind and Rain," *HW*, 495)

Hardy does not romanticize wild nature here. The "creeping moss" is merely an insidious reminder of the destructive forces of time, and man's effort to push back the wilderness is seen as a necessary, if futile, attempt to impose neatness and gaiety on chaos.

Similarly, the most striking feature of Egdon Heath is the barrow, symbol of man's triumph over nature, and Hardy consistently values man's mark upon the natural world: "An object or mark raised or made by man on a scene is worth ten times any such formed by unconscious Nature. Hence clouds, mists and mountains are unimportant beside the wear on a threshold, or the print of a hand."[12]

It was because America lacked the "prints of perished hands" that Hardy found nothing to attract him to the "modern coast" of the United States, which claimed to be "free / From that long drip of human tears" ("On an Invitation to the United States," *HW*, 110). For Hardy, "the beauty of association is entirely superior to the beauty of aspect."[13] So, when he visited the Alps he wrote a poem entitled "The Schreckhorn," which turned out to be a tribute to his friend Leslie Stephen. Similarly, his poem "Zermatt: To the Matterhorn" emphasizes the human tragedy that took place on the slopes of the mountain

[12] Quoted by Florence Emily Hardy, *The Early Life of Thomas Hardy 1840-1891*, p. 153.
[13] Ibid., p. 158.

during the ill-fated Whymper expedition of 1865. In neither poem does Hardy give us any conventional scene-painting. His attitude is similar to that of Morris toward Iceland. The mountains are valued because men lost their lives on them, or "ventured life and limb, / Drawn on by vague imaginings" (*HW*, 322).

It is those imaginings that give life to nature. Hardy specifically rejects the aesthetic quality of scenery in favor of man's subjective vision of nature: "I feel that Nature is played out as a Beauty, but not as a Mystery. I don't want to see landscapes, i.e., scenic paintings of them, because I don't want to see the original realities—as optical effects, that is. I want to see the deeper reality underlying the scenic, the expression of what are sometimes called abstract imaginings."[14] The "deeper reality underlying the scenic" was often supplied by Hardy's sense that the countryside was a mute testimony to history, populated by ghostly forms of past civilizations. The guns that disturb the dead in "Channel Firing" (*HW*, 305), are heard "As far inland as Stourton Tower, / And Camelot, and starlit Stonehenge." Such places derive their special resonance from the mythic kings and druids who still haunt them. Sometimes, indeed, the past overpowers the present, so that the speaker in "By Henstridge Cross at the Year's End" (*HW*, 629) is paralyzed by the weight of ancestral memories:

> Why go the north road now?
> Torn, leaf-strewn, as if scoured by foemen,
> Once edging fiefs of my forefolk yeomen,
> Fallows fat to the plough:
> Why go the north road now?

As he stands "Musing on Whither, and How. . . ." the landscape answers him, rejecting the burden of history and demanding new life:

> "Yea: we want new feet now"
> Answer the stones. "Want chit-chat, laughter:

[14] Ibid., p. 242.

232

Plenty of such to go hereafter
By our tracks, we trow!
We are for new feet now."

Ironically, the new feet will only add to the palimpsest of memories borne by this haunted, humanized landscape.

D. H. Lawrence followed Hardy in responding to nature as a mystery, but when he writes about Hardy he tends to recreate him in his own image. He speaks of the "great background" in Hardy's novels, "vital and vivid, which matters more than the people who move upon it."[15] This sounds like Turner rather than Hardy. Other critics have also stressed Hardy's "pervading sense of the infinitesimal littleness of the human atom in the face of its vast, inanimate, yet somehow sentient, watching, immanent environment."[16] The important point, however, is that Hardy is always aware that if the landscape seems to be sentient it is only because man attributes such a characteristic to it. Even in the Egdon Heath passage, where the landscape comes closest to having an awareness of its own, Hardy continually reminds the reader, by the frequent use of such words as "appeared" and "seemed," that what is being described is colored by the imagination of the observer:

The place became full of a watchful intentness now; for when other things sank brooding to sleep the heath *appeared* slowly to awake and listen. Every night its Titanic form *seemed* to await something; but it had waited thus, unmoved, during so many centuries, through the crises of so many things, that it could only be *imagined* to await one last crisis—the final overthrow. (*Return*, p. 4. My italics.)

Hardy's immense brooding landscapes often seem to dwarf his characters, but it is the characters who are the focal point

[15] D. H. Lawrence, "Study of Thomas Hardy," in *Phoenix*, p. 419.
[16] Lowes, "Two Readings of Earth," *Yale Review*, 15 (1926), 516.

of any scene.[17] Ultimately, the humblest man or woman is of more significance than the bleak moorlands that seem to render the human figure unimportant. This point is made pictorially by the poet himself in some of the drawings that he included in the 1898 edition of the *Wessex Poems*. In the illustration entitled *Her Death and After* (Fig. 14), for example, the scarcely discernible human figures are at the end of a "tunnel" of trees with overarching branches. They are minuscule, but everything in the picture leads to them: they are at the end of the road, and at the vanishing point of the perspective. Similarly, in *She, to Him* (Fig. 15), two small human figures are dwarfed by a backdrop of bleak moorland and vast sky. Yet our eyes are constantly drawn away from the immense nullity of the surroundings to focus on the evidence of man's presence in the landscape. The figures stand on a road that cuts across the moorland in bold curves, leading to a squat tower on the hill. It is this human artifact that dominates land and sky, and that provides the focal point of the whole scene. The drawing might almost have been used to illustrate a passage from *The Return of the Native* (p. 14), in which Hardy carefully describes the relation between a human figure and the landscape:

There the form stood, motionless as the hill beneath. Above the plain rose the hill, above the hill rose the

[17] My generalization is meant to apply only to Hardy's poems, among which I do not include that lengthy epic in prose and blank verse, *The Dynasts*. However, it is worth noting that Hardy prefaces each scene in *The Dynasts* with a brief prose description of the landscape backdrop against which the action is to be played. These backdrops are usually vast panoramas that reduce the characters to insignificance, so that Napoleon's army retreating from Moscow is seen as a mere caterpillar in a hostile universe. The hostility or indifference of the landscape in *The Dynasts* is also seen as a reflection of the workings of the Immanent Will, against which man is powerless. My own feeling is that *The Dynasts* represents Hardy at his ideological worst. In his poems nature may be seen as indifferent to man, but its reality is conveyed with the immediacy of intimate knowledge. The scenic descriptions in *The Dynasts*, on the other hand, seem to me to be rooted in theory rather than experience.

barrow, and above the barrow rose the figure. Above the figure was nothing that could be mapped elsewhere than on a celestial globe.

Such a perfect, delicate, and necessary finish did the figure give to the dark pile of hills that it seemed to be the only obvious justification of their outline.

The symbolic placing of the figure between the earthly and celestial worlds also expresses man's place in the evolutionary hierarchy. Although merging with the landscape, man has nevertheless created that part of the landscape on which he stands, the barrow, and its artificial elevation thrusts him toward the heavens. He not only shapes nature, but he is that part of nature that has achieved awareness of itself. Whatever meaning or justification nature has is bestowed on it by man. "Nature without man," as Hillis Miller writes, "is the blank, neutral presence of things as they are."[18]

In many of his poems Hardy seems to insist on this blank neutrality of "things as they are." The lovers in "Neutral Tones" (*HW*, 12) are surrounded by mute, insensate things:

We stood by a pond that winter day,
And the sun was white, as though chidden of God,
And a few leaves lay on the starving sod;
　—They had fallen from an ash, and were gray.

With the exception of the phrase "as though chidden of God," these lines have a studied matter-of-factness that seems to guarantee the objectivity of the description. The careful notation of objects and the string of "and's" both imply a detached observer, taking pains to note only the bare facts of the scene. But, as with Tennyson's "Mariana" and many of Rossetti's poems, this apparent detachment is really a poetic device to heighten the emotional effect of the landscape. Under the guise of seeming objectivity, the poet gives us an intensely subjective view of the natural world. This is admitted in the final stanza, since it is the "lessons that love deceives" that

[18] Hillis Miller, *Thomas Hardy: Distance and Desire*, p. 85.

have "shaped" the scene forever in the speaker's mind. The landscape is, as Jean Brooks has pointed out, a "most complete objective correlative of the emotion felt."[19] Even in the first stanza, the line which above all seems to be a flat statement of fact ("They had fallen from an ash, and were gray"), is emotionally loaded. One cannot ignore the ambiguity of "ash"; the emotional meaning, the suggestion of a dying fire and of the gray ashes of declining passion, is more important than the literal meaning, the tree species.

Hardy is not sliding weakly into the pathetic fallacy. The plain and leafy facts are there; the leaves are accurately described, but are only present in the poem because they are perceived as emotionally significant to the speaker. As Hardy himself expresses it, the mind "coalesces with and translates the qualities that are already there, —half hidden, it may be— and the two united are depicted as the All."[20] Hardy's "All" is very different from Swinburne's great god Pan, but there is a similarity in the way in which the two artists perceive the relationship between man and nature: the poet is, for both of them, part perceiver, part creator of the world he describes.

The bleak and wintry setting of "The Voice," with the "Wind oozing through the thorn from norward" (HW, 346), is another example of landscape as objective correlative. But this is also a haunted landscape, in which the woman's voice is fleetingly identified with the "breeze, in its listlessness / Travelling over the wet mead to me here." The "ghost" in this poem is extremely insubstantial, and very much a product of the man's desire for contact with the dead. Like the speaker in Rossetti's "The Blessed Damozel," Hardy's protagonist constitutes the beloved voice out of every sound. The two poems, products of entirely different poetic temperaments, are, in most respects, scarcely comparable. Rossetti's blessed damozel has a warm sensuality missing in the insubstantial

[19] Brooks, *Thomas Hardy: The Poetic Structure*, p. 70.
[20] Hardy, *The Early Life*, p. 243.

wraith in Hardy's poem. But Rossetti allows himself two mo-
ments of doubt that come close to Hardy in feeling:

> Surely she leaned o'er me—her hair
> Fell all about my face. . . .
> Nothing: the autumn fall of leaves.

And later:

> Ah sweet! Even now, in that bird's song,
> Strove not her accents there,
> Fain to be hearkened?
>                 (RW, 4)

These are bracketed off from the rest of the poem, and they
give the point of view of the lonely lover on earth. But the
bulk of the poem gives her point of view, and she is a very
real woman in a very real heaven. Hardy, by comparison,
maintains a radical skepticism about the existence of the ghost,
and he never postulates a heaven. We are earthbound with
the man, "faltering foward, / Leaves around me falling." For
him, the woman is "ever dissolved to wan wistlessness," her
voice one with the plaintive note of the wind. She is part of
the natural world, but also gives meaning to that world.

The same sort of reciprocal relationship exists between man
and nature in "The Figure in the Scene" (HW, 476). The
speaker describes how he sketched a scene with the figure of
the woman in the foreground. Rain drifts across the landscape,
obliterating the division between the figure and the scene, and
even blurring the outlines of the drawing itself. The woman
would seem to have become an insignificant part of the natural
world, "Seated amid the gauze / Of moisture, hooded, only
her outline shown, / With rainfall marked across." And yet
the place has no significance without her: "her rainy form is
the Genius still of the spot." In a companion poem, "Why
did I sketch" (HW, 477), the speaker vows never to give
landscape such painful meaning again:

If you go drawing on down or cliff
    Let no soft curves intrude
    Of a woman's silhouette,
But show the escarpments stark and stiff
    As in utter solitude;
    So shall you half forget.

But only "half forget," perhaps. In other poems the ghosts are more insistent, refusing to be omitted from the scene. The ghosts of "In Front of the Landscape" (*HW*, 303-305), for example, thrust themselves between the landscape and the speaker, who is "Plunging and labouring on in a tide of visions." Through the "eddies" of this tide "there glimmered the customed landscape," feebly reduced to "a ghost-like gauze." Internal landscape is more important than external in this poem; the ghosts are produced by the mind, and they actually prevent the protagonist from seeing the real world around him:

What were the infinite spectacles featuring foremost
    Under my sight,
Hindering me to discern my paced advancement
    Lengthening to miles;
What were the re-creations killing the daytime
    As by the night?

The speaker moves through this mental landscape like a "dull form that perambulates, seeing nought / Round him that looms."

Sometimes he tries to escape from the ghosts by seeking a landscape untouched by human associations, such as that described in "Wessex Heights":

There are some heights in Wessex, shaped as if by
    a kindly hand
For thinking, dreaming, dying on, and at crises
    when I stand,
Say, on Ingpen Beacon eastward, or on Wylls-Neck
    westwardly,

I seem where I was before my birth, and after
death may be.
(*HW*, 319)

This is one of the rare poems in which Hardy does use a
natural scene as a retreat from the troubled life of the plains
and the towns. Only on the Heights can he escape from the
"figure against the moon," or the "phantoms having weird
detective ways" that track him in the towns. But there is no
suggestion that on the Heights he comes into contact with
nature as a benign, restorative power. The value that the Wes-
sex Heights have is a purely negative one: he is safe from his
ghosts there because these are hills "Where men have never
cared to haunt, nor women have walked with me." There is
nothing for the mind, creator of ghosts, to work on in this
forsaken spot.

The impulse to flee, which this poem represents, is very
different from versions of that impulse found in other Vic-
torian poets. It has nothing in common with the aesthetic
withdrawal from the world that we see in Tennyson's "Palace
of Art," and even less with the temptations of languid ease
offered by the Lotos Eaters. The Wessex Heights are perhaps
slightly closer to Obermann's "stern Alpine dell," but Hardy's
protagonist is not driven to escape by a generalized romantic
despair. Nor is he a Scholar-Gipsy, fleeing the corruption of
modern life. His ghosts are very personal and specific, gen-
erated by his own memories. Moreover, Arnold's landscapes
of retreat always offer some kind of womblike protection.
Hardy's bleak honesty drives him to barren, exposed land-
scapes, which, like the hills and rocks of Arnold's "Resigna-
tion," seem to "bear rather than rejoice" (*AW*, 100). How-
ever, Hardy does not allow himself to turn the landscape into
such an overt symbol of endurance. It has no message for
man, and the only comfort it offers is that it is too antisocial
to harbor ghosts. The final paradox might be that even on
these lonely hills the protagonist does not really escape from
his ghosts, since the poem, ostensibly about the Wessex Heights,

is actually filled with vivid recollections of the "ghost at Yell'ham Bottom chiding loud" and the "ghost in Froom-side Vale, thin-lipped and vague." These insistent presences, crowding into the poem, make the final declaration that the "ghosts then keep their distance; and I know some liberty" sound like a piece of savage irony. Since the ghosts are in the mind, the speaker carries them with him wherever he goes, and they are most firmly with him when he is congratulating himself on having escaped them.

In many of the *Poems of 1912-13* the protagonist actively seeks out the ghosts, and he does so by returning to specific "haunted" landscapes. The Cornish coast, associated with memories of his courtship of his first wife, Emma, in general evokes happy memories. In "After a Journey" (*HW*, 349), the ghost is not "thin-lipped" and vindictive, but warmly voluptuous with "nut-coloured hair, / And gray eyes, and rose-flush coming and going." He confronts her "across the dark space" of time, asking what she now has to say of their past. By way of an answer, the ghost simply leads him to one of the spots most closely associated with their early happiness, the waterfall. The place itself, and the memories it evokes, must stand as the only answer she can give. There can be no comment on the years of unhappiness and division that followed. Time changes all, but the relative permanence of a particular place confers a kind of immortality on certain events associated with it.

The association, as Hardy clearly recognizes, is bestowed by man; nature remains indifferent. In "At Castle Boterel" (*HW*, 351-52), the steep hill evokes an event in the past:

> Primaeval rocks form the road's steep border,
>     And much have they faced there, first and last,
> Of the transitory in Earth's long order;
>     But what they record in colour and cast
>         Is—that we two passed.

There is perhaps a faint echo here of Wordsworth's Simplon Pass passage. Hardy's primeval rocks bordering the steep road are also "types and symbols of Eternity, / Of first and last, and midst, and without end" (*Prelude* VI.640). But the echo, if it is intentional, works ironically. Hardy carefully avoids the apocalyptic, rapt tone of the Wordsworth passage; the flat, prosaic tone of "And much have I faced there, first and last," deliberately deflates the rocks as romantic symbols. They are important only because they have given permanence to a particular human event by registering themselves on his memory.

For Hardy, as for Swinburne, the sea was often a symbol of freedom, but only because of its association with the wild, free girl he had loved:

O the opal and the sapphire of that wandering western
sea,
And the woman riding high above with bright hair
flapping free—
("Beeny Cliff," *HW*, 350)

The free girl turned into the discontented wife, and now lies "In a noiseless nest / No sea beats near" (*HW*, 342). But her spirit remains the genius of the place and draws the man back to see the "ghost-girl-rider" who "still rides gaily / In his rapt thought" (*HW*, 354).

Donald Davie has made the point that each of the three major landscapes presented in this series of poems is associated, not merely with ghosts and memories, but with "some one particular moral proclivity or principle. Max Gate is the landscape of treason. Boscastle (Beeny Cliff, St. Juliot) is the landscape of loyalty and love"; the third landscape, Plymouth, is, according to Davie, "the questionable, the problematic location,"[21] somewhere between the other two. For Davie, Hardy's landscapes are emblematic. William Buckler perhaps goes even further when he states that the landscapes of the 1912-13 poems are "of the mind, and the drama enacted [is]

[21] Davie, "Hardy's Virgilian Purples," *Agenda*, 10, Nos. 2 & 3 (1972), 147.

an internal one."[22] A similar point about the landscapes of Hardy's later novels has been made by Andrew Enstice.[23]

These represent valuable insights, and a useful antidote to the manufacturers of tourist guides to the Hardy country. But there may be a tendency among modern critics, aware of later developments in poetry, to overstress the mental, introspective quality of Hardy's landscapes. Hardy knows that the moral dimension of a particular scene is conferred upon it by the mind, and that it exists for the perceiver only through a veil of memories and associations. But he also knows that there is an objective reality out there that has its own existence, independent of and indifferent to man. This balance between outward reality and inner imagining is very carefully maintained, although its proportions shift from one poem to the next. In "Under the Waterfall" (*HW*, 335-37), the outward reality is insisted upon. The memory of the picnic by the waterfall is always evoked by the physical act of plunging his arm into cold water, and the remembered day has the same kind of actuality. The place is described with a finicky attention to detail, because the reality of the scene guarantees the reality of the love itself:

Hence the only prime
And real love-rhyme
That I know by heart,
And that leaves no smart,
Is the purl of a little valley fall
About three spans wide and two spans tall
Over a table of solid rock,
And into a scoop of the self-same block.

A further guarantee of the reality of the memory is the drinking glass lost by the lovers on that day, and still lodged in a crevice of the rock. Like the memory, it has been "opal-

---

[22] Buckler, "The Dark Space Illumined: A Reading of Hardy's 'Poems of 1912-13,' " *Victorian Poetry*, 17 (1979), 106.
[23] Enstice, *Thomas Hardy: Landscapes of the Mind*.

ized" by time, but "its presence adds to the rhyme of love /
Persistently sung by the fall above."

The reality of the outward scene is also stressed in "Where
the Picnic Was" (HW, 357-58). On a bleak, wintry day the
speaker climbs the hill to "scan and trace" the spot where
they picnicked one summer:

Now a cold wind blows,
And the grass is gray,
But the spot still shows
As a burnt circle—aye,
And stick-ends, charred,
Still strew the sward
Whereon I stand.

The charred and gritty remains act both as an enduring re-
minder of past happiness, and as a symbol of its transience.

The reality enshrined for the protagonist in the drinking
glass, the waterfall, or the few burnt sticks, is a reality for
him alone, and Hardy is aware of this. In "The Phantom
Horsewoman" (HW, 353-54) he shifts his point of view to
that of an outsider observing the man who "comes and stands /
In a careworn craze, / And looks at the sands." The sights
that "they say" he sees are clearly in his own mind:

Of this vision of his they might say more:
    Not only there
    Does he see this sight,
    But everywhere
    In his brain—day, night,
    As if on the air
    It were drawn rose-bright—
    Yea, far from that shore
Does he carry this vision heretofore.

Sometimes the protagonist is overcome by the bleak reali-
zation that the place associated with his love is just a place,
and that the woman haunts it no longer:

HARDY

What if still in chasmal beauty looms that wild
   weird western shore,
The woman now is—elsewhere—whom the ambling
   pony bore,
And nor knows nor cares for Beeny, and will
   laugh there nevermore.
("Beeny Cliff," *HW*, 351)

Even when he explores a landscape rich with memories, as in
"After a Journey" (*HW*, 349), he is aware of a part of the
scene that remains detached from his associations, oblivious
of the "ghost" he follows:

Ignorant of what there is flitting here to see,
The waked birds preen and the seals flop lazily.

It is this double perspective that gives even the most im-
passioned of Hardy's love poems a tinge of irony. The in-
trospective dreamer is always balanced by the ironist and
skeptic. So, in "The Shadow on the Stone" (*HW*, 530), the
protagonist imagines that he sees the shadow of "a well-known
head and shoulders," but he refuses to turn his head "lest my
dream should fade." The ghost that he tracks down patiently,
with faltering footsteps, is a tantalizingly diffuse presence,
"Facing round about me everywhere" (*HW*, 349), but always
evading him. Like Tennyson, Hardy uses places to evoke vivid
memories of the dead, but he never establishes the kind of
ecstatic communion in which "The dead man touched me
from the past, / And all at once it seemed at last / The living
soul was flashed on mine" (*TW*, 946). In spite of the ghosts
that crowd into his poems, Hardy is too much of a rationalist
to accept their reality outside his own imagination.

Hardy's attitude to his "ghosts" is paralleled by his treat-
ment of external nature. He combines a stubborn clinging to
outward appearances and simple facts with an ability to use
those facts emotionally, even mythically. In "Neutral Tones"
this was achieved simply by making the landscape into an
objective correlative for the emotion of the speaker. In "The
Darkling Thrush" (*HW*, 150) the significance of the landscape

244

is more obviously pointed, and the poet even makes use of such devices as personification: "Frost was spectre-gray"; "land's sharp features." The language is emotionally loaded: the "eye of day" is "weakening" and the wind sounds a "death-lament." But this reading of nature is still rooted in a close and accurate observation of the real world: "The tangled bine-stems scored the sky / Like strings of broken lyres." The first line gives a factual description of the natural scene, the second pushes it in the direction of symbolism. However, this division is in the end false, since even in the first line Hardy has suggested pain, sterility, and frustration. The facts of the landscape are filtered through the bleak perceptions of an observer who is unaware of any cause for rejoicing. He sees the "sharp features" of the land as "The Century's corpse outleant," and the cloudy sky as a crypt. The view of nature given here is not merely unromantic, it is antiromantic. No frost will perform its secret ministry on this winter's evening, and no gentle breeze will awaken the "broken lyres" of the tangled stems.

The poem, written as the epitaph of the nineteenth century, is in fact the epitaph of the great Romantics, not of the Victorians. As David Perkins has pointed out, Hardy's thrush, flinging "his soul / Upon the growing gloom," has its counterparts in the poetry of Keats and Shelley, and although it seems a feeble descendant of their immortal birds, it may ultimately be a more hopeful symbol:

> For if the aging thrush can sing while subject as much to the burden of life as anything else—and while lacking, in this wintry landscape, all the Eden-like props with which the romantics surround their bird-symbols—the implication is that mortal joy, though rare, is certainly being attained.[24]

Hardy deliberately refuses to give his bird the mythic qualities of Shelley's skylark ("Bird thou never wert"), or of Keats's nightingale ("No hungry generations tread thee down"). His

[24] Perkins, "Hardy and the Poetry of Isolation," *English Literary History*, 26, No. 1 (1959), 263.

thrush is plainly mortal, "aged," and "frail, gaunt, and small." But by insisting on these qualities, Hardy creates a new myth to replace the romantic one. It is a myth that has proved useful for the twentieth century, but it was forged in the doubting and despairing consciousness of the Victorians. It is a myth, like Swinburne's, based on the acceptance of certain bleak truths, and on a refusal to accept any kind of illusory comfort. The plain sense of things as they are must generate whatever frail hope man is to gain from the world. Hardy's bird symbol, like his landscapes, is an example of the "chastened sublime."

The landscape of "The Darkling Thrush" is painfully solitary, but it is not really antisocial. Hardy never uses even the wildest landscape to romanticize solitude. With very rare exceptions, his protagonists do not go to nature to escape or withdraw from society. If they are lonely figures that is their misfortune, and the landscape is always seen from the point of view of human need, which may be the basic, physical needs of the laborers who toil on it, or the emotional needs of the wandering figure who peoples it with his own ghosts. But in any case, scenery in Hardy's poems is finally dead. Landscape is not something "out there" to be viewed by a detached observer. Instead, man is part of the landscape, being molded by natural forces, but also conferring upon those forces their emotional, moral, and intellectual significance.

# CONCLUSION

It might be possible to reach a fair degree of consensus on what constitutes a "typically romantic landscape." Such a landscape, one imagines, would inevitably contain lakes and mountains, or wooded glens and rocky crags, and it would almost certainly be wild and solitary. Is it possible to describe an equally typical Victorian landscape? We have seen that the Victorian poets produced landscapes that range from enclosed bowers to wind-swept seacoasts. Such a range reflects the complexity of the age, and underlines the difficulties inherent in making any generalizations about the period.

Nevertheless, some general trends have emerged during the course of this study. There is certainly a movement in the poetry of the period away from mountain scenery as a source of inspiration, and there is a steady decline in the cult of the picturesque. Nor, with the exception of Swinburne, did the Victorian poets seek out the terror associated with the sublime; they tended to view the wilderness as a barren wasteland, or as an evil forest to be avoided. In retreating from the wilder and more rugged types of romantic scenery, however, they did not all move in the same direction. Two major directions might be identified, one of which is toward men and society, while the other is toward isolation or refuge.

The movement toward men and society, which we have seen as a characteristic of the later Tennyson, and of Morris and Browning, is traceable in part to the Victorian social conscience, which was particularly strong in Morris. But it was also the result of a declining interest in mere scenery. As early as 1818, Keats had written, "Scenery is fine—but human nature is finer";[1] this sentiment would certainly have been

[1] Letter to Benjamin Bailey, March 1818, in *Letters of John Keats*, p. 87.

endorsed by Browning, and when Morris visited Iceland it was not primarily to view the scenery. His chief concern was with the effects of such a landscape on the men and women who had to endure its rigors.

To take account of how man relates to the landscape is also a political act, and this is most clearly shown in Morris's socialist utopia, set in a pastoral landscape. But it might be more generally claimed that one of the most important cultural developments to take place during the nineteenth century was that landscape, as an art and as a concept, gradually became more democratic. The art of landscape as developed during the eighteenth century was aristocratic, whether it meant the art of landscape gardening, in which whole villages were sometimes moved to improve the view, or the art of admiring a picturesque view. At its best, the eighteenth-century landscape garden was designed as much to facilitate meditation as for visual effect, but the appeal was to a highly educated and sophisticated mind, a point made by John Dixon Hunt:

> But landscape gardens like Stowe and Hagley Park provided above all contexts for meditation where the mind was allowed an illusion of creative power. Though natural effects were managed ('finished') by art and even augmented by temples, statues, and inscriptions, the associative power of garden scenes upon the mind initiated patterns of thought in suitably responsive visitors. The Elysian Fields with its Temple of Ancient Virtue, satirically set off next door with a ruined Temple of Modern Virtue, and both facing the Temple of British Worthies across the waters of the 'Styx', were a scene designed to foster reflections.[2]

Such a garden was obviously designed to appeal to a more select group of people than the crowd that collects in Sir Walter Vivian's park in *The Princess* to marvel at the mechanical fountains and to ride on the steamboats. In *The Prin-*

---

[2] Hunt, *The Figure in the Landscape*, p. 142.

*cess*, ladies and gentlemen still gather to admire the view, but they gaze at it with a greater awareness that the landscape is lived in, and has a political and social significance. Morris, as we have seen, takes this development further, seeing landscape almost entirely from the point of view of human usefulness, and looking forward to an England that is a garden tilled by social equals, unlike the garden of "rulers and the ruled" (*TW*, 843) that we are shown in *The Princess*.

Hardy was neither a socialist nor a utopian, but in many ways his England was even more democratic than Morris's. This is the result of a major shift in point of view. Landscape in Hardy is never something to be viewed by ladies and gentlemen as an aesthetic experience, with or without social implications. Nor is it seen from the point of view of the social reformer, who looks at the landscape with a certain detachment, seeking to change it. In the end the social reformer may occupy almost as elite a position as the aristocrat. Hardy's point of view is that of the common man. Indeed, "view" becomes an inappropriate term, since landscape ceases to be viewed and is experienced directly by the men and women who labor in its fields or trudge its highways.

The movement toward a humanized landscape represents a strong trend in Victorian poetry, but it is balanced by a counter movement, away from society and into landscapes of refuge and retreat. In the early Tennyson the refuge may be a tropical island paradise, the palace of art, or a garden of the mind; in Arnold it is most typically the forest glade, and in Rossetti it is the enclosed, hushed bower. Such landscapes imply a basic need for protection and isolation, but they carry with them the perils of claustrophobia, solipsism, and unbearable loneliness. Sometimes the retreat was to an essentially internal landscape, and in such landscapes the Victorian poets often discovered the horrors of the subconscious. In the end, Tennyson rejected the landscape of refuge, and Rossetti identified the bower with the pit of death. Browning too, explores the deep hollow in the woods and retreats in horror. Only Arnold managed to preserve his forest glade as a place without sinister associations. His retreats are, as Gerard Joseph writes, "magic cirques facilitating the memory of lost innocence, restorative sanctuaries from the world's girdling hum."[3] One might suggest that all Arnold's subconscious fears were projected outward onto the father figure, who beckons him on up the stern path of duty, or who unwittingly kills his son in "Sohrab and Rustum." Deep within himself Arnold remains the happy, innocent child, and the landscape of the buried life contains no horrors or lurking monsters. It is an imaginary garden without toads.

The desire to creep into an enclosed space was not shared by Swinburne, whose wild seascapes represent a rediscovery of the sublime. Of all the Victorian poets, it is only Swinburne who seeks out the primal terrors of the elements and confronts them joyfully. This might seem to make him a real exception, a true romantic among Victorian romantics, and in certain respects this is so. However, one might also say that Swinburne's desire to plunge into lake or sea, or to become one with the wind, has something in common with the basic impulse that makes Arnold, Rossetti, and the early Tennyson retreat into gardens or woods. In Arnold this impulse springs from the desire to re-enter the world of his childhood and of Wordsworthian nature; in Rossetti it is the desire to find a sanctuary from the world with the "one necessary person"; in the early Tennyson it was largely the desire to cultivate the poetic sensibility in solitude; in Swinburne it is a desire to lose the burden of personality through a union with the cosmos which will result in his rebirth as immortal poet. What all these poets have in common is that they do not treat landscape as something "out there" to be viewed as scenery, nor as an external stimulus to meditation, like the Wye valley in "Tintern Abbey." All of them, in one way or another, wish to become part of the landscape, whether it is seen as having a

[3] Joseph, "Victorian Frames: The Windows and Mirrors of Browning, Arnold, and Tennyson," *Victorian Poetry*, 16 (1978), 77.

protective, womblike function, or whether, like Swinburne's sea, it is fiercely destructive.

This tendency in Victorian poetry to eliminate the gap between observer and landscape may also be seen in both Browning and Hardy. Browning's landscapes tend to be experienced as part of the consciousness of a dramatic character, or, as in "Childe Roland," to become internal landscapes reflecting psychological reality. Indeed, such internal landscapes occur in many Victorian poets. Hardy also depicts scenes through the consciousness of dramatic characters, although even his most thoroughly haunted landscapes have a greater degree of objective, external reality than the fantasy landscape of "Childe Roland." Nor does Hardy's stubborn sense of reality allow him to create the kind of pastoral landscape of refuge beloved by Arnold. Unlike other Victorian poets, he has no desire to lose himself in the landscape by creeping into enclosed spaces, or by diving into the sea. In Swinburne the act of merging with the cosmos is an act of sublime courage granted only to the elect; it is also a means of defeating time. In Hardy there is no act of volition, and man cannot defeat time. Man is simply a part of the landscape because he cannot be otherwise. At the same time, that landscape is also a part of man, haunted by his memories and marked by his toil.[4] Both Swinburne and Hardy might be said, in different ways, to have healed the dichotomy between "men and mountains."

This dichotomy was strongest in the early Victorians, and Tennyson's maid in *The Princess* has a real choice to make between the mountain peaks and the pastoral valleys. The sublime was rejected because it was perceived as humanly diminishing, cold, and barren, and most Victorian poets retreated from the mountains either into the landscape of refuge, or to the social landscape. The sublime landscape recovered

---

[4] In "God's Grandeur," Gerard Manley Hopkins speaks of the land being "smeared with toil." The distaste for what he calls "man's smudge" is obvious, and is not shared by Hardy. Hopkins is a lover of romantic, "unspoilt" nature, but Hardy, surely, has a firmer grasp of the realities of country life. However, such a question demands fuller treatment than I can give here.

by Swinburne is not humanly diminishing, because the poet discovers his true self by surrendering to it. However, this is not a solution open to everyone. Running through Victorian poetry is another type of sublime landscape that is more subdued than Swinburne's, and that might be termed the landscape of endurance. It is first found in Arnold's "Resignation," which in turn may be traced back to the more somber landscapes of Wordsworth. It reappears in Morris's Iceland, and finds its most powerful expression in the chastened sublimity of Hardy's bleak moors. Emily Brontë's Yorkshire moors might be quoted as another version of this landscape. This form of the sublime is chastened partly because it does not provide the kind of ecstasy and enthusiasm associated with the romantic sublime. It is also sobered by the same realization that had finally come to Ruskin, turning him from "mountains to men": that these barren scenes are not merely a delight for the tourist, but must be seen in terms of the human lives to which they form a background. It might be said, therefore, that the social concerns of the Victorians, and their essential human compassion, are reflected even in their most apparently antisocial landscapes.

# LIST OF WORKS CONSULTED

Abrams, M. H. "The Correspondent Breeze: A Romantic Metaphor." *Kenyon Review*, 19 (1957), 113-30.

Appleton, Jay. *The Experience of Landscape*. London: John Wiley, 1975.

Armstrong, Isobel. "Browning and the 'Grotesque' Style." In *The Major Victorian Poets: Reconsiderations*. Edited by Isobel Armstrong. Lincoln: University of Nebraska Press, 1969, pp. 93-123.

Arnold, Matthew. *Poems*. Edited by Kenneth Allott. 2nd ed. by Miriam Allott. New York: Longman, 1979.

———. *The Poetical Works of Matthew Arnold*. Edited by C. B. Tinker and H. F. Lowry. London: Oxford University Press, 1950.

Auden, W. H. *The Enchafèd Flood, or The Romantic Iconography of the Sea*. New York: Random House, 1950.

Axton, W. F. "Victorian Landscape Painting: A Change in Outlook." In *Nature and the Victorian Imagination*. Edited by U. C. Knoepflmacher and G. B. Tennyson. Berkeley and Los Angeles: University of California Press, 1977, pp. 281-308.

Ball, Patricia. *The Central Self: A Study in Romantic and Victorian Imagination*. London: Athlone, 1968.

Barbier, Carl Paul. *William Gilpin: His Drawings, Teaching, and Theory of the Picturesque*. Oxford: Clarendon, 1963.

Barrell, John. *The Dark Side of the Landscape: The Rural Poor in English Painting 1730-1840*. Cambridge: Cambridge University Press, 1980.

———. *The Idea of Landscape and the Sense of Place, 1730-1840: An Approach to the Poetry of John Clare*. Cambridge: Cambridge University Press, 1972.

Baudelaire, Charles. *Les Fleurs du Mal.* Edited by Ernest Raynaud. Paris: Garnier, n.d.

Baum, Paull F. *Tennyson Sixty Years After.* Chapel Hill: University of North Carolina Press, 1948.

Beach, Joseph Warren. *The Concept of Nature in Nineteenth-Century English Poetry.* New York: Macmillan, 1936.

Becht, Ronald E. "Matthew Arnold's 'Switzerland': The Drama of Choice." *Victorian Poetry,* 13 (1975), 35-45.

Blake, William. *The Poems.* Edited by W. H. Stevenson and David V. Erdman. London: Longman, 1971.

Bloom, Harold. *A Map of Misreading.* New York: Oxford University Press, 1975.

———. *The Ringers in the Tower.* Chicago: University of Chicago Press, 1971.

Bonnerot, Louis. *Matthew Arnold: Poète.* Paris: Didier, 1947.

Boos, Florence Saunders. *The Poetry of Dante G. Rossetti: A Critical Reading and Source Study.* The Hague: Mouton, 1976.

Bradbury, Malcolm, and David Palmer, eds. *Victorian Poetry.* London: Edward Arnold, 1972.

Bradley, A. C. *A Commentary on Tennyson's "In Memoriam."* 3rd ed. London: Macmillan, 1920.

Brooks, Jean. *Thomas Hardy: The Poetic Structure.* London: Elek, 1971.

Browning, Elizabeth Barrett. *The Complete Works.* 6 vols. New York: Crowell, 1900; rpt. New York: AMS, 1973.

———. *The Poetical Works.* Cambridge Edition, with an introduction by Ruth M. Adams. Boston: Houghton Mifflin, 1974.

Browning, Robert. "An Essay on Percy Bysshe Shelley." In *Victorian Poetry and Poetics.* 2nd ed. Edited by Walter E. Houghton and G. Robert Stange. Boston: Houghton Mifflin, 1968. First published in 1852 as the introduction to twenty-five *Letters of Shelley.*

———. *The Works of Robert Browning.* Edited by F. G. Kenyon. 10 vols. London: Smith, Elder & Co., 1912.

Buckler, William E. "The Dark Space Illumined: A Reading

254

of Hardy's 'Poems of 1912-13.' " *Victorian Poetry*, 17 (1979), 98-107.

Buckley, Jerome H. *Tennyson: The Growth of a Poet.* Cambridge: Harvard University Press, 1960.

Burke, Edmund. *A Philosophical Enquiry into the Origin of Our Ideas of the Sublime and Beautiful.* 2nd ed. London, 1759; rpt. New York: Garland, 1971.

Burnet, Thomas. *The Sacred Theory of the Earth.* London: 1681-1689; rpt. Carbondale: Southern Illinois University Press, 1965.

Bush, Douglas. *Matthew Arnold: A Survey of His Poetry and Prose.* New York: Macmillan, 1971.

———. *Mythology and the Romantic Tradition.* 1937; rpt. New York: Pageant, 1957.

Calhoun, Blue. *The Pastoral Vision of William Morris.* Athens: University of Georgia Press, 1975.

Carlyle, Thomas. *Sartor Resartus.* 1836; rpt. London: Dent, 1967.

Carr, Arthur J. "Tennyson as a Modern Poet." In *Critical Essays on the Poetry of Tennyson.* Edited by John Killham. London: Routledge and Kegan Paul, 1960, pp. 41-64.

Chadwick, G. F. *The Park and the Town: Public Landscape in the Nineteenth and Twentieth Centuries.* New York: Praeger, 1966.

Chiasson, E. J. "Tennyson's 'Ulysses'—A Re-interpretation." In *Critical Essays on the Poetry of Tennyson.* Edited by John Killham. London: Routledge and Kegan Paul, 1960, pp. 164-73.

Christ, Carol T. *The Finer Optic.* New Haven: Yale University Press, 1975.

Church, Alfred J. *The Laureate's Country: A Description of Places Connected with the Life of Alfred Lord Tennyson.* London: Seeley, 1891.

Clark, Kenneth. *Landscape into Art.* London, 1949; rpt. London: Penguin, 1966.

Clifford, Derek. *A History of Garden Design.* London: Faber & Faber, 1962.

Combe, William. *The Tour of Doctor Syntax, In Search of the Picturesque. A Poem.* 4th ed. London: Ackermann's Repository of Arts, 1813.

Comley, Nancy R. "Marvell, Tennyson and 'The Islet': an Inversion of Pastoral." *Victorian Poetry,* 16 (1978), 270-74.

Cook, Eleanor. *Browning's Lyrics: An Exploration.* Toronto: University of Toronto Press, 1974.

Creese, Walter L. "Imagination in the Suburb." In *Nature and the Victorian Imagination.* Edited by U. C. Knoepfl-macher and G. B. Tennyson. Berkeley and Los Angeles: University of California Press, 1977, pp. 49-67.

Crews, Frederick C. *The Sins of the Fathers: Hawthorne's Psychological Themes.* New York: Oxford University Press, 1966.

Culler, A. Dwight. "Arnold and Etna." In *Victorian Essays: A Symposium.* Edited by Warren D. Anderson and Thomas D. Clareson. Ohio: Kent State University Press, 1967.

―――. *Imaginative Reason: The Poetry of Matthew Arnold.* New Haven: Yale University Press, 1966.

―――. *The Poetry of Tennyson.* New Haven: Yale University Press, 1977.

Dahl, Curtis. "A Double Frame for Tennyson's Demeter?" *Victorian Studies,* 1 (1958), 356-62.

―――. "The Victorian Wasteland." In *Victorian Literature.* Edited by Austin Wright. New York: Oxford University Press, 1961, pp. 32-40.

Davie, Donald. "Hardy's Virgilian Purples." *Agenda,* 10, Nos. 2-3 (1972), 138-56.

―――. *Thomas Hardy and British Poetry.* London: Routledge and Kegan Paul, 1973.

DeVane, William Clyde. *A Browning Handbook.* 2nd ed. New York: Appleton-Century-Crofts, 1955.

―――. "The Landscape of *Childe Roland.*" *PMLA,* 40 (1925), 426-32.

Devlin, Francis Patrick. "Tennyson's Use of Landscape Imagery." Ph.D. dissertation, University of Indiana, 1968.

Dickens, Charles. *Dombey and Son*. Edited by H. W. Garrod. London: Oxford University Press, 1950.

Doughty, Oswald. *A Victorian Romantic: Dante Gabriel Rossetti*. 2nd ed. London: Oxford University Press, 1960.

———, and J. R. Wahl, eds. *Letters of Dante Gabriel Rossetti*. 4 vols. Oxford: Clarendon Press, 1965.

Drew, Philip, ed. *Robert Browning: A Collection of Critical Essays*. London: Methuen, 1966.

Dyson, A. E. "The Last Enchantments." *Review of English Studies*, NS 8 (1957), 257-65.

Eggenschwiler, David Lee. "Arcadian Myth in the Poetry of Tennyson and Arnold." Ph.D. dissertation, Stanford University, 1965.

Eggers, J. Philip. *King Arthur's Laureate: A Study of Tennyson's 'Idylls of the King.'* New York: New York University Press, 1971.

Ellison, R. C. " 'The Undying Glory of Dreams': William Morris and the 'Northland of Old.' " In *Victorian Poetry*. Edited by Malcolm Bradbury and David Palmer. London: Edward Arnold, 1972, pp. 139-75.

Enstice, Andrew. *Thomas Hardy: Landscapes of the Mind*. New York: St. Martin's Press, 1979.

Fabricant, Carole. "Binding and Dressing Nature's Loose Tresses: The Ideology of Augustan Landscape Design." *Studies in Eighteenth-Century Culture*, 8 (1979), 109-35.

Feingold, Richard. *Nature and Society: Later Eighteenth-Century Uses of the Pastoral and Georgic*. New Brunswick, N.J.: Rutgers University Press, 1978.

Fitzgerald, Edward. "Some Recollections of Tennyson's Talk from 1835 to 1853." In *Tennyson and His Friends*. Edited by Hallam, Lord Tennyson. London: Macmillan, 1911, pp. 142-47.

Fleissner, R. F. "*Percute Hic*: Morris' Terrestrial Paradise." *Victorian Poetry*, 3 (1965), pp. 171-77.

Fleming, G. H. *Rossetti and the Pre-Raphaelite Brotherhood.* London: Rupert Hart-Davis, 1967.

Fletcher, Pauline. "Romantic and Anti-Romantic Gardens in Tennyson and Swinburne." *Studies in Romanticism*, 18, No. 1 (1979), 81-97.

Ford, George H. "Felicitous Space: The Cottage Controversy." In *Nature and the Victorian Imagination.* Edited by U. C. Knoepflmacher and G. B. Tennyson. Berkeley and Los Angeles: University of California Press, 1977, pp. 29-48.

―――. *Keats and the Victorians: A Study of His Influence and Rise to Fame, 1821-1895.* New Haven: Yale University Press, 1944.

Forsyth, R. A. "The Myth of Nature and the Victorian Compromise of the Imagination." *English Literary History*, 31 (1964), 213-40.

Fredeman, W. E. *Pre-Raphaelitism: A Bibliocritical Study.* Cambridge: Harvard University Press, 1965.

Frye, Northrop. *Anatomy of Criticism.* Princeton: Princeton University Press, 1957.

Fuller, Jean Overton. *Swinburne: A Critical Biography.* London: Chatto and Windus, 1968.

Fulweiler, Howard W. "Tennyson and the 'Summons from the Sea.' " *Victorian Poetry*, 3 (1965), 25-44.

Golder, Harold. "Browning's *Childe Roland.*" PMLA, 39 (1924), 963-78.

Gottfried, Leon. *Matthew Arnold and the Romantics.* London: Routledge and Kegan Paul, 1963.

Greg, W. W. *Pastoral Poetry and Pastoral Drama.* London: Bullen, 1906.

Gunn, Thom. "Hardy and the Ballads." *Agenda*, 10, Nos. 2 & 3 (1972), 19-46.

Hardy, Florence Emily. *The Early Life of Thomas Hardy 1840-1891.* New York: Macmillan, 1928.

―――. *The Later Years of Thomas Hardy 1892-1928.* New York: Macmillan, 1930.

Hardy, Thomas. *The Complete Poems of Thomas Hardy.* Edited by James Gibson. London: Macmillan, 1976.

———. *The Return of the Native.* London: Osgood, 1895.

Harris, John. *The Garden: A Celebration of One Thousand Years of British Gardening: the Guide to the Exhibition Presented by the Victoria and Albert Museum.* London: New Perspectives, 1979.

Harris, Wendell V. "Where Late the Sweet Birds Sang: Looking Back at the Victorians Looking Back at the Romantics Looking Back . . ." *Victorian Poetry,* 16 (1978), 167-75.

Harrison, Frederic. *My Alpine Jubilee, 1851-1907.* London: Smith, Elder and Co., 1908.

Harrison, Martin. *Pre-Raphaelite Paintings and Graphics.* London: Academy Editions, 1971.

Henderson, Philip, ed. *The Letters of William Morris to His Family and Friends.* London: Longmans, 1950.

———. *Swinburne: The Portrait of a Poet.* London: Routledge and Kegan Paul, 1974.

———. *Tennyson, Poet and Prophet.* London: Routledge and Kegan Paul, 1978.

———, ed. *William Morris: His Life, Work and Friends.* New York: McGraw-Hill, 1967.

Hipple, W. J. *The Beautiful, The Sublime, and The Picturesque in Eighteenth-Century British Aesthetic Theory.* Carbondale: Southern Illinois University Press, 1957.

Hixson, Jerome C. "Cauteretz Revisited." *Tennyson Research Bulletin,* 2 (1975), 145-49.

Hoare, Dorothy M. *The Works of Morris and Yeats in Relation to Early Saga Literature.* Cambridge: Cambridge University Press, 1937.

Hollis, Valerie. "Landscape in the Poetry of Tennyson." Ph.D. dissertation, Bryn Mawr, 1966.

Hollow, John Walter. "Singer of an Empty Day: William Morris and the Desire for Immortality." Ph.D. dissertation, Rochester, 1969.

———. "William Morris and the Judgment of God." *PMLA,* 86 (1971), 446-51.

Hopkins, Gerard Manley. *The Poems of Gerard Manley Hopkins.* 4th ed. Edited by W. H. Gardner and N. H. Mackenzie. London: Oxford University Press, 1967.

Hopkins, R. Thurston. *Thomas Hardy's Dorset.* London: Cecil Palmer, 1922.

Howard, Ronnalie. *The Dark Glass: Vision and Technique in the Poetry of Dante Gabriel Rossetti.* Athens: Ohio University Press, 1972.

Hughes, R. E. "Browning's 'Childe Roland' and the Broken Taboo." *Literature and Psychology,* 9 (1959), 18-19.

Hunt, John Dixon. *The Figure in the Landscape: Poetry, Painting, and Gardening during the Eighteenth Century.* Baltimore: Johns Hopkins University Press, 1976.

―――. "The Poetry of Distance: Tennyson's 'Idylls of the King.' " In *Victorian Poetry.* Edited by Malcolm Bradbury and David Palmer. London: Edward Arnold, 1972, pp. 89-121.

―――. *The Pre-Raphaelite Imagination 1848-1900.* Lincoln: University of Nebraska Press, 1968.

Hussey, Christopher. *The Picturesque: Studies in a Point of View.* New York: Putnam, 1927.

Hyams, Edward. *The English Garden.* London: Thames and Hudson, 1964.

Irvine, William, and Park Honan. *The Book, the Ring, and the Poet: A New Biography of Robert Browning.* New York: McGraw-Hill, 1974.

Jack, Ian. *Browning's Major Poetry.* Oxford: Clarendon, 1973.

James, D. G. *Matthew Arnold and the Decline of English Romanticism.* Oxford: Clarendon, 1961.

Jamison, William A. *Arnold and the Romantics.* Copenhagen: Rosenkilde and Bagger, 1958.

Johnson, E.D.H. "The Lily and the Rose: Symbolic Meaning in Tennyson's *Maud.*" *PMLA,* 64 (1949), 1222-27.

Johnson, Wendell Stacy. "D. G. Rossetti as Painter and Poet." *Victorian Poetry,* 3 (1965), 9-18.

―――. "Memory, Landscape, Love: John Ruskin's Poetry

and Poetic Criticism." *Victorian Poetry*, 19 (1981), 19-34.

Joseph, Gerard. "Victorian Frames: The Windows and Mirrors of Browning, Arnold, and Tennyson." *Victorian Poetry*, 16 (1978), 71-87.

Jump, John D., ed. *Tennyson: The Critical Heritage*. London: Routledge and Kegan Paul, 1967.

Keats, John. *The Complete Poems*. Edited by Miriam Allott. London: Longman, 1970.

———. *Letters of John Keats*. Selected by Frederick Page. London: Oxford University Press, 1954.

Keith, W. J. *The Poetry of Nature: Rural Perspectives in Poetry from Wordsworth to the Present*. Toronto: Toronto University Press, 1980.

Kemp, Edward. *How to Lay Out a Garden*. 3rd ed. New York: Wiley & Son, 1894.

Killham, John, ed. *Critical Essays on the Poetry of Tennyson*. London: Routledge and Kegan Paul, 1960.

———. *Tennyson and "The Princess": Reflections of an Age*. London: Athlone, 1958.

Kincaid, James R. *Tennyson's Major Poems: the Comic and Ironic Patterns*. New Haven: Yale University Press, 1975.

King, Roma. *The Focusing Artifice: The Poetry of Robert Browning*. Athens: Ohio University Press, 1968.

Knight, G. Wilson. "The Scholar Gipsy." In *Neglected Powers: Essays on Nineteenth and Twentieth Century Literature*. London: Routledge and Kegan Paul, 1971, pp. 231-42.

Knoepflmacher, U. C. "Dover Revisited: The Wordsworthian Matrix in the Poetry of Matthew Arnold." *Victorian Poetry*, 1 (1963), 17-26.

———, and G. B. Tennyson, eds. *Nature and the Victorian Imagination*. Berkeley and Los Angeles: University of California Press, 1977.

Kocmanová, Jessie. "The Poetic Maturing of William Morris." *Brno Studies in English*, 5 (1964), 9-222.

WORKS CONSULTED

Landow, George P. *The Aesthetic and Critical Theories of John Ruskin.* Princeton: Princeton University Press, 1971.
Lang, Cecil Y., ed. *The Swinburne Letters.* 6 vols. New Haven: Yale University Press, 1962.
Lawrence, D. H. *The Complete Poems.* 3 vols. London: Heinemann, 1957.
———. "Study of Thomas Hardy." In *Phoenix: The Posthumous Papers of D. H. Lawrence.* 1936; rpt. London: Heinemann, 1961, pp. 398-516.
———. *Women in Love.* London: Heinemann, 1954.
Layard, George Somes. *Tennyson and His Pre-Raphaelite Illustrators: a Book about a Book.* London: Stock, 1894.
Levine, George. "High and Low: Ruskin and the Novelists." In *Nature and the Victorian Imagination.* Edited by U. C. Knoepflmacher and G. B. Tennyson. Berkeley and Los Angeles: University of California Press, 1977, pp. 137-52.
———. *The Realistic Imagination: English Fiction from Frankenstein to Lady Chatterley.* Chicago: University of Chicago Press, 1981.
Lewis, C. S. "William Morris." In *Rehabilitations and Other Essays.* 1939; rpt. New York: Books for Libraries Press, 1972, pp. 35-55.
Lindsay, Jack. *William Morris: His Life and Work.* London: Constable, 1975.
Lorsch, Susan E. "Algernon Charles Swinburne's 'Evening on the Broads': Unmeaning Landscape and the Language of Negation." *Victorian Poetry,* 18 (1980), 91-96.
Lourie, Margaret A. "Below the Thunders of the Upper Deep: Tennyson as Romantic Revisionist." *Studies in Romanticism,* 18, No. 1 (1979), 3-27.
Lowes, John Livingstone, "Two Readings of Earth." *Yale Review,* 15 (1926), 515-39.
Lowry, Howard Foster, ed. *The Letters of Matthew Arnold to Arthur Hugh Clough.* London: Oxford University Press, 1932.

262

McGann, Jerome J. *Swinburne: An Experiment in Criticism.* Chicago: University of Chicago Press, 1972.

McGhee, Richard D. " 'Thalassius': Swinburne's Poetic Myth." *Victorian Poetry,* 5 (1967), 127-36.

Mack, Maynard. *The Garden and the City.* Toronto: University of Toronto Press, 1969.

Mackail, J. W. *The Life of William Morris.* 1899; rpt. New York: Blom, 1968.

McLuhan, H. Marshall. "The Aesthetic Moment in Landscape Poetry." In *English Institute Essays.* Edited by Alan S. Downer. New York: Columbia University Press, 1952, pp. 168-81.

————. "Tennyson and Picturesque Poetry." In *Critical Essays on the Poetry of Tennyson.* Edited by John Killham. London: Routledge and Kegan Paul, 1960, pp. 67-85.

McSweeney, Kerry. "Swinburne's 'A Nympholept' and 'The Lake of Gaube.' " *Victorian Poetry,* 9 (1971), 201-16.

Malins, Edward. *English Landscaping and Literature 1660-1840.* London: Oxford University Press, 1966.

Manwaring, Elizabeth. *Italian Landscape in Eighteenth Century England: A Study Chiefly of the Influence of Claude Lorrain and Salvator Rosa on English Taste 1700-1800.* New York: Oxford University Press, 1925.

Marvell, Andrew. *The Poems and Letters of Andrew Marvell.* Edited by H. M. Margoliouth. 3rd ed. Oxford: Clarendon, 1971. Vol. I.

Marx, Leo. *The Machine in the Garden: Technology and the Pastoral Ideal in America.* New York: Oxford University Press, 1964.

Maxwell, Donald. *The Landscape of Thomas Hardy.* London: Cassell, 1928.

Mégroz, R. L. *Dante Gabriel Rossetti: Painter Poet of Heaven in Earth.* London: Faber and Gwyer, 1928.

Meisel, Martin. " 'Half Sick of Shadows': The Aesthetic Dialogue in Pre-Raphaelite Painting." In *Nature and the Victorian Imagination.* Edited by U. C. Knoepflmacher and

G. B. Tennyson. Berkeley and Los Angeles: University of California Press, 1977, pp. 309-40.

Merchant, Ramona. "Pippa's Garden." *Studies in Browning and His Circle*, 2, No. 2 (1974), 9-20.

Miller, Betty. *Robert Browning: A Portrait*. New York: Scribner's, 1952.

Miller, J. Hillis. *The Disappearance of God: Five Nineteenth-Century Writers*. Cambridge: Harvard University Press, 1963.

——. *Thomas Hardy: Distance and Desire*. Cambridge: Harvard University Press, 1970.

Milton, John. *The Poems of John Milton*. Edited by John Carey and Alastair Fowler. London: Longman, 1968.

Morris, William. *The Collected Works*. Edited by May Morris. 24 vols. London: Longmans, 1910-1915.

Mustard, Wilfred P. *Classical Echoes in Tennyson*. New York: Macmillan, 1904.

Nicolson, Harold. *Swinburne*. New York: Macmillan, 1926.

——. *Tennyson: Aspects of His Life, Character and Poetry*. London: Constable, 1923.

Nicolson, Marjorie Hope. *Mountain Gloom and Mountain Glory: The Development of the Aesthetics of the Infinite*. Ithaca, N.Y.: Cornell University Press, 1959.

Noyes, Russell. *Wordsworth and the Art of Landscape*. Bloomington: Indiana University Press, 1968.

Oberg, Charlotte H. *A Pagan Prophet: William Morris*. Charlottesville: University Press of Virginia, 1978.

Orr, Mrs. Sutherland. *Life and Letters of Robert Browning*. London: Smith, Elder, 1891.

Parris, Leslie. *Landscape in Britain c. 1750-1850*. London: Tate Gallery, 1973.

Pater, Walter. *Appreciations: With an Essay on Style*. 1889; rpt. London: Macmillan, 1911.

——. "Demeter and Persephone." In *Greek Studies*. 1895; rpt. London: Macmillan, 1910, pp. 81-151.

Pattison, Robert. *Tennyson and Tradition*. Cambridge: Harvard University Press, 1979.

Paulin, Tom. *Thomas Hardy: The Poetry of Perception*. London: Macmillan, 1975.

Peck, John. "Hardy and the Figure in the Scene." *Agenda*, 10, Nos. 2 & 3 (1972), 117-25.

Perkins, David. "Hardy and the Poetry of Isolation." *English Literary History*, 26, No. 1 (1959), 253-70.

Piehler, Paul. *The Visionary Landscape: A Study in Medieval Allegory*. London: Edward Arnold, 1971.

Pinion, F. B. *A Hardy Companion: A Guide to the Works of Thomas Hardy and Their Background*. New York: St. Martin's Press, 1968.

Pope, Alexander. *Poetical Works*. Edited by Herbert Davis. London: Oxford University Press, 1966.

Pooton, Lawrence III. "Browning and the Altered Romantic Landscape." In *Nature and the Victorian Imagination*. Edited by U. C. Knoepflmacher and G. B. Tennyson. Berkeley and Los Angeles: University of California Press, 1977, pp. 426-39.

Preyer, Robert. "Tennyson as an Oracular Poet." *Modern Philology*, 55 (1958), 239-51.

Priestley, F.E.L. *Language and Structure in Tennyson's Poetry*. London: Andre Deutsch, 1973.

Rader, Ralph Wilson. *Tennyson's "Maud": The Biographical Genesis*. 1963; rpt. Berkeley and Los Angeles: University of California Press, 1978.

Rawnsley, Willingham. "Tennyson and Lincolnshire." In *Tennyson and His Friends*. Edited by Hallam, Lord Tennyson. London: Macmillan, 1911, pp. 8-32.

Raymond, Meredith B. " 'The Lake of Gaube': Swinburne's Dive in the Dark and the 'Indeterminate Moment.' " *Victorian Poetry*, 9 (1971), 185-99.

Raymond, W. *The Infinite Moment and Other Essays in Robert Browning*. Toronto: University of Toronto Press, 1965.

Reed, John R. *Perception and Design in Tennyson's "Idylls of the King."* Athens: Ohio University Press, 1969.

Ricks, Christopher. *Tennyson*. New York: Macmillan, 1972.

Riede, David G. *Swinburne: A Study of Romantic Mythmaking*. Charlottesville: University Press of Virginia, 1978.

———. "Swinburne's 'On the Cliffs': The Evolution of a Romantic Myth." *Victorian Poetry*, 16 (1978), 189-203.

Robertson, David. "Mid-Victorians amongst the Alps." In *Nature and the Victorian Imagination*. Edited by U. C. Knoepflmacher and G. B. Tennyson. Berkeley and Los Angeles: University of California Press, 1977, pp. 113-36.

Robson, W. W. "The Dilemma of Tennyson." In *Critical Essays on the Poetry of Tennyson*. Edited by John Killham. London: Routledge and Kegan Paul, 1960, pp. 155-63.

Roper, Alan. *Arnold's Poetic Landscapes*. Baltimore: Johns Hopkins University Press, 1969.

———. "The Moral Landscape of Arnold's Poetry." *PMLA*, 77 (1962), 289-96.

Rosenberg, John D. *The Darkening Glass: A Portrait of Ruskin's Genius*. London: Routledge and Kegan Paul, 1963.

———. *The Fall of Camelot: A Study of Tennyson's 'Idylls of the King.'* Cambridge: Harvard University Press, 1973.

———. "Swinburne." *Victorian Studies*, 11 (1967), 131-52.

———. "Tennyson and the Landscape of Consciousness." *Victorian Poetry*, 12 (1974), 303-10.

Rossetti, Christina. *The Complete Poems of Christina Rossetti*. Vol. I. Edited by R. W. Crump. Baton Rouge: Louisiana State University Press, 1979.

———. *The Poetical Works*. Edited by W. M. Rossetti. 1904; rpt. New York: Georg Olms, 1970.

Rossetti, Dante Gabriel. *The House of Life: A Sonnett Sequence by Dante Gabriel Rossetti*. Edited by Paull F. Baum. Cambridge: Harvard University Press, 1928.

———. *Poems*. Edited by Oswald Doughty. London: Dent, 1957.

———. *The Works of Dante Gabriel Rossetti*. Edited by William Michael Rossetti. London: Ellis, 1911.

Rossetti, William M. *Dante Gabriel Rossetti: His Family-Letters with a Memoir*. London: Ellis, 1895.

Rowse, A. L. *Matthew Arnold, Poet and Prophet.* London: Thames and Hudson, 1976.

Ruskin, John. *The Works of John Ruskin.* Edited by E. T. Cook and Alexander Wedderburn. 39 vols. London: Allen, 1903-1912.

Russell, George W. E., ed. *Letters of Matthew Arnold 1848-1888.* 2 vols. New York: Macmillan, 1896.

Ryals, Clyde de L. *From the Great Deep: Essays on 'Idylls of the King.'* New York: Ohio University Press, 1967.

————, ed. *Nineteenth-Century Literary Perspectives: Essays in Honor of Lionel Stevenson.* Durham, N.C.: Duke University Press, 1974.

Sambrook, James, ed. *Pre-Raphaelitism: A Collection of Critical Essays.* Chicago: University of Chicago Press, 1974.

Sendry, Joseph. " 'In Memoriam' and 'Lycidas.' " *PMLA,* 82 (1967), 437-43.

Shairp, J. C. *On Poetic Interpretation of Nature.* New York: Hurd and Houghton, 1877.

Shaw, W. David. *Tennyson's Style.* Ithaca: Cornell University Press, 1976.

Sheppard, Paul, Jr. "The Cross Valley Syndrome." *Landscape,* 10, No. 3 (1961), 4-8.

Sonstroem, David. *Rossetti and the Fair Lady.* Middletown, Conn.: Wesleyan University Press, 1970.

Southworth, James Granville. *The Poetry of Thomas Hardy.* New York: Columbia University Press, 1947.

Spector, Stephen J. "Rossetti's Self-Destroying 'Moment's Monument': 'Silent Noon.' " *Victorian Poetry,* 14 (1976), 54-58.

Spencer, Jeffry B. *Heroic Nature: Ideal Landscape in English Poetry from Marvell to Thompson.* Evanston, Ill.: Northwestern University Press, 1973.

Spenser, Edmund. *The Poems of Spenser.* Edited by J. C. Smith and E. De Selincourt. 1912; rpt. London: Oxford University Press, 1959.

Staley, Allen. *The Pre-Raphaelite Landscape.* Oxford: Clarendon, 1973.

Stange, G. Robert. "Tennyson's Garden of Art: A Study of *The Hesperides.*" In *Critical Essays on the Poetry of Tennyson.* Edited by John Killham. London: Routledge and Kegan Paul, 1960, pp. 99-112.

———. "Tennyson's Mythology: A Study of *Demeter and Persephone.*" *English Literary History,* 21 (1954), 67-80.

Stein, Richard L. *The Ritual of Interpretation: The Fine Arts as Literature in Ruskin, Rossetti, and Pater.* Cambridge: Harvard University Press, 1975.

Stephen, Leslie. *The Playground of Europe.* London: Longmans, 1871.

———. "A Substitute for the Alps." *National Review,* 23 (1894), pp. 460-67; rpt. in *Men, Books, and Mountains.* Minneapolis: University of Minnesota Press, 1956, pp. 203-12.

Stevens, Wallace. *The Collected Poems.* London: Faber, 1945.

Stevenson, Lionel. "The 'High-Born Maiden' Symbol in Tennyson." In *Critical Essays on the Poetry of Tennyson.* Edited by John Killham. London: Routledge and Kegan Paul, 1960, pp. 126-36.

———. *The Pre-Raphaelite Poets.* Chapel Hill: University of North Carolina Press, 1972.

Stewart, Stanley. *The Enclosed Garden: The Tradition and the Image in Seventeenth-Century Poetry.* Madison: University of Wisconsin Press, 1966.

Stone, Donald D. *The Romantic Impulse in Victorian Fiction.* Cambridge: Harvard University Press, 1980.

Strachey, James, ed. *Works of Sigmund Freud.* London: Hogarth Press, 1953.

Surtees, Virginia. *The Paintings and Drawings of Dante Gabriel Rossetti (1828-1882): A Catalogue Raisonné.* 2 vols. London: Oxford University Press, 1971.

Swinburne, Algernon Charles. *The Complete Works of Algernon Charles Swinburne.* Edited by Sir Edmund Gosse and T. J. Wise. 20 vols. London: Heinemann, 1925-1927.

———. *Poems and Ballads, Atalanta in Calydon.* Edited with

an introduction and annotation by Morse Peckham. New York: Bobbs-Merrill, 1970.

Talon, Henri A. "Dante Gabriel Rossetti, peintre-poète dans *La Maison de Vie*." *Études anglaises*, 19, No. 1 (1966), 1-14.

Tennyson, Alfred. *Poems*. London: Edward Moxon, 1857.

———. *The Poems of Tennyson*. Edited by Christopher Ricks. London: Longman, 1969.

Tennyson, Charles. *Alfred Tennyson*. New York: Macmillan, 1949.

Tennyson, Hallam. *Alfred Lord Tennyson: A Memoir by His Son*. 2 vols. London: Macmillan, 1897.

———, ed. *Tennyson and His Friends*. London: Macmillan, 1911.

Tinker, C. B. and H. F. Lowry. *The Poetry of Matthew Arnold: A Commentary*. London: Oxford University Press, 1940.

Townsend, Francis G. *Ruskin and the Landscape Feeling: A Critical Analysis of His Thought During the Critical Years of His Life, 1843-56*. Illinois Studies in Language and Literature, Vol. 35, No. 3. Urbana: University of Illinois Press, 1951.

Trilling, Lionel. *Matthew Arnold*. New York: Norton, 1939.

Turner, James. *The Politics of Landscape: Rural Scenery and Society in English Poetry 1630-1660*. Oxford: Blackwell, 1979.

Vallance, Aymer. *William Morris, His Art, His Writings, and His Public Life*. London: G. Bell & Sons, 1897.

Walters, John Cuming. *In Tennyson Land*. London: George Redway, 1890.

Watson, J. R. *Picturesque Landscape and English Romantic Poetry*. London: Hutchinson, 1970.

Welby, T. Earle. *A Study of Swinburne*. New York: George H. Doran, 1926.

———. *The Victorian Romantics 1850-1870*. London: Gerald Howe, 1929.

Williams, Merryn. *Thomas Hardy and Rural England*. London: Macmillan, 1972.

Williams, Raymond. *The Country and the City*. New York: Oxford University Press, 1973.

Willoughby, John. "Browning's 'Childe Roland to the Dark Tower Came.' " *Victorian Poetry*, 1 (1963), 291-99.

Wordsworth, William. *Poetical Works*. Edited by Thomas Hutchinson. London: Oxford University Press, 1969.

Yeats, W. B. "The Happiest of the Poets." In *Ideas of Good and Evil*. London: Macmillan, 1903.

# INDEX

INDEX

Browning, Robert (*cont.*)
114; "Essay on Shelly," 112,
114; "A Face," 113; "The Flow-
er's Name," 126-127; "Fra
Lippo Lippi," 113; "A Gram-
marian's Funeral," 114; "Home-
Thoughts from Abroad," 101;
"Ivàn Ivanovitch," 108-109; "La
Saisiaz," 103-105; "Love Among
the Ruins," 119-120; "Meeting
at Night," 116-117; "My Last
Duchess," 114; *Paracelsus*, 124;
"Parting at Morning," 117; *Pau-
line*, 109-112, 114, 132, 154,
230; "Pippa Passes," 105-107,
115, 116; "Porphyria's Lover,"
114, 193; *The Ring and the
Book*, 106, 114-116; "Serenade
at the Villa," 127-128; "Sibran-
dus Schafnaburgensis," 125;
"Two in the Campagna," 117-
119; "Up at a Villa—Down in
the City," 102-103, 178;
"Women and Roses," 125-126
Buckler, William, 241-242
Buckley, Jerome, 37, 70n
Burke, Edmund, 3n, 12
Burnet, Thomas, 174
Bush, Douglas, 18n, 42
Byron, George Gordon, Lord, 3,
18-19, 25, 50, 88, 215

Caine, Hall, 161
Calhoun, Blue, 165, 185
Carlyle, Thomas, 35, 202
Carr, Arthur J., 65n
Chadwick, G. F., 11n
Chaucer, Geoffrey, 192
Chiasson, E. J., 30n
Christ, Carol, 122, 134
Church, Alfred J., 50n
Clare, John, 15
Claude (Lorrain), 14, 20, 118, 135
Clifford, Derek, 9n, 10
Clough, Arthur Hugh, 79-80, 82,

91, 94, 104
Coleridge, Samuel Taylor, 183
Combe, William, 6
Comte, Auguste, 229
Constable, John, 14, 15, 135
Cook, Eleanor, 105
Creese, Walter, 189
Crews, Frederick, 13
Culler, Dwight, 49, 75-76, 82, 84n,
85, 89-90, 98, 104n

Dahl, Curtis, 131, 200
Darwin, Charles, 123, 124, 229,
230
Davie, Donald, 224n, 241
Denham, Sir John, 14
DeVane, Robert, 129-130
Dickens, Charles, 11, 160
Doughty, Oswald, 153
Dyson, A. E., 93

Ellison, R. C., 176
Enstice, Andrew, 242

Fabricant, Carole, 13
Feingold, Richard, 15n
Fitzgerald, Edward, 34
Ford, George H., 8, 13, 43, 148,
153n, 163n, 167
Freud, Sigmund, 12, 110n
Frye, Northrop, 4n
Fulweiler, Howard, 33

Gainsborough, Thomas, 15
Gilpin, William, 6, 12
Golder, Harold, 129
Gottfried, Leon, 72
Gunn, Thom, 228n

Hallam, Arthur, 21, 23-24, 26, 46,
63-66, 221
Hardy, Thomas, 94, 143, 224-246,
249, 251-252
——"After a Journey," 240, 244;
"At Castle Boteril," 240-241;

272

274

Swinburne, Algernon C. (*cont.*)
174, 195-196; "Neap-Tide,"
210; "A Nympholept," 219-221;
"On the Cliffs," 209; "Thalas-
sius," 207-209; "Tristram and
Iseult," 214-219; "The Triumph
of Time," 204-206; "The Two
Dreams," 192-194
Talon, Henri, 148
Tennyson, Alfred, 13, 19-71, 72,
77, 81, 89, 93-94, 98, 100, 102,
108, 113, 114, 124, 125, 127,
133, 135, 155, 156, 158, 163,
165, 166, 168, 170, 179, 187,
191, 194, 199-201, 204, 209,
214, 218, 221, 229, 235, 239,
244, 247, 249-251; and Mable-
thorpe, 35, 50; and Somersby,
50, 63-66; illustrations for the
Moxon *Tennyson*, 136-140
——"Adeline," 52; "Aylmer's
Field," 58-60; "Balin and
Balan," 38-39; "Break, break,
break," 35; "Come down, O
maid," 24-27, 41, 42, 53, 68;
"Come into the garden, Maud,"
53, 54; "Crossing the Bar," 32;
"The Day Dream," 61; "The
Death of Oenone," 44; "Demeter
and Persephone," 200-201; "A
Dream of Fair Women," 55-56;
"Enid and Geraint," 37-38;
"Enoch Arden," 58, 60-62, 66,
102; "The Gardener's Daugh-
ter," 61-63, 102; "Gareth and
Lynette," 39-40; "Here often,
when a child," 35; "The Hesper-
ides," 48n; "The Holy Grail,"
28, 30-32, 36-37, 77; *Idylls of
the King*, 28, 30-32, 36-41, 55,
59, 77, 93, 108 (and see individ-
ual titles); "I have led her home,
my love," 56; *In Memoriam*, 23-
24, 32-33, 35-36, 63-66, 244;

"In the Valley of the Cauteretz,"
22-23; "The Kraken," 33-34, 98;
"The Lady of Shalott," 50-51,
68, 136-139; "Locksley Hall,
Sixty Years After," 71n; "The
Lotos-Eaters," 26-27, 44-47,
124, 199-200, 204, 239; "The
Lover's Tale," 19-21, 44; "Mar-
garet," 52-53; "Mariana," 50-
51, 60, 70, 72, 102, 114, 136,
138, 168, 185, 235; *Maud*, 53-
58, 60-62, 66-70, 93, 155, 158,
170, 230 (and see individual ti-
tles); "Maud has a garden of
roses," 54; "The Mermaid," 33;
"The Merman," 33, 98; "Ode to
Memory," 49; "Oenone," 21-22,
42-45, 221; "Oh! That 'Twere
Possible," 53; "On Sublimity,"
19; "The Palace of Art," 41, 50-
51, 138-140, 239; "The Passing
of Arthur," 32; "The Poet's
Mind," 48n, 49-51; *The Prin-
cess*, 24-27, 41-42, 53, 66-70,
187, 248-249, 251; "Recollec-
tions of the Arabian Nights," 48-
49; "The Sea-Fairies," 33; "Sir
Galahad," 27-28; "Tithonus,"
46-47; "Ulysses," 29-30, 32
Tennyson, Charles, 50n
Tennyson, Hallam, 19, 34
Theocritus, 42, 95
Trilling, Lionel, 84
Turner, James, 14-15
Turner, J.M.W., 5, 113, 160, 211,
216, 218, 226, 233

Versailles, 9, 10, 13
Virgil, 42, 95

Walters, John Cuming, 50n
Welby, T. Earle, 147-148
Williams, Raymond, 13, 15, 54-55
Willoughby, John, 165-166

INDEX

Wordsworth, William, 4, 9, 21, 23-
24, 72-74, 77, 79, 83, 88-89,
101, 106, 107, 121, 129, 161,

209, 230, 240-241, 250, 252

Yeats, W. B., 225

Library of Congress Cataloging in Publication Data

Fletcher, Pauline, 1938-
  Gardens and grim ravines.

  Bibliography: p.
  Includes index.
  1. English poetry—19th century—History and
criticism.    2. Landscape in literature.    3. Nature in
literature.    I. Title.
  PR595.L27F56    1983        821'.8'0936        82-24130
  ISBN 0-691-06556-X